Design by Justine Strasberg

Jim A

Text by Christopher Finch

RANDOM HOUSE   NEW YORK

The Art, the Magic, the Imagination

enson

THE WORKS

This book
is dedicated to
Tom and Joan Dunsmuir and to the
memory of Richard Hunt. —C.F.

RANDOM HOUSE
Creative Director—Rochelle Udell ❋ Art Director—Mary Maguire
❋ Project Manager—Janis Donnaud ❋ Production Supervisors—
Kathy Rosenbloom, Della Mancuso ❋ Production Editor—Beth Pearson
❋ Editorial Assistants—Sarah Parr, Rebecca Beuchler

JIM HENSON PRODUCTIONS
Creative Director—Jane Leventhal ❋ Editorial Director—Louise Gikow
❋ Photo Editor—Francesca Olivieri ❋ Creative Consultant—Cheryl Henson
❋ Research Associates—Karen Falk, Danielle Obinger, Craig Shemin
Special thanks to Jane Henson and Frank Oz

Copyright ©1993 by Jim Henson Productions, Inc.

All rights reserved under International and Pan-American Copyright Conventions.
Published in the United States by Random House, Inc., New York,
and simultaneously in Canada by
Random House of Canada Limited, Toronto.

All permissions to reproduce illustrations and lyrics appear on pages 250-51.

Library of Congress Cataloging-in-Publication Data

Finch, Christopher.
Jim Henson: the works / Christopher Finch.—1st ed.
p.   cm.
ISBN 0-679-41203-4
1. Henson, Jim. 2. Puppeteers—United States—Biography.
I. Title.
PN1982.H46F56   1993
791.5'3'092—dc20   92-50152
[B]

Manufactured in China
11 12 13 14

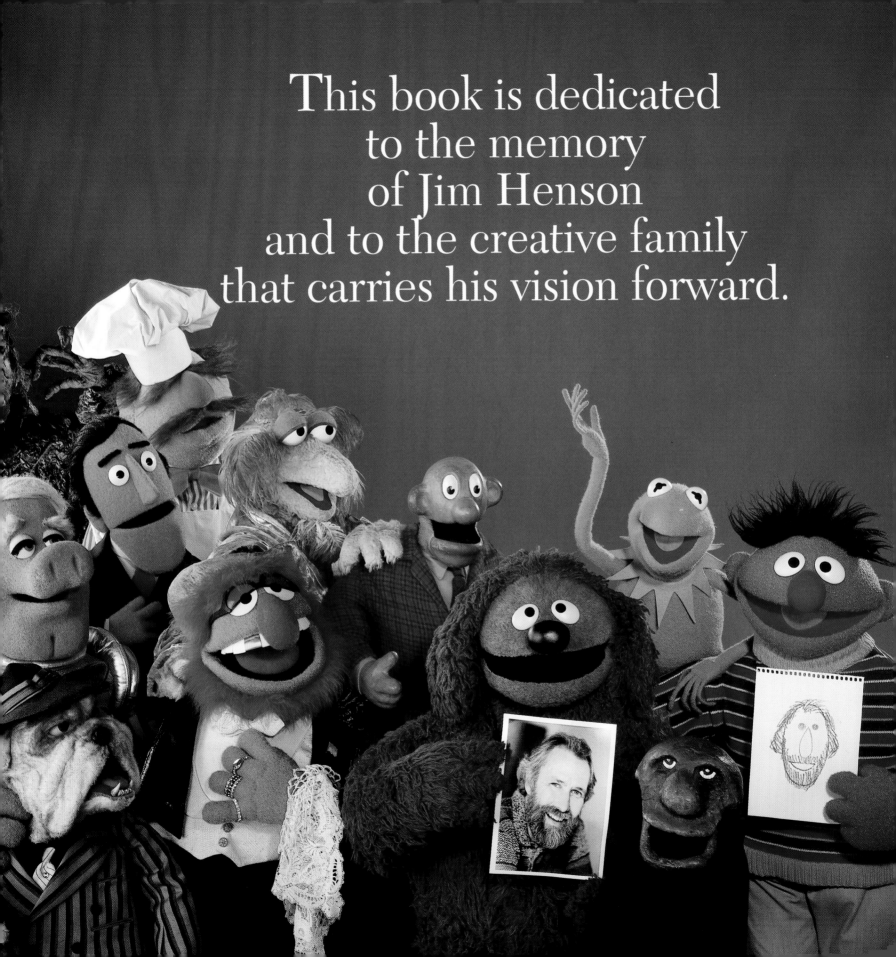

This book is dedicated
to the memory
of Jim Henson
and to the creative family
that carries his vision forward.

INTRODUCTION

When asked to write this introduction, I didn't realize how difficult it would be to put thoughts and feelings into words that would express what Jim Henson meant to me and millions of other people. Perhaps my difficulty stemmed from the fact that I have also seen Jim's work through the eyes of others. Long before I met him I admired him, and after we met and worked together I came to love his art, his spirit, his humanity. But unless you have had the experience of sitting in a village in war-ravaged Guatemala, or a humble, boxlike room in the wretched South African township of Alexandra, or in a dust-covered hovel on a Native American reservation, or in the tin shacks that house the thousands who live desperate lives in East Kingston, Jamaica, or the teeming *favelas* of Rio de Janeiro, or in an overcrowded, below-poverty-level dwelling in a ghetto in New York, Chicago, or Detroit, among people whose lives are dominated by their bitter struggle for existence and some bit of dignity, unless you've seen from these places the looks on the faces of small children as they watched *Sesame Street* or the Muppets, you'll never really understand what Jim and his colleagues have done for millions of chil-

HARRY BELAFONTE appeared with these exotic characters during his rendition of "Turn the World Around" on *The Muppet Show*.

dren all over the world, children who would have never smiled, nor dared to dream, had it not been for Jim Henson. I come from those places; I know these faces. Through them I came to fully appreciate Jim.

This book is not just a voyage into the life of a popular American personality. If it were just that it would still be, in many ways, worthy of its existence. But in these pages there is much to discover about this remarkable man and the doors of joy and freedom of expression he opened to all who partook in his short journey in an all-too-short life.

HARRY BELAFONTE on the set with Animal and Kermit.

Jim might not have happened in quite the same way were it not for the love and distinctive contributions made by his grandmother, called, simply, Dear; his wonderful wife, Jane Nebel; and people like Jerry Juhl, Joan Ganz Cooney, Don Sahlin, Bonnie Erickson, and certainly Frank Oz and David Lazer and a handful of others. They all had vision. But I'm sure all would admit that it was Jim who made the overwhelming difference. Jim was their vision's visionary.

What is so wonderfully curious is that Jim Henson's social and spiritual environment was not at all uncommon. As you read his story you will find his early years interesting, filled with their fair share of average America, with sad moments and many humorous ones. But nothing about his formative years or early adolescence prepares us for the genius that would erupt.

If nothing in the environment can be directly credited for who and what he became, then where did it come from? Where did he get "it"?

In my search for the answer I looked at the milestones of chance and coincidence that touched his life. I have talked with people whom he encountered and whose offerings he drew upon to fulfill his objectives. I looked in many places and could find no settling answer. Then I realized, after reading this book, that I could never have found the answer. The "it" I was looking for cannot be found in a place or an incident. The answer is simple. Jim Henson was blessed. He was one of those rare persons who, despite whatever life does or does not offer, will stand out as the brightest stars in their galaxy. And he was just that—this prince turned frog.

At his eulogy at St. John the Divine, as we listened to his wife, Jane, and their children, Lisa, Cheryl, Brian, John, and Heather, speak, as we watched Big Bird walk down the aisle, and as Kermit and all the Muppets gathered together in their song of goodbye, all who were present understood clearly that Jim would never be lost to us.

I am forever grateful for my friendship with David Lazer. He helped my wife, Julie, and me understand the Muppet family with far greater intimacy than we may have otherwise been afforded. If this were not an introduction, I would take the time to tell you an intriguing story about an old English circus manager's wagon and its mysterious disappearance somewhere in the English countryside. Those of you who know David should one day ask him to tell you this wonderful tale.

I also take this opportunity to say how grateful I am to have been touched by the talent and the humanity of all the men and women in the Muppet family with whom I worked. Breaking bread with them, laughing with them, creating with them, was one of the better encounters I have had.

I hope you enjoy this man's story.

— HARRY BELAFONTE

How do you write about someone who did so much and who meant so much to you? All I can do is put down some remembrances and feelings.

People recall Jim in many different ways. What I remember and still feel about him is his strength. His strength of character, his strength of vision, his strength of will.

He would travel to New York, London, Toronto, Los Angeles…our main areas of production over the years. He would travel back and forth, constantly working. He always worked harder than anyone else in the company. But he would never complain about how tired he was or how he was shouldering so much. Never. He would always find something positive about it. He loved his work.

But Jim was no workaholic. I always marveled at how, given his heavy schedule, he could relax and play. He seemed to appreciate life so much. Every aspect of it. He would go on a balloon trip with friends, drinking champagne while drifting over the French countryside. He would take a group of us, first class, on the QE2 to London to shoot *The Muppet Show*. He would rent a boat with family and friends and sail around the islands. He loved taking walks or flying kites on Hampstead Heath in London, or a really good meal, or an evening with friends.

I've never known anyone like Jim. He had a strength and a sweetness, a stillness and a savvy. He was the most giving man I've ever known. He had a great generosity of spirit, of time, of money for other people. He valued quality work, but being a good human being was just as important to him.

He was head of a large company with offices in three cities. He was the father of five children. He was a performer, a writer, a producer, a television director, a motion picture director, a businessman, a creator, a visionary. And with all this he always managed to have fun.

JIM HENSON AND FRANK OZ perform Kermit and Piggy in *The Muppet Movie*.

During a recording date he would feel responsible for keeping things moving, so he would be the serious one while we performers clowned around between takes. He would often get impatient with us, which usually meant he would quietly clear his throat and shift his weight on his stool. That's when we knew we should get to work. But then he couldn't help himself and he would join in the silliness until he

JIM AND FRANK take up somewhat precarious positions during an early shoot.

cried from laughter. And then he would look at his watch and bring us back on course. But he always had a gift for allowing chaos and, through the chaos, guiding us to a better result.

Sitting next to me in our countless taxi trips and airplane rides, Jim would talk to me about the future, about the new projects that excited him and what he hoped to do with them and who could best help him bring them about. I remember years ago, during one of those talks, he said to me that he just wanted to "do good stuff." As he became more successful he saw that he also had opportunities to do good for people, too. He wanted to make a difference.

In Thornton Wilder's *Our Town*, the dead in the cemetery speak of the living, saying about them that "they don't understand." Well, Jim understood. He loved his family. He loved his work. He loved us. He loved and appreciated life. He understood.

— FRANK OZ

Over the years, television has produced a few individuals blessed with the ability to touch our hearts, our minds, and our lives with their vision. It's not so much that these special people march to a different drummer, but that they carry their own orchestras around with them in their heads. And when we allow them to play their tunes, the sound reverberates for generations. They make us think and they make us laugh.

Such a special individual was my friend Jim Henson.

My first connection with Jim came from the fact that he was a great admirer of my father, Edgar Bergen. They were both soft-spoken, sensitive, creative people. And the man who gave us Charlie McCarthy was always the first to acknowledge the genius of the man behind Kermit the Frog and all the other Muppets. Jim dedicated *The Muppet Movie* to my father, and I was one of the first guests to perform in the now legendary *Muppet Show*.

Who can talk about Jim without bringing up another connection—the one that extended in all his bright green innocence from Jim's right arm—the sane and sensible savant of the swamps, Kermit the Frog.

KERMIT and Candice Bergen.

The story of Jim Henson begins at a local television station in Washington, D.C., where he worked with his wife, Jane. Jim's first connection with the public was made with a five-minute nightly show called *Sam and Friends*. From there, the idea that was to become the Muppets grew to include a group of individuals who were only too happy to commit themselves to the childlike sophistication of Jim Henson. Together they expanded the boundaries of their art, giving life to a host of characters that have become as familiar and as lovable as members of our own families.

With the passage of time, Jim continued to refine his vision, introducing new characters to the already overflowing menagerie of furrier-than-life creatures. And no matter how large the Muppet organization became, how intense the schedule, Jim was always there in the middle of things: guiding, encouraging, inspiring, and perfecting the vision.

A real breakthrough came for Jim in 1969 when the Children's Television Workshop started an experiment in education for preschoolers called *Sesame Street*. In 1976 the world welcomed *The Muppet Show*, a program that went on to have a global impact. This was followed by *Fraggle Rock*, the multi-Emmy-winning *Muppet Babies*, and the highly imaginative *Jim Henson Hour*.

In *The Muppet Movie*, Kermit expressed for Jim the optimism and the hope that formed the underlying theme of all his work. Here's how he put it:

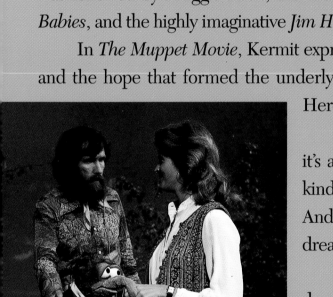

JIM and Candice with the Great Gonzo.

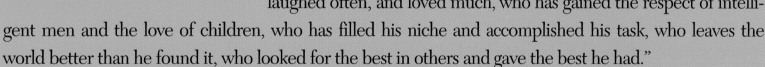

CHARLIE McCARTHY and Edgar Bergen.

"I've got a dream, too, but it's about singing and dancing and making people happy. That's the kind of dream that gets better the more people you share it with. And, well, I've found a whole bunch of friends who have the same dream. And it kind of makes us like a family."

Jim made us all like a family because we were drawn into his dream. We'll continue to be fans and faithful followers and family because we know he leads us to the best of places. Writer Robert Louis Stevenson wrote, "That man is a success who has lived well, laughed often, and loved much, who has gained the respect of intelligent men and the love of children, who has filled his niche and accomplished his task, who leaves the world better than he found it, who looked for the best in others and gave the best he had."

That sounds like a perfect description of my friend Jim Henson.

— CANDICE BERGEN
From a speech about Jim Henson made during the 1990 Emmy Awards ceremony

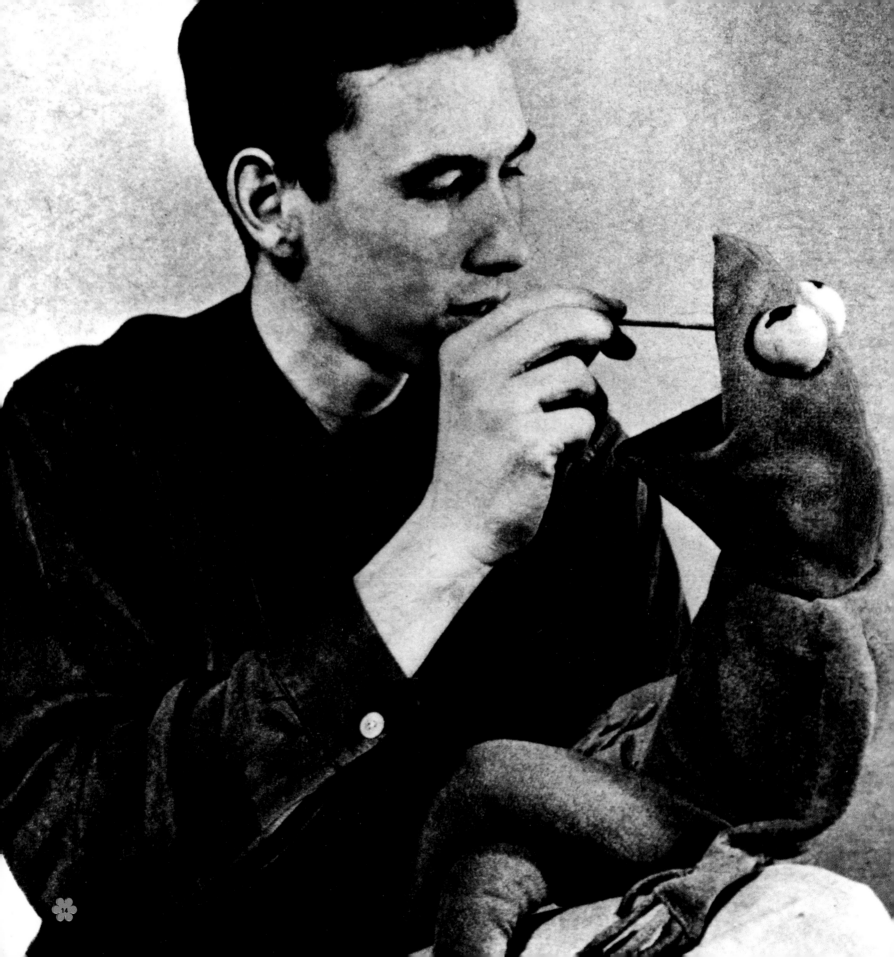

CHAPTER ONE

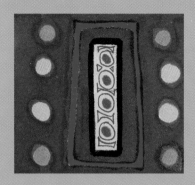

Jim Henson was not quite eighteen when his puppeteering stint at WTOP ended and he auditioned for WRC-TV, Washington's NBC owned and operated station. WRC would remain his home base for the next seven years—from 1954 until 1961.

Among the first of his assignments at WRC was *Afternoon*, a magazine show aimed at housewives. This marked his first collaboration with Jane Nebel—the woman who later became his wife.

"They would have a cooking segment," Jim later recalled. "They'd have news, they'd have a local combo, and they'd do fashion shows with models, so it was a fairly large operation—and we were part of that."

"I think we were put on the show to do spots for children," Jane remembers. "But we were college students amusing ourselves, and we did these wild things with the puppets, lip-synching to Stan Freberg records—like his takeoff on 'Banana Boat'—and things like that. I guess it had a quality of abandon and nonsense and of being somewhat experimental. In any case, somebody at the station decided to take these little pieces and try them in a choice time slot."

The station's idea was for a five-minute show that would be screened twice a day, at 6:25 P.M. (immediately before *The Huntley-Brinkley Report*) and at 11:25 P.M. (immediately before *The Tonight Show*, then hosted by Steve Allen).

"We were handed the best imaginable audiences," says Jane Henson. "Everyone followed *Huntley-Brinkley*, and Steve Allen was extremely popular as well. It was an incredible break, and I never did know for sure who was responsible for it."

Jim's new show was called *Sam and Friends*. It made its debut on May 9, 1955, and ran till

A YOUNG JIM HENSON refurbishes an early version of Kermit, one of the first of his Muppet creations. At this point, Kermit was not yet a frog.

Professor Madcliffe

Kermit

Jane

Henrietta

Jim

Harry

Moldy
Hay

Sam

Scoop

Hank

Omar

Yorick

Mushmellon

Icky Gunk

WHEN JIM HENSON'S groundbreaking TV show
Sam and Friends was at the peak of its success, he
posed with his wife-to-be, Jane Nebel, and a group of
the characters they performed on the show or in
commercials. The puppets were already very much in
the familiar Muppet style.

Wilkins

Wontkins

SAM—THE NOMINAL STAR of *Sam and Friends*—was a primitive version of the basic kind of hand and rod Muppet that Jim Henson devised in the mid-fifties. He had the face of a prizefighter, with protruding Clark Gable ears, a W. C. Fields nose, and permanently astonished eyes. Like a well-designed cartoon character, he derived some of his personality from his features. But Jim's manipulation of Sam—a tilt of the head to find an appropriate eye focus, a bounce to a song—completed the picture.

December of 1961, winning a local Emmy in 1958 and establishing a devoted following for the Hensons' repertory of humorous creations, which were known from the first as the Muppets—and included a simple, green, lizardlike character called Kermit. (Jane Henson recalls that the name *Muppet* was actually an amalgam of the words *puppet* and *marionette*…although Jim later insisted that he chose the name simply because he liked the sound of it.)

Sam and Friends provided an ideal apprenticeship for Jim, since it enabled him to function as inventor, director, and set designer in addition to filling his basic roles as puppet builder and performer. Producers of earlier puppet programs on television had simply placed a camera in front of a traditional puppet theater and shot the proceedings from the viewpoint of someone sitting in the audience. Jim quickly realized that his real theater was the television set in the viewer's home. Like the movie screen, the television screen was a magic window you could open onto any world you chose. Like cartoon characters, puppets could go anywhere and do anything you could imagine.

And Jim Henson had a fertile imagination.

Television cameras of that time were equipped with revolving turrets fitted with lenses of different focal lengths. Jim soon learned that he could employ these lenses to create a variety of illusions involving spatial perceptions. Using a wide-angle lens, for instance, he could make a puppet appear to be a great distance from the camera,

JANE HENSON

Jane Henson was Jim Henson's first working partner. She recalls that from the very beginning, it was the medium of television itself that fascinated Jim. "In his spare time he'd be in the control room, trying to understand what was going on. And the technicians loved teaching him because he really learned his lessons well. He couldn't wait to try out the things he was learning on *Sam and Friends*. He would tell the technicians that he'd like to try this or that, and then it would become a team thing. The atmosphere in the studio was very relaxed because in the beginning, we were lip-synching to records. There was no live sound…so there was no need to be completely quiet. We could talk as we worked, and if something went especially well, the crew would applaud. If something went wrong, we'd laugh anyway."

DESIGNED BY JIM, the titles of *Sam and Friends* (*near left*) demonstrate that the show's creator had little respect for the proprieties of television graphics. In fact, the entire show was an exercise in benevolent irreverence. Its gentle anarchy was emphasized by the fact that it was juxtaposed, in both of its two daily broadcasts, with the NBC network news—a time slot that also gave it enormous exposure. The fanciful vehicle occupied by a trio of the show's regulars (*far left*) is typical of the props built by Jim during the *Sam and Friends* period. In those days, Jim did just about everything short of operating the camera. He not only designed, built, and performed the Muppets, he also devised the skits they appeared in, constructed the props, and painted the backgrounds.

then rush into close-up with the speed of an express train. All that was involved was an arm movement of two or three feet—the lens did the rest. Jim's use of television cameras to animate his characters transformed the art of puppetry.

In order to capitalize on their innovative use of the television screen, Jim and Jane taught themselves to work while watching the puppets on a television monitor. This wasn't easy, because the image on the TV screen is reversed; when the puppeteer moves a character to the right, the character moves to the left on the screen. It was a skill worth perfecting, however, because for the first time, it enabled them to see not only their own performances as they were happening, but also exactly what the audience would see.

The ability to view his work through his audience's eyes led Jim to develop a style of puppet that was extremely flexible and wonderfully expressive in television close-ups. Although some of the *Sam and Friends* puppets, including Sam himself, were made from relatively hard materials, Jim soon began to experiment with softer substances like foam rubber. The original Kermit (who was not yet a frog) was constructed by Jim in 1955 from a spring coat abandoned by his mother and two halves of a Ping-Pong ball.

"…Kermit started out as a way of building, putting a mouth and covering over my hand," Jim later explained. "There was nothing in Kermit outside of the piece of cardboard—it was originally cardboard—and the cloth shape that was his head. He's one of the simplest kinds of puppet you can make, and he's very flexible because of that …which gives him a range of expression. A lot

JERRY JUHL

Although he would eventually become head writer of *The Muppet Show*, Jerry Juhl was hired to replace Jane Henson as a performer and general factotum. "I met Jim Henson in 1961. By then, the Muppets already had a cult following with a reputation for bizarre, slightly dangerous comedy. Yet Jim seemed so utterly *normal*. He had driven across the country in a shiny new station wagon with his wife, Jane, and baby Lisa. They looked as average and suburban as actors in a Chevrolet commercial.

"After a while, Jim asked me to come see his puppets. We walked out to the station wagon. He unlocked the tailgate and opened a large black box. The things he brought out of that box seemed to me to be magical presences, like totems—but funnier: an angry creature whose whole body was a rounded triangle; a purple skull named Yorick; a green froglike thing. One after the other, Jim pulled them from the box, put them on his hand, and brought them to life. Who *was* this Henson guy? These things weren't even puppets—not as I had ever seen or defined them. This guy was like a sailor who had studied the compass and found that there was a fifth direction in which one could sail. When he offered me a berth on the ship, I signed on."

FROM THE VERY BEGINNING of his career, Jim Henson employed the classic Muppet style of hand and rod puppet, but he also experimented with every other kind of puppet. At the *far right*, Jerry Juhl (partially hidden) and Jim operate a squad of rather stiff characters whose movements are controlled from beneath by an array of rods and levers. The odd-looking fellow winking at the audience (*near right*) was known as Nobody—perhaps because he had no body. Suspended from a frame about three feet high, his moving parts were made of white string and were animated by almost invisible threads attached to the fingers of a pair of gloves worn by the puppeteer.

of people build very stiff puppets—you can barely move the thing—and you can get very little expression out of a character that you can barely move. Your hand has a lot of flexibility to it, and what you want to do is to build a puppet that can reflect all that flexibility."

Over the years, Jim used everything from elaborate marionettes to simple finger puppets. But Kermit is an example of one of the classic Muppet types of puppet: the combined hand and rod puppet. The puppeteer places one hand inside the character's head, controlling head movements by pivoting that hand from the wrist and operating the mouth with fingers and thumb. The puppeteer uses his or her other hand to operate two almost invisible rods that control the character's hands. Occasionally, the puppeteer is assisted in this by a second puppeteer.

At first, there was no live sound on *Sam and Friends*; the Muppets lip-synched to songs such as the Louis Prima and Keely Smith version of "That Old Black Magic." This featured Kermit, wearing a short, dark wig, and Sam, whose manic action transformed the mood. But as Jim became more confident, he began to try his hand at writing sketches, which also meant using his own voice on television for the first time. These sketches included parodies of television shows such as Ed Murrow's *Person to Person* and even *The Huntley-Brinkley Report*. In 1957, the Muppets also began to star in commercials, providing Jim with new sources of creative inspiration as well as a significant new source of income.

In 1958, Jim Henson took a leave of absence from *Sam and Friends*, temporarily relinquishing the show to Jane Nebel and Bob Payne, an old high school acquaintance of

WITH HIS FIRST SERIOUS TELEVISION EARNINGS, Jim purchased this 1956 white T-Bird convertible. (He also bought his mother a color TV set, then still an expensive novelty, and an electric organ.) The photograph was taken outside the Hensons' home in Hyattsville. Jane Henson feels that it was probably snapped with all of the Henson extended family looking on from the driveway, laughing and cheering Jim (and Sam) on. "After all," she says, "Sam had made it all possible."

Commercial Days

Jim and Jane Henson broke into the field of commercials in 1957 when they began to make local spots for Wilkins Coffee. Eventually they would make more than 300 commercials for this sponsor alone. These early commercials, like many of those that followed, were short—lasting just seven seconds—and very much to the point. They starred a couple of characters called Wilkins and Wontkins—Wilkins being the character who will drink Wilkins Coffee, of course, and Wontkins being the character who won't. Wilkins would suggest that Wontkins should try a cup of Wilkins Coffee. Wontkins, being a negative type, would not only ignore this suggestion but actively show his disdain for Wilkins Coffee. Wilkins (the character, not the coffee) would respond by blowing Wontkins to pieces or otherwise obliterating him. (In one instance, Wontkins played against type by accepting a cup of coffee and pretending to enjoy it. At the end of the commercial, however, he asked for his bribe.)

The fact that Wilkins and Wontkins were stylized puppet characters made this kind of behavior acceptable. The fact that the situations Jim thought up were always comical made the commercials memorable...especially since they were being shown in an era when the idea of the humorous commercial was a novelty.

"Till then," Jim once explained, "the agencies believed that the hard sell was the only way to get their message over on television. We took a very different approach. We tried to sell things by making people laugh. Bob and Ray were doing the same thing at about the same time in the New York market, doing funny spots for Piels beer, but we were definitely in the vanguard."

Jim's irreverent attitude to salesmanship quickly drew attention from other sponsors. Soon the production of commercials had become an important and lucrative activity for the Muppets. Between 1957 and 1969, when *Sesame Street* brought them a new level of fame (and they stopped creating commercials because of Jim's concerns about the characters doing a children's show at the same time they were selling products), the Muppets made an almost unbelievable number of advertising spots for products like Royal Crown Cola, Community Coffee, Wilson's Certified Meats, Purina Dog Chow, Ivory Snow, Gleem toothpaste, La Choy Chow Mein, and IBM.

THE NEXT generation of Muppet commercials gave rise to many characters who would be of considerable importance to the future of the Henson brand of puppetry. The most significant of these would be Rowlf the Dog, but there were others: a monster that devoured a computer in an IBM coffee break spot turned out to be a precursor of *Sesame Street*'s Cookie Monster. The La Choy Dragon, who went berserk in a supermarket in another commercial, was enormously important in being the first full-body Muppet character—a larger than life-size Muppet with a performer inside. This made him the forerunner of many more famous Muppets such as Big Bird.

Making commercials was of significance to Jim and his growing Muppet team in a number of different ways. Commercials supplied income, of course, but they also provided valuable experience and the opportunity to further explore the technical side of puppetry. *Sam and Friends* had been shot live in a television studio, as were most of the Muppets guest shots in the early years. The commercials, on the other hand, were generally made on film, which offered Jim the chance to master a new medium. The resulting experimentation involved everything from the use of new materials to the search, on Don Sahlin's part, for an invisible stitch that would permit a character's head to be sewn together without the seams being visible on screen.

THE LA CHOY DRAGON was a spectacular fire-breathing creature who placed considerable demands upon the skills of the Muppet performers. Here Jim Henson (hidden), Frank Oz, and Jerry Juhl guide the dragon—minus its lower limbs—through a moment of bravura pyrotechnics while Don Sahlin stands ready with the fire extinguisher. With his orange skin and fuchsia scales, the La Choy Dragon is a good example of the way in which Jim and Don, as designer and builder, used the relatively new medium of color television to create even more visually whimsical characters.

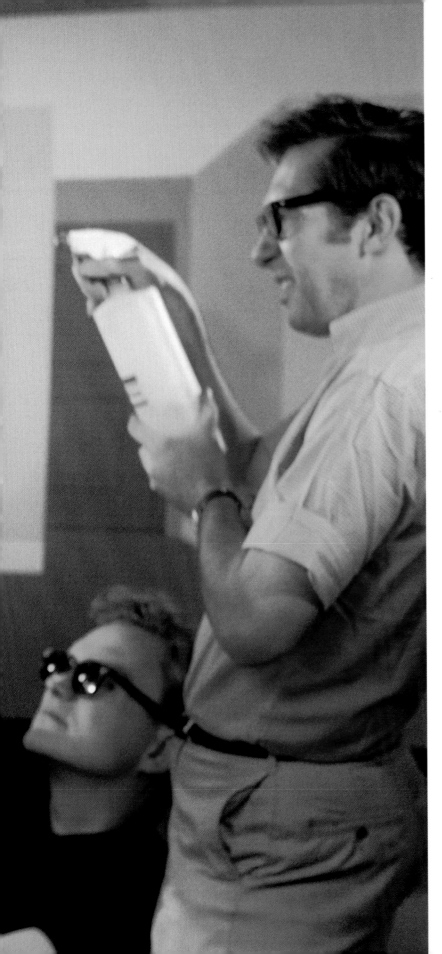

Jim's. This allowed Jim to travel in Europe, and there he discovered the world of traditional puppetry.

Everywhere he went, he looked up puppeteers, and was soon full of admiration for their artistry. The young man who had looked upon puppetry as a "means to an end" was beginning to change his mind. Returning to Washington, he took over the reins of *Sam and Friends* once more. He also set about the task of planning an elaborate European-style production of *Hansel and Gretel* for a live audience, an attempt to work in the classical style that he had seen abroad. The production became—by his own later account—ridiculously overcomplicated, and he ultimately abandoned it.

Bob Payne left *Sam and Friends* soon after Jim's return (he would continue to work intermittently with the Henson workshop team over the years) but remembers clearly how exciting it felt to work with the Muppets at the start. "Jim's philosophy was, 'If we can make it work, we'll use it,'" Bob explains. "He never fell back on stale devices—partly because he didn't know any."

By then, the show was being seen in key time slots in a major market, which led to the Muppets being asked to perform guest spots on network programs such as *The Tonight Show* and *The Today Show*. By then, too, Jim was married and the father of a daughter, Lisa. Lisa was just eight weeks old when she was driven to Detroit, where her parents attended the 1960 Puppeteers of America convention. There they met Burr Tillstrom and other puppetry greats.

Jim was on top of the world. He was a young, successful man with a wife, a child, and a Rolls (albeit a secondhand one), and he had already appeared on network television. So heady was he that he did something alien to his rather shy nature. On a lark, he allowed Burr Tillstrom to drive him down to the center of Detroit while Jim performed Kermit out the top of the car through the sun roof. As Jane recalls, "What with the Rolls and the new baby, we made quite an impression—without particularly intending to."

DON SAHLIN

For more than a decade, Don Sahlin was the Muppets' top designer/builder. He worked very closely with Jim, who remembered his time with Sahlin fondly. "The way Don and I used to work, I would generally do a little scribble on a scrap of paper—which Don would regard with a certain reverence as being the 'essence' which he was working toward. The work was a pleasant cooperative effort during which we would talk about the character and often change it quite a bit....Don had a very simple way of working—reducing all nonessential things and homing in on what was important....[He] had more to do with the basic style that people think of as 'the Muppets' than anybody else.

"I loved the way Don played. Throughout his life he would play—pick up some bit of feathers and attach a long rubber band to it, stretch it down the hall, and release it as you came into the room. Or he'd pose a puppet on the john. He had this sense of playfulness that he actually used, and inspiration would come out of the free-release moments."

Don's playfulness affected everyone—Jim included. Knowing that Jim worked late, Don once set up an elaborate practical joke in their 53rd Street office. If Jim were to open the bathroom door in the middle of the night, the shower curtain would part, revealing a giant, monstrous face. As it turned out, Jim may or may not have used the bathroom that night; he never said a word about Don's prank to anyone.

Among those who noticed were Mike and Frances Oznowicz, parents of Frank Oz and well-known puppeteers in their own right. The following year, when the convention was held in California, the Hensons had the opportunity to see Frank in action.

By now Jane was pregnant with their second daughter, Cheryl, and had decided to retire from performing. Jane had made a major contribution to the evolution of the Muppets. If Jim had been the innovator, Jane had proven herself a gifted performer who helped originate the basic Muppet style. Finding her replacement would not be an easy task.

At the California convention, Jim was tremendously impressed with the Oznowiczes' son. Jim would have hired him on the spot, but Frank was still in high school. Instead Jim signed up another talented California puppeteer and writer, Jerry Juhl, who had acquired valuable television experience performing a children's show on a San Jose station.

Jerry would eventually become a key figure in the Henson organization as head writer for *The Muppet Show* and other projects, but in 1961 he was needed primarily for his performing abilities, filling in for Jane during the last few months of *Sam and Friends'* remarkable run. In all probability the show could have continued for another six or seven years, but Jim Henson—just twenty-six years old—had decided to move on to new goals.

By 1962, the Muppets were virtually regulars on *The Today Show* and frequent guests on other network programs, while becoming increasingly well known for their witty and irreverent commercials.

The frequency of their trips to New York was making it more and more likely that Jim would consider relocating to Manhattan. In April of that year, they participated in the pilot for a proposed network comedy series called *Mad, Mad World*. In June, Jim videotaped an ambitious little puppet drama called *Tales of the Tinkerdee*, the precursor of many future projects. National fame seemed within his grasp and the move to New York had become inevitable.

For a while, the Henson family rented an apartment in the Beekman Place building where Burr Tillstrom lived. With a growing family (Lisa and Cheryl were followed by Brian and John, and eventually by Heather), the Hensons soon needed more space; they bought a house in Greenwich, Connecticut, in January 1964. But the Muppets' business headquarters—two modest rooms and a bathroom—remained in Manhattan, in a building on East 53rd Street. It was there that the team of Jim Henson and Jerry Juhl was expanded to include two more key members: Don Sahlin and, finally, Frank Oz.

Even before he joined the Muppets, Don Sahlin was known as a highly gifted American puppet designer and builder. He would prove to be an invaluable asset to the growing Henson organization.

Toward the end of 1962, Jim called Don in to create Rowlf the Dog, initially built for a Purina Dog Chow commercial. In 1963, Don joined the still tiny Muppet staff on a full-time basis, bringing his own brand of eccentricity to an already zany atmosphere. He liked to frighten people and would, for example, rig detonators to explode in their desks.

Don also excelled at solving technical problems and his mechanical bent carried over into his hobbies, which in turn often fed back into his work. There was no better example of this than the environment for mice Don created a few years later in the New York workshop.

"Bonnie Erickson's [a Muppet designer's] boyfriend worked for Sloan-Kettering Hospital," puppeteer Dave Goelz remembers, "and he would liberate mice every now and then, save them from being experimented on, and give them the dubious advantage of surviving in our shop…they all lived in an aquarium on somebody's desk—on Don's desk, I guess…we had seven at one time and they would all sleep together. It was beautiful to watch.

"Don devised a ride for them, made out of a clear plas-tic sphere with a little hole cut in it that a mouse could climb through. And Don had put lines and pulleys all up and down the ceiling so that he could lower the sphere into the mice's cage, and when one of them would climb into the sphere, he would raise it and pull on another line so that the mouse would go traveling down to somebody else's desk. Then he would lower the sphere and the mouse would get out. It was a regular little tram service.

"Later he created an aerial highway all over the shop. It went to chandeliers—there was one over my desk—and it went up to the top of cupboards, and down to people's desks, so the mice could move around on their own, travel-ing in a Slinky. It was like a mouse freeway."

The style of puppet Don had been best known for was actually quite removed from the typical Muppet as devel-oped by Jim Henson. But Don loved Jim's ideas and dis-played an intuitive gift for interpreting them. The puppets Jim had built for *Sam and Friends* were simple and expres-sive. Don would simplify Muppets still further—almost to the point of abstraction—while somehow making them even more expressive. His singular talents would come to the fore with the puppets he created for *Sesame Street*, but they were amply present from Rowlf onward.

Having graduated from high school, Frank Oz joined the Muppets just six months after Don. This was supposed to be a temporary stay for Frank before college, but he proved so indispensable that any thought of continuing his education was soon discarded. Jerry Juhl continued to per-form, but with Frank's arrival he was able to spend more time on his writing, which would prove to be his real métier.

Frank hadn't performed much with hand puppets, so he had to develop new skills. He trained on the job—work-ing a great deal with Jane Henson, experimenting endlessly with character development, and practicing in front of a mirror to perfect his lip-synch technique. Jim had waited a long time to do voices, and so would Frank—in his case,

THE LETTER "T" SPEAKS WITH A DISTINGUISHED ENGLISH ACCENT

WHEN YOU ASK FOR TEA, MAKE SURE IT'S WILKINS TEA.

THE LETTER "O"

OH?

DRAWN BY JIM HENSON, this storyboard is a typical example of the way an early Muppet commercial was laid out for client approval before

THE LETTER "Y"

WHY?

"T":

BECAUSE WILKINS
TEA IS... (UGH!)
TOPS!
[OTHER LETTERS SLIDE IN]

going in front of the cameras. In those days, Jim would supply all the voices himself and also be responsible for the sound effects.

BUILT for *Tales of the Tinkerdee*, Tamanilla Grinderfall was a striking addition to the Muppet family. Tamanilla was the only character that Jerry Juhl actually performed.

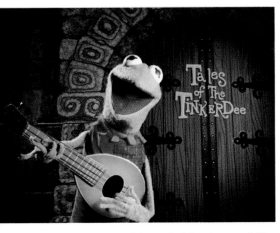

IN THE SUMMER of 1962, the Muppet team traveled to Atlanta to shoot a show called *Tales of the Tinkerdee*. Jerry Juhl, who helped write the script and also performed one of the main characters— Tamanilla Grinderfall— explains that *Tinkerdee* was a children's show. "It was a pilot for a half-hour series we were trying to get onto the networks. Tinkerdee was a fairy tale kingdom and Kermit narrated the story in song. He had a lute (*above*), and you'd see him on little grassy knolls singing the narration we had written in the form of quatrains with god-awful puns and hideous rhymes, which he performed to very sweet, lilting music. That's how we made the transitions from one scene to the next....The whole show was strongly influenced by *Rocky and Bullwinkle*, and it was really just half an hour of one-line jokes. We'd done those kind of gags before, on *Sam and Friends* and when we did guest spots, but this was the first time we'd stretched them to fill thirty minutes."

Tamanilla—or "Tammy," as she was popularly known— was built by Jim.

four years. Soon, though, he was performing characters to a voice track prerecorded by Jim and assisting Jim with characters like Rowlf, who required two puppeteers.

Rowlf would become the first Muppet to be elevated to national stardom when he became a regular on ABC's *The Jimmy Dean Show*, which ran for three seasons, from 1963 to 1966. In every show, Rowlf would do a spot with country & western singer Dean in which they exchanged banter and occasionally sang together. Instead of miming to prerecorded sound tracks, Jim had to learn to interact in character with a live performer. It was an important experience, and Jim had expert teachers in the form of the veteran writers who scripted the show.

"They would work with me in terms of performance and the delivery of punch lines," he later remembered. "Buddy Arnold was an old-fashioned sock-'em joke person, and you can learn a lot from those guys. You learn to put the funniest word at the end of the punch line, and you learn to deliver that line clean and sharp. If you stumble on your phrase, you've killed your laugh and the audience never knows it....So *Jimmy Dean* was great from a point of view of learning the craft, and Rowlf was the first solid, fully rounded personality we did."

Humor had always been Jim's forte, but the wild humor of *Sam and Friends* had been totally spontaneous. With *Jimmy Dean* he learned a more disciplined kind of comedy. One of his greatest strengths was that he was able to blend that kind of discipline into later projects, such as *The Muppet Show*, without ever losing the freshness and spontaneity that made *Sam and Friends* so innovative.

By the time *The Jimmy Dean Show* ended, Rowlf was receiving a huge amount of fan mail, and Jim Henson had attained an enviable position in show business. But guest spots—even permanent ones—and commercials were not enough for Jim and his growing family of puppeteers.

They wanted more.

Rowlf

PSYCHOLOGICAL PROFILE:

The first fully rounded character performed by Jim Henson, the piano-playing Rowlf is wonderfully down-to-earth, with a dry, self-deprecating sense of humor. With his permanently surprised eyes, almost like a pair of fried eggs, Rowlf is a master of the double take. At the same time, his quick-wittedness makes him very believable when he ad-libs or fires off a quirky aside.

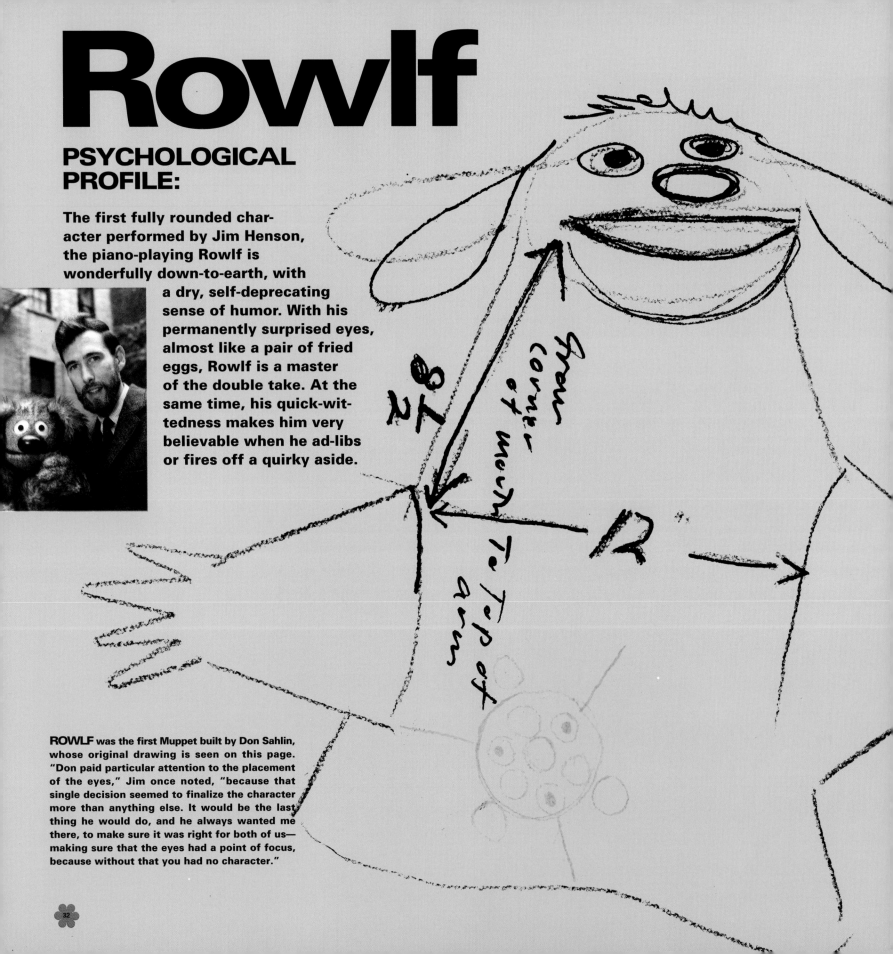

ROWLF was the first Muppet built by Don Sahlin, whose original drawing is seen on this page. "Don paid particular attention to the placement of the eyes," Jim once noted, "because that single decision seemed to finalize the character more than anything else. It would be the last thing he would do, and he always wanted me there, to make sure it was right for both of us— making sure that the eyes had a point of focus, because without that you had no character."

SINCE *The Jimmy Dean Show* required Rowlf to work with the show's live star, special sets had to be built that took their difference of size into account, anticipating the kind of set-building challenge that would be faced at the time of *The Muppet Show*.

Broadcast by ABC from 1963 to 1966, *The Jimmy Dean Show* provided the Muppets, in the person of Rowlf, with their first regular, prime-time exposure. Performed by Jim Henson, usually with the assistance of Frank Oz, Rowlf was featured every week in a seven- or eight-minute segment during which he would chat with the show's star (*above*) about everything from politics to medicine—the tone being folksy in a knowing, Will Rogers kind of way. Rowlf had a way of gently upstaging the star with apparently ad-libbed quips (which were in fact scripted) and with exaggerated facial reactions to his own bad puns. He would also be called upon to sing from time to time, presenting an interesting challenge to Jim who, though musical, did not think of himself as possessing silver vocal cords. On at least one occasion, a special guest star—Lassie—was brought in to interact with Rowlf, who during the run of the show became so popular that eventually he was receiving more fan mail than Jimmy Dean himself. When Dean played Las Vegas, Rowlf was there with him, giving Jim valuable stage experience. In addition, Rowlf's tenure on *The Jimmy Dean Show* gave Jim the opportunity to develop Rowlf's character over a period of time. *Below* are three early sketches of Rowlf drawn by Jim. The one on the *right* obviously won out.

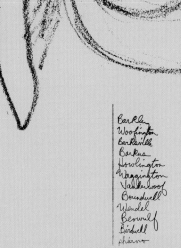

UNLIKE MOST early Muppets, Rowlf was designed as a live hand puppet. The principal performer (Jim), who operated the head and mouth, also "wore" Rowlf's right paw, while an assistant puppeteer had his or her hand in Rowlf's left paw. When Rowlf played the piano—a skill he could perform because of his "live hands"—Jim operated the head while another puppeteer operated both paws. This list of possible names for Rowlf was written by Jim.

IN THE MUPPETS' first New York office, on East 53rd Street, Jim sprawls on a Charles Eames chair in what Jane Henson recalls as "a typical pose." The photograph dates from the mid-sixties.

FRANK OZ

Destined to become Jim Henson's key performing partner and the man who gives life to characters as diverse as Grover, Cookie Monster, Fozzie Bear, and Miss Piggy, Frank Oz arrived in New York in 1963. "It was August. I was nineteen years old, and Jim had asked me to come to work with him part time in New York. I walked up those narrow stairs and opened the door to the Muppets studio—two small rooms, a nook for the secretary, Carol, and a bathroom. Don Sahlin worked in the back workshop next to Jim's animation stand and opposite the big Yorick head that stared down at the people below on East 53rd Street. Jerry Juhl had a desk in the front room next to the Ampex tape machine. Opposite Jerry's desk there was a dart board on the closet door with lots and lots of holes on the door. Above the dart board hung the papier-mâché moose head that would light up. There was a big black chair and ottoman. Jim's chair. He would sit on it or lie in it working on character or script ideas.

"This is the room where Jim, wearing his bright flowered ties and speaking just above a whisper, would hold meetings with clients. This is where Don Sahlin would try his practical jokes. This is where Jim and I and Don and Jerry would hear that Kennedy had been shot. This is where we'd eat the deli sandwiches with those funny-tasting East Coast pickles. For the kid from Oakland, everything here was new and strange and exciting and adult."

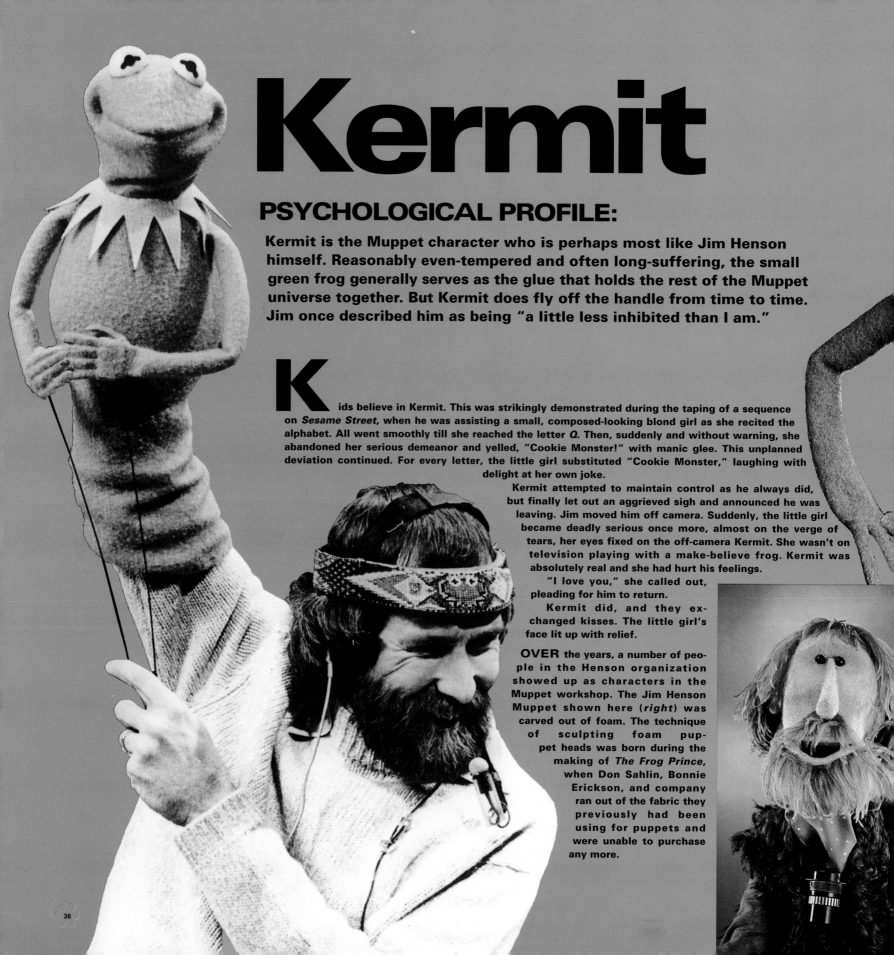

Kermit

PSYCHOLOGICAL PROFILE:

Kermit is the Muppet character who is perhaps most like Jim Henson himself. Reasonably even-tempered and often long-suffering, the small green frog generally serves as the glue that holds the rest of the Muppet universe together. But Kermit does fly off the handle from time to time. Jim once described him as being "a little less inhibited than I am."

Kids believe in Kermit. This was strikingly demonstrated during the taping of a sequence on *Sesame Street*, when he was assisting a small, composed-looking blond girl as she recited the alphabet. All went smoothly till she reached the letter *Q*. Then, suddenly and without warning, she abandoned her serious demeanor and yelled, "Cookie Monster!" with manic glee. This unplanned deviation continued. For every letter, the little girl substituted "Cookie Monster," laughing with delight at her own joke.

Kermit attempted to maintain control as he always did, but finally let out an aggrieved sigh and announced he was leaving. Jim moved him off camera. Suddenly, the little girl became deadly serious once more, almost on the verge of tears, her eyes fixed on the off-camera Kermit. She wasn't on television playing with a make-believe frog. Kermit was absolutely real and she had hurt his feelings.

"I love you," she called out, pleading for him to return.

Kermit did, and they exchanged kisses. The little girl's face lit up with relief.

OVER the years, a number of people in the Henson organization showed up as characters in the Muppet workshop. The Jim Henson Muppet shown here (*right*) was carved out of foam. The technique of sculpting foam puppet heads was born during the making of *The Frog Prince*, when Don Sahlin, Bonnie Erickson, and company ran out of the fabric they previously had been using for puppets and were unable to purchase any more.

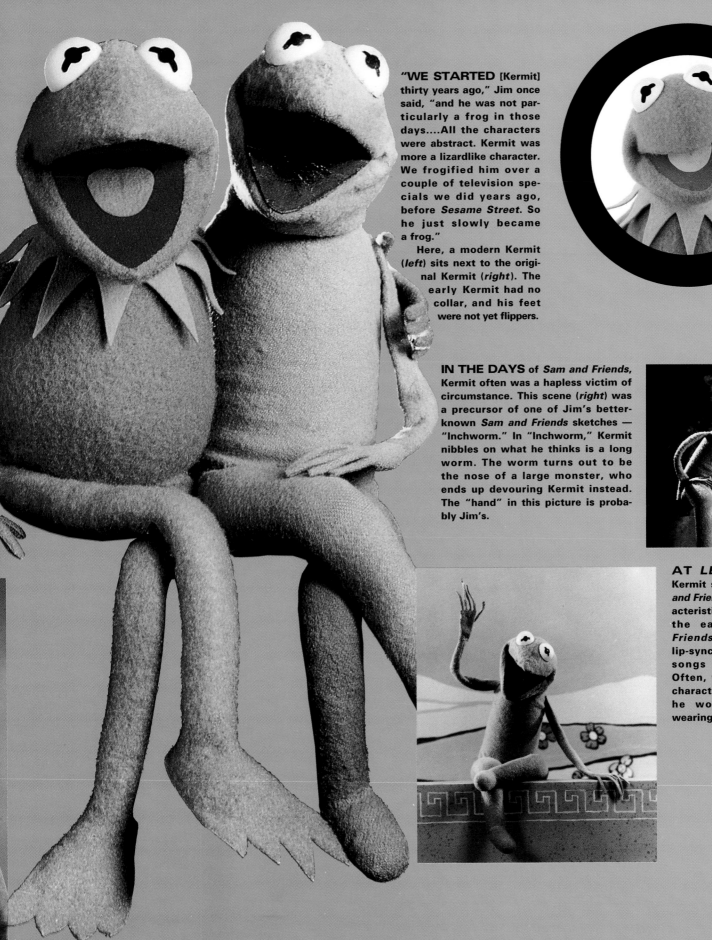

"WE STARTED [Kermit] thirty years ago," Jim once said, "and he was not particularly a frog in those days....All the characters were abstract. Kermit was more a lizardlike character. We frogified him over a couple of television specials we did years ago, before *Sesame Street*. So he just slowly became a frog."

Here, a modern Kermit (*left*) sits next to the original Kermit (*right*). The early Kermit had no collar, and his feet were not yet flippers.

IN THE DAYS of *Sam and Friends*, Kermit often was a hapless victim of circumstance. This scene (*right*) was a precursor of one of Jim's better-known *Sam and Friends* sketches — "Inchworm." In "Inchworm," Kermit nibbles on what he thinks is a long worm. The worm turns out to be the nose of a large monster, who ends up devouring Kermit instead. The "hand" in this picture is probably Jim's.

AT *LEFT*, an early Kermit sits on the *Sam and Friends* set in a characteristic pose. During the early *Sam and Friends* years, Kermit lip-synched to popular songs of the day. Often, when a female character was needed, he would show up wearing a blond wig.

CHAPTER TWO

While Rowlf the Dog was bringing the Muppets into the entertainment mainstream by way of *The Jimmy Dean Show,* Jim Henson was also pursuing a quite different set of goals—goals that would perhaps surprise some of the people who thought of him solely as an entertainer.

In the late fifties, Jim had bought a 16-mm Bolex camera and a secondhand animation stand and had begun to experiment with taking the work he had been creating in his art classes and bringing it to life. "I started painting on a sheet of paper placed under the lens on the bed of the animation stand," he later explained. "I would just paint a couple of strokes and take a frame or two of film, and I would be able to watch this painting evolve and move. From that time on I lost interest in…straight painting as such because the aspect of movement in animation was so much more fascinating."

It was not only animation that intrigued Jim but filmmaking in general. He was already familiar with working in film by the late fifties and early sixties because many of his commercials were shot in that medium. During that time, he also made a number of brief movies in which standard narrative devices were replaced by sequences of images that presented a story in ways that were sometimes surreal, sometimes almost abstract.

"In those days," he once explained, "I used to think in terms of having two careers going—two threads that I was working on at the same time. One was accepted by the audience and was successful, and that was the Muppets. The other was something I was very interested in and enjoyed very

JIM HENSON launching himself into the unknown in a scene from his short film *Timepiece* (1965), which was nominated for an Academy Award.

much, but it didn't have any commercial success—which didn't bother me because I got so much pleasure from working on those noncommercial projects....I thought of myself as an experimental filmmaker back then, and I was interested in the visual image and all [the] different ways of using it."

The first of Jim's major experimental works was *Timepiece*, an ambitious short begun in the spring of 1964, soon after the Henson family had moved to Greenwich. The movie was written, directed, and produced by Jim, who also performed the leading role.

As the title suggests, *Timepiece* is about time. Although its method isn't logical and its message is always oblique, it might be described as a surrealistic fable about man entrapped by time. There are suggestions that the protagonist has perhaps suffered a breakdown as a consequence of his slavery to the time clock, but to describe the movie in such literal terms is to miss the whole point. It is also about dislocations in time, time signatures in the musical sense, time as a philosophical concept, and so on. Even more than that, it is an exercise in orchestrating images for their own sake in an effort to present a purely aesthetic experience that can be compared to a prelude by Chopin or a collage by Picasso.

Jim's approach to making this movie was, in fact, very much like making a collage, except that his disparate images unfold in time rather than being presented simultaneously on a single sheet of paper. The film begins with Jim as a hospital patient, morose in bed, being treated by a physician whom we see only from the back. Jim escapes and undergoes a series of adventures and encounters that are knit together by a steady rhythmic pulse on the sound track. This starts as a heartbeat and is transformed in various ways as the action evolves. At one moment it is the clicking of high heels, at another the sound of a typewriter, at another a drumbeat, and repeatedly the ticking of a clock, so that the

pattern of sound is constantly measuring time in one way or another. Images are cut to this rhythmic undercurrent. Traffic signals change on the beat, characters on pogo sticks bounce to the beat, and all the while the protagonist seems in flight from the realities of time.

He sheds his hospital clothes for leopard skins and swings through the trees like Tarzan. A polite dinner turns into a wild banquet as the protagonist and his wife, now in period clothes, tear ravenously at food in a parody of a famous scene from Tony Richardson's film version of *Tom Jones*. When they continue their meal in a nightclub, the wife is transformed into a stripper. Later the protagonist becomes a Wild West gunslinger who, in a *High Noon* showdown, shoots the Mona Lisa. He is sent to jail, escapes, and, after running through a graveyard, is suddenly catapulted into the air and sprouts pterodactyl-like wings. Eventually he ends up back in the hospital bed and in the final shot the audience learns that patient and doctor are one and the same person.

Of course, this was a Jim Henson film, so the rather bizarre material was handled with a light and almost whim-

IN DECEMBER OF 1964, the Muppets—booked onto *The Jack Paar Show*—were called to NBC Studios in Radio City for a 10 A.M. rehearsal. Because things were running late, however, it turned out that the Muppets weren't needed on the set until 4 P.M.. To pass the time, Jim Henson, Frank Oz, Don Sahlin, and Jerry Juhl turned their attention to a utilities closet in their dressing room. "We opened the door," Jerry recalls, "expecting it to lead somewhere, but instead it was just this shallow closet with a maze of pipes....We had nothing to do, and Don had brought paints because we were performing something that needed touch-ups, so one thing led to another and we started decorating the pipes. It was Jim's idea—a typical Jim idea—and as the whole thing got more elaborate, one of us hopped in a cab and brought more material from the workshop. People at the studio began to hear about this crazy closet and started stopping by, asking if they could take pictures. At some point, late in the afternoon, there was a knock on the door and a voice outside said, 'Hello, I'm Charlton Heston. Could I see your closet?' Since practical jokes weren't unknown in our world, we yelled back, 'Yeah, sure, you're Charlton Heston.' And, of course, it was Charlton Heston."

By air time, Frank Oz remembers, even Jack Paar had heard about the closet and insisted on taking a camera back into the dressing room to show what these "crazy Muppet people" had done. The decorated closet survives to this day.

sical touch; and parts of the movie are very funny indeed. Screened for the first time at the Museum of Modern Art in May of 1965, *Timepiece* enjoyed an eighteen-month run at one Manhattan movie theater and was nominated for an Academy Award (although Frank Oz recalls that Jim voted for another short which he thought was better than his!).

In retrospect, *Timepiece* is significant in that it an-nounced the ambitions that would lead, in the eighties, to movies like *The Dark Crystal* and *Labyrinth*. It was also a demonstration of Jim's sure grasp of the film medium. Propelled by a rapid series of jump cuts that anticipated the kind of editing that would be favored by producers of music videos two decades later, *Timepiece* exemplified a stylistic approach that was emblematic of the sixties.

"Richard Lester did *A Hard Day's Night* at about the same time I was doing *Timepiece* and I just loved what one could do with the montaging of visual images...," Jim once

said. "I was also playing with a flow-of-consciousness form of editing, where one image took you to another image and there was no logic to it but your mind put it together....I've always felt that the visual image is very powerful—music and image together, I guess. Those two things work on one level for me, while the spoken word and dialogue work at a much shallower level."

Among his other roles on *Timepiece*, Jim was his own stunt man, and the flying sequence required him to take a leap from a six-meter diving board into a swimming pool. It

was only after he got up on the high board, Jerry Juhl recalls, that Jim realized he'd never jumped from that kind of height before.

"When he climbed to the top of the ladder, he was suddenly absolutely terrified," Jerry says. "He was in tails or a tuxedo or something like that. It was this whole elaborate setup and he couldn't just say no. So he went ahead and jumped. We never even knew

THIS SPIR-
ITED drawing
was made by
Jim Henson to
decorate the
proposal for a
never-produced
television
special that
would have
costarred the
Muppets and
Tonight Show
host Johnny
Carson.

that he had been scared until it was all over."

"Jim would never have jumped off that diving board on his own," Jane Henson adds. "But he was a lot more courageous where his work was concerned."

Jim's other notable experimental productions of the sixties—*Youth '68* and *The Cube*—were both made for television and aired as segments of an NBC series of occasional specials with the generic title "Experiments in Television." Taped in December of 1967 and aired the following spring, *Youth '68* is a "collage" documentary that attempts to present a picture of American youth in the period between the first Haight-Ashbury "Summer of Love" and the catharsis of the Woodstock Festival. Fast-moving and underscored with rock music, it has the same kind of kinetic energy as *Timepiece*, even though the reality-based subject matter is very different.

The Cube was a more ambitious production. An avant-garde television drama written by Jerry Juhl and Jim and directed by Jim, it was produced and aired in 1969 (though it had been conceived three years earlier). Jerry remembers it as one of a number of projects the pair of them collaborated on during the period.

"Jim and I periodically worked on movie ideas. Sometimes we got a story idea, not knowing if it was for a television special or a feature. We did treatments for a number of things, several of which were in the general fantasy genre that showed up much later in Jim's treatment for *The Dark Crystal*....I can't remember the genesis of *The Cube*, but I know the inspiration for the piece was Jim's. It was definitely his kind of project....We worked out plot and character together, and we collaborated on some scenes, but some I'd write and pass to him, and some he'd write and pass to me. Then we'd sit down and work together again.

"[Jim's] inspiration for *The Cube*," Jerry continues, "came more from exploring the possibilities of television.... We were just reaching the point with videotape editing

where you could play with it and get novel results, though the equipment was crude by today's standards. It was really a matter of shooting film-style on videotape, but the possibilities seemed exciting to us, and especially to Jim."

The Cube is a stripped-down absurdist exercise in which, for reasons the audience is not made privy to, an un-named man (played by Richard Schaal) has been imprisoned in a pristine white, completely symmetrical room (the cube of the title). For all intents and purposes he is sealed in this room—unable to leave—even though dozens of other characters can get in and out without difficulty. During the course of the film, he is pestered by a variety of unhelpful characters, including a woman who claims to be his wife, a sinister hotel manager, an interior decorator (who wants to turn the cube into a showpiece), a handyman, and various doctors and scientists. At one point a cocktail party invades the cubicle, but the "prisoner" is cut off from it by an invisible barrier. Nothing is what it seems. A woman turns out to be a man and when, at the end, the prisoner

thinks he has finally returned to reality, he cuts himself and bleeds strawberry jam.

Like *Timepiece*, *The Cube* is leavened with humor but, also like *Timepiece*, it gives notice of Jim's "serious" side, which would reappear in the eighties. In fact this serious side disappeared only from the point of view of public exposure. There were always serious projects on the back burner, but they were eclipsed for a decade and more by the success of the Muppets. And because Jim was always so enthusiastically preoccupied with whatever he was working on at the time, some of his ideas would simply become submerged for a while, only to reappear later, as Jerry Juhl remembers.

"I was in London in 1985 while Jim was shooting *Labyrinth*. I walked out onto this giant soundstage and there was this huge set—the M. C. Escher maze used at the climax of the movie. Jim came down from a ladder and I re-

minded him that we had talked about using an Escher maze in a proposal we had worked on twenty years earlier. He had absolutely no recollection of it. We actually went back and found the treatment, but he still didn't remember. The idea had just sort of percolated into his subconscious and reemerged years later. That was so typical of Jim. He always said he didn't have a good memory, but in fact he always hung on to useful ideas until they were needed."

Jim's most unexpected project of the sixties had nothing to do with either puppets or television. This was Cyclia, intended as a three-dimensional *son et lumière* environment in which music, projected film imagery, and special effects were to be combined to create a new kind of aesthetic experience. For economic reasons (and because he thought it would be fun) Jim conceived of presenting this new experience in the form of a nightclub that, if it had been realized, would have been a spectacular forerunner of the multimedia discos of the late seventies and eighties.

"The idea began," Jane Henson recalls, "during the first wave of psychedelia. Jim went to see Jefferson Airplane and was very intrigued with it—the light shows and the psychedelic graphics. His idea was for an environment with multiple screens. Images would be projected onto the screens, and the screens themselves would be somewhat organic, so as to transform the images. There would be images projected onto bodies, too—dancers in white costumes—and strobe lights and music. And Jim had also planned a transparent floor that would be in different layers and would be programmed to pulsate in time with the music. That's been done since, of course, but at the time it was a new idea."

Jim Henson's diaries reveal that he was shooting film for Cyclia as early as October of 1966, and in February of the following year he talked to the management of the El Morocco club in New York about the possibility of installing Cyclia there. Nothing came of that or of other plans for Cyclia, but still Jim and his team continued to prepare for

IN *THE MUPPET MUSICIANS OF BREMEN,* Bremen is a hamlet in Louisiana, rather than a city in Germany. This gave Jim the opportunity to draw on his memories of his Mississippi boyhood.

ORIGINALLY BUILT for *Tales of the Tinkerdee,* Tamanilla Grinderfall (*below* and *right*) returned to play a major role in *The Frog Prince,* one of several fairy tales turned inside-out by the Muppets. In these lighthearted spoofs, tradition was tossed aside in favor of wisecracks and anachronisms.

the day it might open. "I shot thousands and thousands of feet of sixteen-millimeter film for Cyclia," Frank Oz recalls. "There were supposed to be sixteen projectors, so we would have needed a tremendous amount of material. Jim would take me down to the Village, and we'd look in on these little discos to see what was happening. Then I'd go out and shoot more film. Jim actually asked me to be his film editor. I didn't know film at all at that time, but he taught me and encouraged me—convinced me I could do it. It's where I got the first experience that enabled me to become a movie director."

"When you didn't have anything else to do," Jerry Juhl remembers, "you'd grab this old Bolex and go out and shoot something. If it had been raining, Frank and I might drive over to New Jersey to shoot reflections in wet streets. Then we would take a piece of music and stay up all night editing to it. At one point, Jerry Nelson [another of the principal puppeteers] and I experimented with projecting images onto smoke produced with dry ice. It worked

pretty well, but we realized it wouldn't be very practical in a club setting."

In part Cyclia was a product of Jim Henson's restless imagination, and of his ability to reflect the mood of the times. But it also grew out of his dissatisfaction with the opportunities that were being offered him as a puppeteer.

"Except for *Jimmy Dean*," Jane Henson explains, "there were just commercials and guest spots on other people's shows, and in the end these were frustrating because they provided no opportunity for character development.... The Muppets were pretty well liked by then. All of the big shows were ready to at least listen to our ideas, and when they had an opening they'd put us on. But nobody was prepared to give the Muppets a show of their own, and Jim began to feel maybe he should be looking in another direction."

In practice, the Muppets had taken on a momentum that had become almost independent of Jim Henson. Their frequent guest appearances on programs such as *The Ed*

ONE OF THE OUTCOMES of the Muppets' frequent guest spots on *The Ed Sullivan Show* was their involvement in a Christmas special—*The Great Santa Claus Switch*—produced by Ed Sullivan's company and aired in 1970. In the picture *below*, the indefatigable maestro of the Sunday night variety show is dwarfed by Thog, one of the largest Muppets ever built.

THE MUPPET fairy tales mixed humans and puppets indiscriminately. In *Hey Cinderella!*, for example, the King was represented by a puppet while his son and heir—Prince Arthur Charlie—was played by human actor Robin Ward (*above*).

SPLURGE—a giant, full-body character from *Hey Cinderella!* who loves radishes. This purple, shaggy monster is one of the forerunners of full-body Muppet characters like Big Bird and Thog.

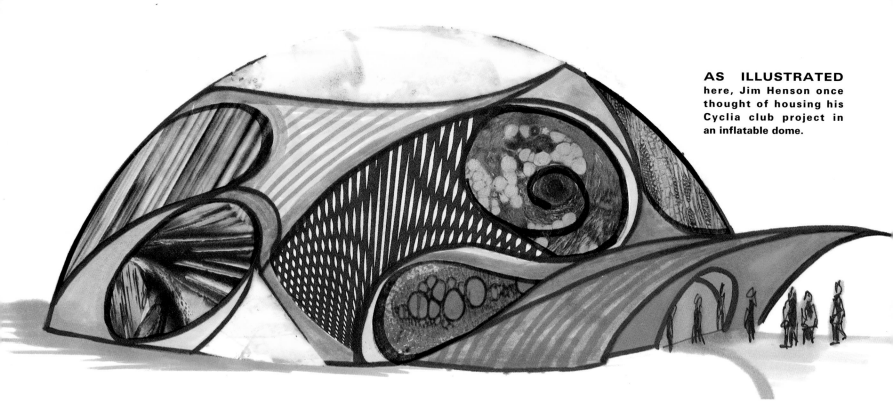

AS ILLUSTRATED here, Jim Henson once thought of housing his Cyclia club project in an inflatable dome.

AMONG THE LEAST KNOWN of Jim Henson's projects are two innovative television shows, *Youth '68* and *The Cube*—broadcast by NBC television in 1968 and 1969, respectively—and Cyclia, an experimental discothèque/nightclub that occupied a good deal of Jim's creative energy during the 1960s.

Youth '68 was an ambitious attempt to use the documentary form to present an impressionistic image of young America at a moment when a revolution in everything from music to clothes to political attitudes was spreading through a whole generation. Hippies, radicals, and straight-looking college students were given the chance to speak for themselves. So were their elders. Both sides came out with the expected clichés and with a few words of wisdom. This was interspersed with "psychedelic" footage and with glimpses of young Americans— from draftees to rock stars—in a variety of settings. With Bob Dylan and The Who on the sound track, the show progressed in a series of jump cuts that lent it a kinetic excitement.

The Cube (black and white photo and *collage)* was an avant-garde drama

THE CUBE

written by Jim and Jerry Juhl and directed by Jim. The cube of the title refers to a white cubicle in which a nameless man has been imprisoned. It slowly becomes apparent that he is perhaps imprisoned not in an actual cube at all, but in his own mind—that the cube is, in fact, himself. The show has something of the same mood as the absurdist comedies of Eugène Ionesco with a dash of *The Twilight Zone* thrown in for good measure.

As for Cyclia (*color illustrations*), this was very much a product of the psychedelic era, but it was conceived on a grand scale and in many ways looked forward to the multimedia discos of the eighties and to the era of MTV videos. Jim's concept included the use of multiple projectors and screens that would permit the creation of an elaborate visual environment of shifting images. Thousands of feet of film were shot to this end, but Cyclia was never realized. Cyclia Enterprises—incorporated in 1967—was abandoned in 1970. All that survives today are some notes, a few reels of film, and the Jim Henson sketches reproduced here.

Sullivan Show caught the attention of Jon Stone and Tom Whedon, two young writer-producers who in 1964 sold a pilot to ABC for what was intended to be a weekly, Saturday-morning children's show.

"The idea," explained Jon, "was to tell the story of *Cinderella* over six months with a cliffhanger at the end of each show. These cliffhangers would depend on the fact that everybody knows the story so that, for instance, Cinderella runs from the ball and as she descends the marble steps you hear this crunch of breaking glass. Then next week you pick up the story from that point, like the old movie serials.

"Tom and I had seen the Muppets, and we'd met Jim but never worked with him. The pilot was conceived with the Muppets in mind—live actors and Muppets, and also in-between characters who were part human, part animated mask."

The Muppets were engaged and the pilot shot in October of 1965. ABC did not schedule the series, but Jim had seen potential in the idea of taking a fairy story and giving it a modern twist, and a couple of years later he managed to revive the idea in the form of a one-hour special, which was shot in Toronto in 1968 and shown on ABC in 1970.

Modified by Jon Stone and Tom Whedon from their original pilot, with music by Joe Raposo, and directed by Jim, *Hey Cinderella!* is by far the most ambitious Muppet production of the period. It retells the famous story in period costume but with scores of deliberate anachronisms, especially in Stone and Whedon's clever dialogue. The most remarkable thing about the production, however, is the way in which it combines Muppets and human actors. Cinderella herself is human. Her two stepsisters, on the other hand, are puppets. Musicians at the palace ball are humans with Muppet heads, while Cinderella's dog, Rufus, is a Muppet at times but in at least one scene is represented by a real dog.

Kermit is present as a mildly cynical commentator on the action who is pressed into service as Cinderella's coachman. He is aided and abetted by Splurge, a hulking creature and one of the first of the Muppet full-body characters.

Thanks to the fractured logic of the script and to good performances and production values, the show was enough of a success that it led directly to two other Toronto-produced fairy tales that went under the heading of *Tales from Muppetland—The Frog Prince* and *The Muppet Musicians of Bremen. The Frog Prince*, which for the first time featured Kermit as a frog, was very much in the same idiom as *Hey Cinderella! The Muppet Musicians of Bremen* was somewhat different in that it totally ignored the usual fairy tale setting and instead transformed Bremen into a hamlet in the Louisiana bayous where a quartet of downtrodden barnyard animals triumphed over evil and got to play some pretty good Dixieland music.

The show was different from either of its predecessors in other respects as well. Its setting was far less derivative and the characters were distinctly original rather than comic glosses on traditional fairy tale types. The biggest technical success of the show was using soft foam puppet heads in conjunction with human actors to represent the villains. The heads were made by Bonnie Erickson, who had been hired by the Henson organization as a free-lance costume designer during *The Frog Prince*. So flexible and convincing were these heads that Dick Smith, the dean of special effects makeup artists, was certain that the Muppet team had learned some new makeup trick and called Jim to congratulate him.

By the time these shows were broadcast, however, the Henson team—and Jon Stone and Joe Raposo too—had gone on to something else. This new venture would become one of the most significant television series of all time and make the Muppets famous around the world.

THE NUMBER 3 (*right*) is from a counting series designed and animated by Jim Henson for *Sesame Street*.

REEL #-VTR1-4562 VTR2-7819

| SHOW. | ITEM: | TAKE: |

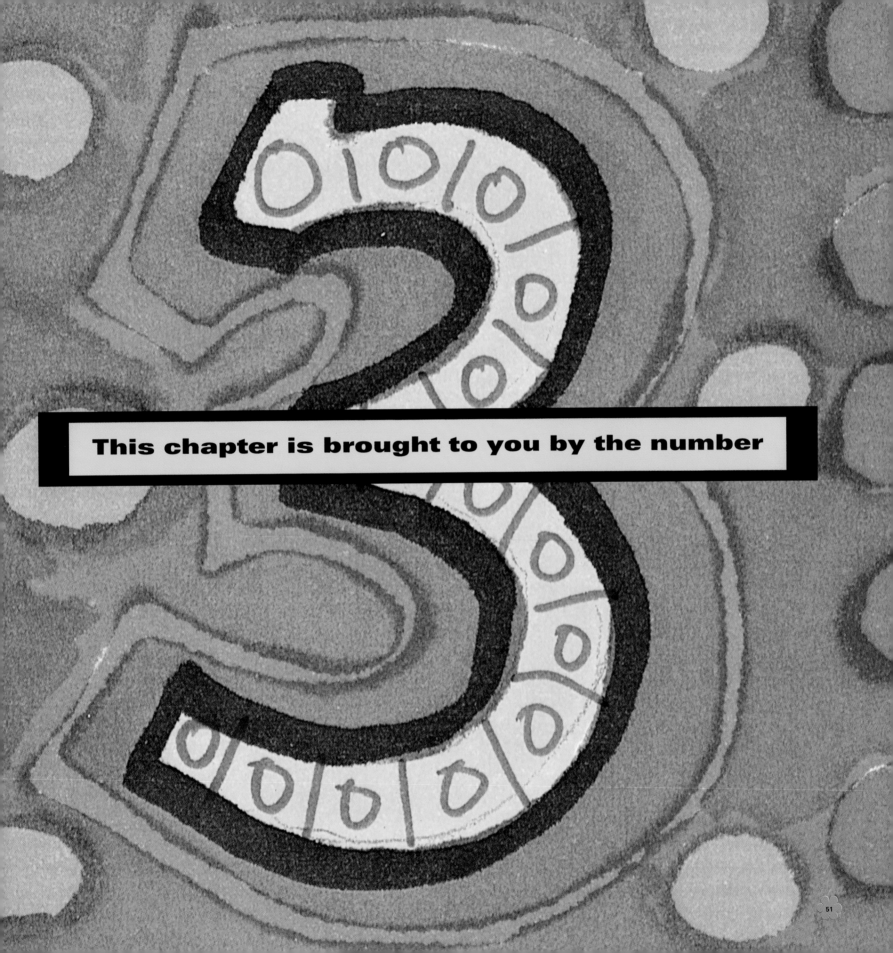

This chapter is brought to you by the number

In 1966, while *The Jimmy Dean Show* was in its final season, the Carnegie Institute initiated a study of children's television that paid particular attention to how the medium could be used to reach out to underprivileged inner-city youngsters. Heading up the study was Joan Ganz Cooney, on leave of absence from her position as a producer of news and documentaries at WNET, New York's public television station. She had been chosen for the job precisely because she was not a professional educator, though she did have a bachelor's degree in education.

Joan Cooney found that almost all of the fare then being offered to children on television was condescending and vacuous. She proposed that public television supply something more substantial. The result, after a period of fund-raising, was the establishment of the Children's Television Workshop (CTW), which in 1968 began to assemble a team of people to produce an as-yet-unnamed show for preschoolers. Among those hired was Jon Stone, who—along with Dave Connell and Sam Gibbon—would be one of three producers of the show.

As the show began to take form, a series of three-day seminars was held in Boston at which educators and other experts presented their views. It was at those seminars that Joan Cooney met Jim Henson.

Cooney had first become aware of Jim Henson a couple of years earlier when a friend had taken her to see a screening of Muppet commercials. She found them hilariously funny but had forgotten about them until Jim's name was brought up in connection with what was then still called *The Preschool Educational Television Show*. The basic proposal mentioned puppets as a possible ingredient of the show, and it was Jon Stone who suggested the Muppets.

WHEN *SESAME STREET* WAS LAUNCHED, in November 1969, it brought to the world a radically new concept of children's programming and a whole new gang of Muppets. Shown here is a 1983 photograph of Big Bird flanked by various *Sesame Street* Muppets, among them Oscar the Grouch, Cookie Monster, Ernie, Bert, the Count von Count, Sherlock Hemlock, and Grover.

JOAN GANZ COONEY began to look at children's television under the auspices of the Carnegie Institute. She found herself appalled by the lack of worthwhile programming. Her study led directly to the formation of the Children's Television Workshop and the production of *Sesame Street*. She first met Jim Henson at a seminar about the show.

"This was during the period of the Weathermen. There had been bombings and so on, and we knew there were some people who didn't like what we were doing. I was sitting up front with some CTW people, and this man came in, dressed in what appeared to me to be hippie clothes with a hippie beard....He walked into the back of the room and sat there, ramrod straight, just staring ahead, rows and rows from the rest of us. I whispered to Dave Connell, 'How do we know that man isn't going to kill us?'

"'It isn't very likely,' Dave said. 'That's Jim Henson.'"

"I asked Jon," says Cooney, "who we should talk to if Jim Henson wasn't available. He said that if that was the case then we would make do without puppets. That's how strongly he and the other producers felt about it."

In fact, Jim was not quick to accept the invitation. His work at that point—*Timepiece*, *The Cube*, his commercials—was more adult. In all probability he had doubts about becoming involved with a children's show, even though Cooney's proposal emphasized the need to entertain adults as well as kids. His final decision, Cooney believes, may have been influenced by the events of the day.

"It was at this time that Martin Luther King and Robert Kennedy were killed, and I think that affected many people, including Jim. There was a feeling in the air that something had to be done, and while the show was not aimed solely at poor children or inner-city children, they were the bull's-eye of the target....I don't think Jim was particularly involved with social issues—we never discussed them—but like others who came aboard at that period, he was certainly responding to the prevailing social climate."

According to Jane Henson, her husband had some additional reasons for becoming part of the project.

"Jim agreed to do *Sesame Street* because it gave him the opportunity to work on a wide variety of things—puppetry, animation—and also because of our children. It was through them that he had begun to realize that children could be a very sophisticated audience."

Through Jon Stone, Jim finally indicated that he was disposed to joining the project, and it was this that brought him an invitation to the Boston seminar. Soon he was working enthusiastically with Jon Stone and the other producers—and with Joe Raposo, who had been appointed musical director—developing ideas and characters for the show. His efforts were primarily directed toward the puppet segments, of course, but the producers also tapped his filmmaking talents to devise animated and live-action sequences.

By the time the pilot was ready for taping, in July of 1969, there was still no name for the show. The situation was so desperate, in fact, that Jon Stone had to write a special Muppet sketch to be performed at the news conference announcing the show—a sketch making fun of the difficulties everyone was experiencing with the search for a title.

In a set designed to look like a network boardroom, Muppets were seated at a long conference table.

"It's a show for kids," said one Muppet, "so why don't we call it *The Kiddie Show*?"

"Too vague," argued another. "This is a show for very small preschoolers, so why don't we call it *The Little Kiddie Show*?"

"Still pretty vague," protested a third. "How about *The Itty-Bitty Little Kiddie Show?*"

"But we want to reach inner-city children," another Muppet chimed in. "Let's call it *The Inner-City, Itty-Bitty Little Kiddie Show.*"

At the last moment, someone—nobody seems to remember quite who—came up with the name *Sesame Street*. Jon Stone thought kids would find the name unpronounceable.

"It goes against everything we're trying to do," he argued. "'Sesame' is a problem word for kids. It doesn't sound the way it looks, and no preschooler is going to get the connection between *Sesame Street* and 'Open Sesame.'"

"Luckily," he says now, "I was outvoted, for which I'm deeply grateful."

Few people would argue with the proposition that *Sesame Street* is the most important children's program in the history of television. The basic premise, proposed by Joan Ganz Cooney, was to create a show that would capitalize on the fact that children were known to love the pace and wit of television commercials, with their slick editing and those jingles that stick in the mind. Why not, Cooney reasoned, use those same techniques to sell learning? Why not create sixty-second video bites that would teach preschoolers to count to ten or jingles that would help them learn the alphabet? The show could even be sponsored by letters and numbers. ("This episode of *Sesame Street* is brought to you by the letters *X* and *Z* and by the number *three*.")

"I wanted a hip, *Laugh-In* type of a show," Cooney explains, "with humor that children would get something out of but that adults and older siblings would enjoy too. I said in my study that *Alice in Wonderland* and all great children's literature is built on several levels, and we would do the same with this program. I also said that we would have four hosts. In that way we could have men and women, blacks, whites, and Hispanics, and we wouldn't get into a situation where a single host could hold us hostage. Then we would

JON STONE—the first head writer for *Sesame Street* and one of the show's principal directors and producers for over twenty-four years—first introduced the Muppets to Joan Ganz Cooney.

"Jim and Jane used to bring the kids to our home in Vermont from time to time, and on one of those occasions, Jim decided to give skiing a try. So we took him over to Stratton Mountain and got him outfitted, and I walked him over to the bunny hill. Later, Jim became an accomplished skier, applying himself to the task with his characteristic determination; but this morning, like every other first-day skier, he spent a lot of time on his backside (and frontside) until he was absolutely covered with snow. It was all over his clothes, in his beard, in his hair; and it's this image that sticks in my memory: this skinny snowman coming at me down that gentle little hill, standing straight up, arms straight out to the sides, poles dangling. I remember telling him he looked like Christ of the Andes, and we both sat down in the snow, laughing. I don't know why we thought it was so funny, but it was."

JOE RAPOSO was another key member of *Sesame Street*'s core group, the show's resident composer. He supplied Jim Henson (in the person of Kermit) with such hit songs as "Bein' Green." Once, Joe described a song he was writing to a *New York Times* reporter as follows: "I want to describe the promise of every morning and the curiosity and hope in every child's face. I would like to think that this theme of hope and wonder is at the root of all my work."

Big Bird

PSYCHOLOGICAL PROFILE:

Charming, loving, stubborn, and intensely curious, the perennially six-year-old Big Bird is a lot like the preschooler watching at home. He doesn't always understand things right away, and when an explanation is offered, he tends to get the wrong end of the stick. This makes more explanations necessary, until finally, he does grasp the point of whatever is under discussion—as does his preschool counterpart.

← eyes blink

7½ ft.

CONCEIVED BY Jim Henson (whose drawings for the character are seen here and on the opposite page) and built by Kermit Love with a head by Don Sahlin, Big Bird is one of the most extraordinary of the *Sesame Street* Muppets. Standing 8'2", he can skate and perform many other feats in which preschoolers take pride.

Preparing to perform, Caroll Spinney first puts on Big Bird's legs and then the basic body costume, which extends from thigh to chin. The neck and head are fitted at the last minute; Caroll sees through a scrim in the neck concealed by feathers. (He sometimes also wears a small video monitor strapped to his chest.) He controls Big Bird's head and mouth movements by placing one hand high above his head in the puppet "skull."

The fact that Big Bird works so well is due in large part to the artistry of Kermit Love, who accepted the challenge of building the 8'2" canary. Love had had extensive experience with puppets as well as with costume design in the legitimate theater when he met Jim Henson in the mid-sixties. "Don Sahlin, with whom I'd worked extensively, said 'You really ought to come and meet Jim Henson. He's very different from you but I think you'll like him. He doesn't have much theater background but he has a lot of experience in video.' So Jim and I had a lovely lunch and I discovered that it was true that we didn't have much in common except, strangely enough, a rapport by nature. Jim asked me to work on a character—the La Choy Dragon—he'd developed. It was kind of theatrical in scale, and once I got involved with that it was easy to go on to other things."

Among these "other things" was Big Bird. "When Big Bird was being developed," Love says, "I kept the image of Jim Henson in mind. I always thought of Jim's stature—he was well over six feet tall—and that loping gait he had when he walked down a hallway. Somehow or other that was what stuck in my mind. And I even envisioned, at first, the person who would perform Big Bird walking backward, so that his knees would bend backward, the way a bird's knees bend. But then I thought, 'That's silly, we're not really creating a bird, we're creating a puppet, so there's really no need to have him walk backward.'"

Caroll Spinney has been with *Sesame Street* from the beginning and performs both Big Bird and Oscar the Grouch.

"I first met Jim Henson at a puppet festival in Sturbridge, Massachusetts, in the summer of 1962. He did a wonderful show of his early, bizarre stuff. It was the best puppet show I had ever seen. I also did my own little show and afterwards, he suggested I come down to New York to 'talk about' the Muppets.

"I never got around to that, but in August of 1969 Jim was in the audience at the Puppeteers of America Festival in Salt Lake. Everything went wrong with my big show, a program that combined puppetry and animation in one theater—[an attempt] to meld the two mediums. After the show, Jim came backstage and said to me, 'I liked what you were trying to do!' Then he said, 'Why don't you come to New York and talk about the Muppets?' That sounded familiar somehow, only this time I asked him what he meant! 'Talk about joining the Muppets,' he explained.

"And so, only a month later, I joined the Muppets and Jim gave me the great privilege of playing Big Bird and Oscar the Grouch."

CAROLL SPINNEY

Jerry Nelson was performing on the radio at nine years of age and later became a puppeteer with Bil and Cora Baird. He worked with the Muppets on an occasional basis from the mid-sixties, becoming a full-time member of the team with the advent of *Sesame Street.*

"The angriest I've ever seen Jim—and I only saw him angry twice in the twenty-something years I knew him—was while we were doing *The Muppet Show.* We used to come in on Sunday mornings to read the script. Then we'd have music rehearsals, and then we'd go look at the sets, and talk about any problems we might have. This particular Sunday, we came in and read the show and there was not one thing [in the script] for me. I just sat there...I didn't read a line. I was very, very upset by this; I was hurt that they hadn't given me one thing to do, and that they had made me come in and sit through the whole read-through. So at the end of it, I very theatrically stood up, walked over to the trash can, dropped the script in it, and walked out.

"Later, Jim called me into his office and said, quietly, 'Don't you ever do that again.' This was the angriest I've ever seen him. Of course, he was right. If I had needed to make that statement, I could have made it to him privately. And it was interesting. Jim himself would never have upbraided me or talked strongly to me while everyone was around. He did it privately...like I should have. Jim was like a Zen master that way...he taught by example."

JERRY NELSON

Richard Hunt—who joined the *Sesame Street* troupe in 1970—quickly proved himself to be a versatile performer with strong musical and vocal talents. Jane Hunt, Richard's mother, remembers exactly how Richard reacted when he first auditioned for Jim.

"Richard had come into New York to see Gus Allegretti, who performed the Mr. Moose and Bunny Rabbit characters on *The Captain Kangaroo Show.* Gus knew the family, and he was one of the reasons that Richard had gotten interested in puppets. Plus, people had been giving Richard puppets all his life, and by the time he was in high school, Richard was doing puppet shows for all my friends' children. So Richard decided he'd ask Gus for a job.

RICHARD HUNT
1951–1992

"When Richard spoke to Gus that day, it turned out that Gus couldn't use him. But Richard had been watching *Sesame Street,* and he realized there might be an opportunity there. So he went to a phone booth, called Henson Associates, and asked them, cold, if they were hiring puppeteers.

"Amazingly, Jim was auditioning people that very day. So Richard went right over to 67th Street. He was ushered into a room, and there were Frank and Jim and Jerry [Nelson] and a box full of puppets. 'They threw a puppet at me and said sit down,' Richard later reported to me. 'It was incredible. We just all talked together! We knew right away we had the same sense of humor....And I think they liked me!...' "

have the animation pieces and the puppet pieces, and that was the basic skeleton of the show."

Sesame Street was to be a truly integrated neighborhood with not only black, white, and Hispanic residents but also more bizarre denizens who seldom show up on census forms. Children would encounter familiar human characters, but also creatures such as they might fantasize about in their wilder flights of imagination.

Jim Henson produced some delightful animated sequences for *Sesame Street*—especially some of the segments he designed to reinforce preschoolers' grasp of numbers—but it was with Big Bird, Oscar the Grouch, Ernie, Bert, Cookie Monster, Grover, Prairie Dawn, Snuffleupagus, Biff and Sully, Don Music, Guy Smiley, Elmo, and the rest that his contribution, and that of his team, became invaluable.

Some of these characters were planned, but Jon Stone

recalls that others emerged quite by accident.

"Cookie Monster grew out of a game-show sketch we had no ending for," he remembers. "Cookie himself was a trunk puppet—a general-purpose monster with no character assigned to him—but we used him in that sketch, and when Frank brought him to life we realized we had something."

Bert and Ernie had a more complex evolution. Joan Cooney remembers that an educational advisor at one of the early seminars had suggested that it would be nice to have a child on the show who got the best of adults. This idea was judged to be politically unacceptable, but it was discussed. Cooney believes that Bert and Ernie evolved out of that concept, with Bert standing in for the stodgy adult figure and Ernie taking on the role of the cocky kid.

In developing characters like Bert and Ernie, Jim and his team were always working within the guidelines set down by CTW's panel of educational advisors, who had provided a curriculum for the series. But Jim and the other performers had the freedom to bring that curriculum to life.

"Often," Jim recalled later, "the material we were given was kind of dry, but Frank and I would play with it and improvise and bring in gags till it worked for us. Sometimes you can make a line funny just by having your character do a double take. But always we did this while staying true to the spirit of what we had been given in the first place...."

Soon, Jim was wholly immersed in *Sesame Street*. "I put aside a few other areas I'd been working on," he said once, "because at that point it was as if the audience wanted *Sesame Street* and it was what I should be putting my time and energy into. Since the beginning, the Muppets have had a sort of life of their own and we—the people who work with them—serve that life, and the audience, and the characters. It's something I don't particularly dictate at all."

When *Sesame Street* premiered on November 10, 1969, one of the Muppets who played a prominent role was Kermit, now definitely a frog, though with a propensity to

FRAN BRILL joined the *Sesame Street* performing staff in 1970. She was the first female puppeteer to work with the Muppets since Jane Henson's retirement almost ten years earlier.

"One of the extraordinary things about Jim was that he was a perpetual student of life. Genius that he was, he was always searching, questioning, exploring. When I first met Jim, in the early years of *Sesame Street*, he was reading the *Seth* books, going to psychics and palm-readers, experiencing transcendental meditation, doing est—whatever was out there. He was judgmental about nothing—open to almost everything. I think he felt that all these 'journeys' were the means to the same end—raising his level of consciousness, deepening his understanding of how all things on earth were related one to another, that every action had a reaction. He told me that for him there was not one right way, but that he took a little something from all of them."

dress up in a variety of costumes. Along with Kermit, Bert and Ernie, and Cookie Monster, the Muppets from the show's first period included Guy Smiley, Grover, the Count von Count, Oscar the Grouch, and Big Bird.

An important factor in the evolution of this range of characters was the fact that Frank Oz had recently been persuaded to be heard. His vocal talents provide the memorable voices for Bert, Grover, and Cookie, among others.

"I had been very self-effacing," Frank says. "In fact, I was just plain scared to do voices. Then a situation came up on the old Al Hirt television series where I finally *had* to do voices. That was just a few months before we started work on *Sesame Street* and I was still pretty insecure with voices when *Sesame Street* began—*very* insecure—but it was a great opportunity for me to blossom, and gradually I got better....The voices were pretty much set from the beginning, but I can easily hear the difference between one of my early *Sesame Street* performances and a later performance of the same character. I can hear that in the early performance I'm

(continued on page 69)

Bert & Ernie

PSYCHOLOGICAL PROFILE:

Ernie is a tease. If Bert wants to sleep, Ernie wants the light on in order to read. Ernie also has a highly developed poetic streak that sometimes confounds his roommate. Who else could have made a hit song out of "Rubber Duckie"?

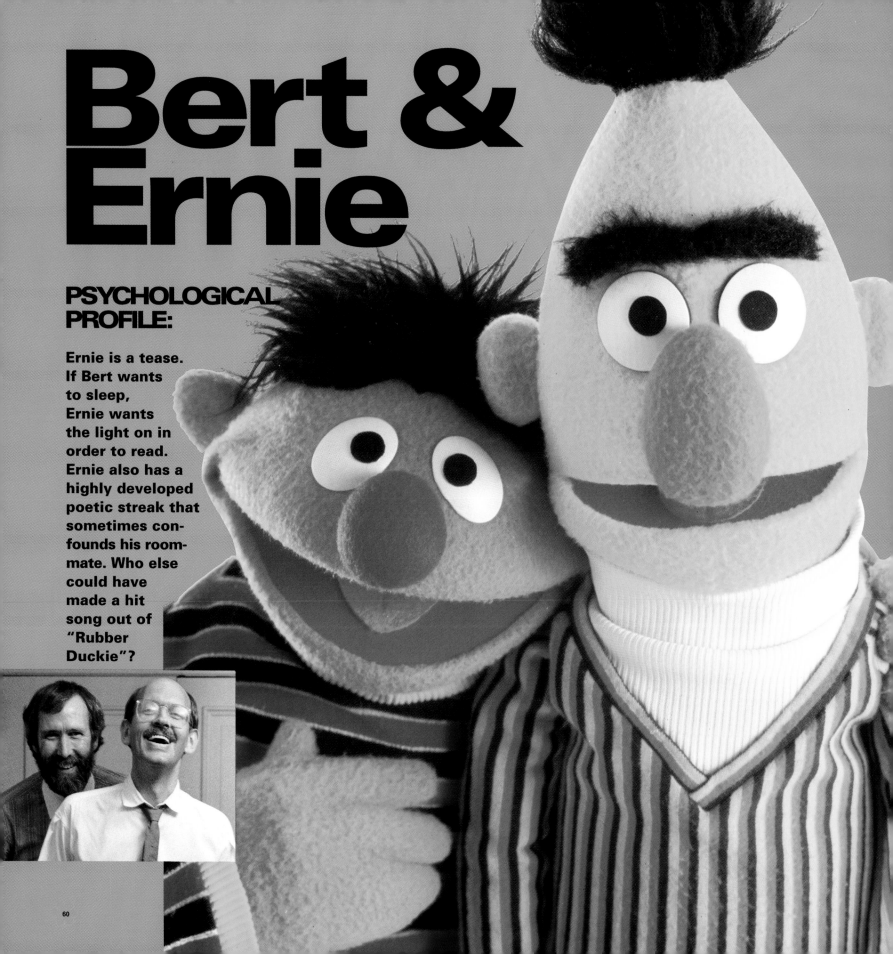

PSYCHOLOGICAL PROFILE:

If Ernie (right) is poetic, Bert is resolutely prosaic. He collects paper clips and is fascinated by the behavior of pigeons. Ernie has a carefree attitude toward the world; Bert is worried about everything. Not surprisingly, Bert and Ernie fight all the time, but they remain the best of friends.

A s performed by Frank Oz and Jim Henson respectively, Bert and Ernie are one of the great comedy teams, worthy of comparison with Laurel and Hardy or Burns and Allen. As built by Don Sahlin, they are classic examples of the eloquently simplified Muppets so characteristic of *Sesame Street*. Frank, in fact, credits Don with defining the two characters through the contrasts he built into them. "The design was so simple and pure and wonderful," says Frank. "You had somebody who is all vertical and somebody who is all horizontal."

For some Muppet aficionados, Bert and Ernie represent the apotheosis of the performance collaboration between Jim and Frank. Surprisingly, they were not sure, at first, which of them would perform which character. "As I recall," says Frank, "we were just playing around with who should do who. I tried Ernie and Jim tried Bert, but it didn't seem to click. Then we went over to the mirror and switched and Jim said, 'I feel a bit more comfortable this way.' And I felt the same, so that's how it happened."

These drawings, probably made by Jim Henson, clearly indicate the difference in character between vertical Bert and horizontal Ernie.

61

Big Bird and Mr. Hooper.

Elmo, a very small and very popular Muppet.

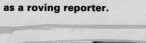

Kermit the Frog on the job as a roving reporter.

Two all-time favorites, Kermit and Cookie Monster.

Telly Monster and a trio of lambs.

Guy Smiley, the ultimate TV host—and, according to Joan Cooney, one of Jim's funniest characters.

Kermit demonstrates his familiarity with other pond-dwellers.

A gaggle of Muppets watches as Ernie takes a bath.

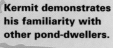

Big Bird admires Luis and Maria's baby.

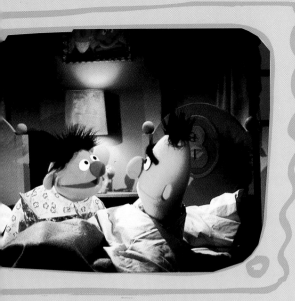

The Count with a quintet of counting enthusiasts.

Snuffy and Big Bird roller-skating in Central Park.

Ernie and Bert in their bedroom.

Placido Flamingo and Homer.

A trio of lovable monsters—Grover, Elmo, and Cookie Monster.

The number 8 as represented in a stop-action counting sequence—"The King of Eight"—produced by Jim Henson.

Prairie Dawn.

SESAME STREET Highlights

Since *Sesame Street* has aired continuously—and daily—since 1969, it would be difficult to assemble a highlight reel. There have been literally hundreds of memorable moments, and everyone has his own particular favorites. It is perhaps more fruitful to contemplate typical moments—types of situations that have been encountered over and over again, with variations, and are still eagerly anticipated by the audience. The Count von Count throwing himself with passion into a counting song, for instance. Kermit, dressed in his soft-brimmed hat and trench coat, heading out onto the street to conduct an interview. Cookie Monster looking sorry for himself after devouring everything in sight. Guy Smiley grinning his manic grin. Elmo looking up at someone's knees. Grover contemplating his latest good deed and congratulating himself on how pleased his mother would be. Big Bird mispronouncing Mr. Hooper's name. Placido Flamingo singing. Oscar grouching.

These are the *Sesame Street* moments that make us all smile.

Three friends.

CAROLY WILCOX joined the Muppet workshop crew during the first season of *Sesame Street* and quickly established herself as a puppet builder of exceptional ability.

"It sometimes seemed to me that all the rest of the business was just to provide Jim the opportunity to puppeteer. He loved puppeteering like a duck loves water. I remember Jim grinning, lying buried under piles of Styrofoam boulders, puppeteering Fred Elf in 'Santa Claus Switch.' *Sesame Street* gave him such scope for wonderfully silly characters: Salvador Dada, Guy Smiley, hippies, Martians—and especially Ernie. Watching Jim's Ernie teasing Frank Oz's Bert and driving him to distraction was to witness unadulterated GLEE!"

SESAME STREET has provided the occasion for a significant number of oversize, full-body puppets, of which Big Bird is the best known. Two other characters to fall into this category are Big Bird's friend Aloysius Snuffleupagus, or Snuffy—the largest *Sesame Street* puppet—and his baby sister, Alice (*left*). While Snuffy is operated by two puppeteers (Marty Robinson, who took over the role during the 1971–72 season, performs Snuffy's front half and voice; Bryant Young is in the rear), Alice is inhabited by one (Judy Sladky), while her eye mechanism is remote controlled.

Making Muppets

With the advent of *Sesame Street*, The Muppet workshop went from being a small room where Don Sahlin could build just about everything with a little help from his friends to being a bustling establishment where Sahlin and Caroly Wilcox needed an ever-growing staff to keep pace with the demands of a daily show.

Besides the regular characters, there was also a constant need for puppets to play one-time-only roles in sketches and musical numbers. Sometimes these were built from scratch, but more often they were adapted from the library of general-purpose puppets which, in the workshop, were variously referred to as trunk puppets, "Anything Muppets" (in the case of *Sesame Street*), and "Whatnots" (a term coined to distinguish these *Muppet Show* puppets from their *Sesame Street* counterparts). These Anything Muppets were (and still are) unadorned puppet torsos and heads that could be turned into anything a script required by adding the right eyes, the right nose, the right wig, the right costume.

Occasionally, too, the show would call for a mechanically elaborate puppet—one rigged to perform some special feat. To oversee this sort of work, Jim brought in the technical wizard Franz "Faz" Fazakas, who had previously been one of the architects of Burr Tillstrom's Kuklapolitan universe. Faz would be the driving force behind everything "technical" that the shop would produce for fourteen years. He would invent eyeballs that moved, servos—magical mitts that enabled puppeteers to control a character's eyes, mouth, or power of locomotion from a distance—and an entirely electronically generated puppet, among other things. He would make it possible for Kermit to ride a bicycle, rats to cook pancakes, and Doozers to build towers all over *Fraggle Rock*.

To accommodate all this activity, the workshop left 53rd Street and relocated in larger premises on 67th Street. The walls were lined with drawers and boxes marked *Big Bird Feathers*, *Large Noses* or *Small Monsters* (*opposite*). Talking lettuce and garrulous loaves of bread shared bench space with musical crabs and lopsided fish. It was a magical place and an appropriate home for the Muppet characters.

THE PUPPETS built for *Sesame Street* represent the apotheosis of what might be called the Don Sahlin style of Muppet puppet. This style was inherited by Caroly Wilcox, who kept it very much alive—though with her own distinctive flair—until the 1991–92 season, when another talented designer, Ed Christie, took over the task. As already noted, Don (seen *above* with Ernie) took Jim Henson's basic approach to puppet building and design and refined it into something that was both simple and sophisticated at the same time. Don's *Sesame Street* Muppets adhere to Ludwig Miës van der Rohe's famous dictum, "Less is more." It is hard to imagine how they could have been simplified any further, yet they can express anything the writers and performers ask of them.

Don placed an enormous emphasis on what has come to be known, in Muppet circles, as "the Magic Triangle"—the shape formed by the set of the eyes in relation to the nose—and the positioning of that triangle on the head. If the eyes and nose are properly placed, the puppet has eye focus and character.

Don was also a master of using the new materials that were becoming available at the time. He was skilled at building or sculpting the basic shape of a head out of sheets or blocks of synthetic foam—giving the puppets the required flexibility for television. But he was equally skilled at using fleece, fake fur, feathers, or flocking to cover the basic shape. His sculptural sense established the overall feel of a character. His sense of color (Bert and Ernie) and texture (Grover) did a great deal to add to that character's expressiveness.

KEVIN CLASH

Although he did not join the Henson organization until the 1984–85 season, Kevin Clash—performer of the immensely popular Elmo—quickly proved himself as a puppeteer of outstanding ability.

"When I was ten years old, I saw *Sesame Street* for the first time, and I knew then and there that I wanted to be a puppeteer with the Muppets. I finally met Jim by working on the *Sesame Street* float in the Macy's Thanksgiving Day Parade and soon after was hired for the show.

"In 1985, we did *The Muppets—A Celebration of Thirty Years*. We were doing a scene that involved over two hundred puppets, and Jim asked all the main puppeteers to help the hundred or so background puppeteers with their performances. Steve Whitmire and I were watching the monitor when we noticed this one little white rabbit in the background of the shot. While all the other puppets were calmly and rhythmically singing to the prerecorded song, this rabbit was hyperactively jumping up and down and shamelessly upstaging the other Muppets. We looked at each other in horror and I told Steve I would talk to Wayne Moss, the floor manager, and have him instruct the rabbit's puppeteer to tone down the wild movement.

"When asked, Wayne gave me a puzzled look and said, 'Are you *sure* you want me to tell that puppeteer to tone down?' I said, 'Of course, he's upstaging everybody else!' Wayne reluctantly spoke the instructions into his walkie-talkie. The puppet slowly sank behind the table as the puppeteer's head slowly rose above it. It was Jim!"

Aloysius
Snuffleupagus

FEW *Sesame Street* characters are more touching than Snuffy, the mastodon-like creature who was first encountered as Big Bird's imaginary friend. Eventually, Snuffy lost his imaginary status because concerns arose about the fact that none of the *Sesame Street* adults believed Big Bird when he talked about Snuffy—and children need to be believed. Here Snuffy is seen with his baby sister, Alice.

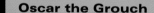

Oscar the Grouch

PRESCHOOLERS know all about grouches—they can be pretty grumpy themselves. That's why they have no difficulty in identifying with Oscar, the ultimate Grouch. To say that Oscar—who lives in a garbage can—is a skeptic is to indulge in understatement. He takes nothing on trust, and he is not shy about expressing his disdain for the mealy-mouthed politeness practiced by the other inhabitants of *Sesame Street*. Somehow, though, he manages to remain a sympathetic character.

ANYONE who has lived with a preschooler knows that at that age kids are preoccupied with monsters, and the *Sesame Street* world is full of them. Some, like Cookie, are apt to lose control, and others, like Oscar, are less than sociable. But all of them are manageable, inhabiting the television world rather than the shadowy recesses of the subconscious. No Muppet exemplifies this nonthreatening aspect of monsterhood better than Telly—a sweet, desperately insecure character whose imagination often is out of control and who constantly and hopelessly seeks Oscar's approval.

Cookie Monster

THIS *Sesame Street* favorite began life as an anonymous Muppet monster. Then he was inserted into a game-show sketch and his insatiable appetite for cookies was revealed to the world. Cookie Monster quickly became the world's most prominent exemplar of instant gratification.

Telly Monster

Some Muppet Favorites

Grover

THE COUNT VON COUNT displays an enthusiastic passion for counting that is unequaled on *Sesame Street*. It can be presumed that the Count is a distant cousin of that other Transylvanian nobleman, Count Dracula; but despite his needle-sharp incisors, he is no threat to sleeping house guests. He will, however, probably count them.

The Count von Count

OCCASIONALLY seen in the guise of Super Grover—the world's most ineffectual and sympathetic superhero—Grover is an infinitely vulnerable, infinitely optimistic soul. Although he possesses a highly developed facility for self-deception, this is balanced by his ingrained honesty. And although he is apt to get carried away by irrelevant trains of thought, he is also capable of delivering pearls of wisdom. In the end, it is Grover himself who describes his personality most accurately when he introduces himself to viewers as "lovable, furry old Grover"—which says it all.

IT HAS BECOME a tradition for *Sesame Street* to go on the road once in a while. Going on the road can mean heading out into New York's Central Park (a stone's throw from the studio and one of Jim Henson's favorite places), or traveling halfway round the world. Some of the locations visited (*clockwise from left*) include the Great Wall of China, Japan, Central Park, Arizona, and Hawaii.

rigid and scared. There's a real difference between the early, monotone, unenergetic Bert and the later lively, energetic Bert. As I got more confidence, the voices changed for the better, and Jim always supported me and gave me the chance to settle down."

Frank's newly discovered voice talents were crucial to the success of both Grover and Cookie Monster. He describes Cookie's voice as "just a regular monster voice," though a demanding one to perform because it has to be made in the throat. Of Grover's voice—virtually the opposite of Cookie's in that it possesses a poignant, almost tentative, edge—Frank says, "It just sort of evolved."

Cookie Monster is the culmination of a generation of omnivorous Muppets that date back to the early days of *Sam and Friends.* For a decade or more, they were generally performed by Jim Henson himself. By the time of *Sesame Street,* however, Frank had inherited the role. As Jon Stone noted, Cookie evolved from a sketch that had no ending till Frank took the bright blue, general-purpose monster puppet from a trunk. The sketch was a quiz show skit and the blue monster, having won a prize, was offered the choice of a trip to Hawaii or a cookie.

Needless to say, he did not pick Hawaii.

For a while, Cookie ate anything and everything. However, he eventually developed his insatiable appetite for cookies—and thus was domesticated into a character children could relate to and deal with.

If Cookie is the embodiment of instant gratification, Grover is an infinitely vulnerable, infinitely optimistic soul who resonates with the child in all of us. His apparent simplicity is deceptive; Frank notes that Grover is perhaps the most rounded character in his repertoire.

Grover always wants to help, although his attempts to do so often backfire. He possesses a highly developed facility for self-deception, leavened by an ingrained honesty. Like most kids, he sometimes fancies himself a superhero but,

like most kids, he also knows at some near-rational level that he isn't one. Over the years, *Sesame Street* viewers have been able to share in Super Grover's fantasies, in which—costumed in cloak and helmet—he flies almost as well as any self-respecting superhero but is apt to crash-land in bushes or trees. In one typical episode, while attempting to break up a fight between two brothers, Super Grover launches into a heartfelt monologue about his beloved Mommy. He becomes so carried away with his train of thought that the brothers become bored with fighting and make up. Seeing this, Super Grover delightedly takes credit for the reconciliation.

"Mommy," he beams, "would be so proud!"

Cookie Monster and Grover are probably the two best-known of the *Sesame Street* monsters—a group that also includes such Muppet favorites as Elmo, Telly, and Herry Monster.

For *Sesame Street,* the Muppets brought monsters to life in such a way as to permit kids to come to terms with the idea of a monster in a safe and nonthreatening way. *Sesame Street* monsters have been tamed without becoming too tame, and they have been put to the task of conveying a vari-

MARTY ROBINSON—who performs Telly, Snuffleupagus, and other favorites—is a mainstay of the *Sesame Street* team.

"It was my fifth audition for the Muppets in as many days...but this time was different; Jim was there. What had begun as a lark was now somewhat intense. At one point in the proceedings, I found Jim standing next to me watching a video playback. 'I saw your work,' he said. 'Hmmm...' Over the years, we all learned to interpret the valuable words of encouragement he had for us.

"I, and the rest of the staff on *Sesame Street*, really appreciated that no matter how many dozens of projects Jim was involved with and the impossible constraints on his time, he always found time to return to us. He'd be there on the floor with the rest of us—sweating, forgetting lines, sore arms and all."

THE NARRATIVE PARTS of the *Sesame Street* show occur on the people-sized sets that are home to the human members of the cast and to the characters like Big Bird, who interact with them on a regular basis. There are also smaller puppet sets that are strictly for Muppet-only segments. It is on these sets that the Count counts bats and cobwebs, Cookie devours brownies, and Placido Flamingo exercises his vocal cords.

The photograph *above*, taken in 1975, shows five performers—Jerry Nelson, Caroly Wilcox, Jim Henson, Frank Oz, and Richard Hunt—on one of the very basic sets used for the Muppet-only segments. As can be seen, the set does not take up a great deal of room, though it is, in fact, a relatively large and complicated set by *Sesame Street* standards. Often Muppet sketches for the show are shot with the puppets posed against a plain illuminated blue screen that permits filmed backgrounds to be inserted by means of video special effects.

Later productions, such as *The Muppet Show*, used far more elaborate sets. Where *Sesame Street* is concerned, however, the simplicity of the settings—like the simplicity of the puppets themselves—is a definite plus, adding greatly to the feeling of innocence that the show embodies.

Jon Stone recalls that he used to direct the Muppet-only segments of *Sesame Street* without pay, just because it was so much fun to be involved with the process. At *left*, Stone calls for action as Frank Oz prepares to put Super Grover through his paces. At *right*, Jim Henson and Jerry Nelson bring Kermit and a smartly outfitted hare to life for a Muppet variation on a well-known fable.

ety of lessons about socially acceptable behavior. Who better, after all, to embody antisocial behavior than a monster? And if a monster learns that it is behaving badly, kids in the audience learn the same thing. What's more, they discover that the monsters they imagine—both within and without—can be brought under control as well. Not that Muppet monsters always misbehave. Sometimes they are there to teach children how to cross the street safely, and sometimes a monster foursome gets together to sing four-part harmony—in praise, of course, of the number 4.

The number 4—along with a host of other digits—is also celebrated by the Count von Count, one of *Sesame Street's* most effective teachers. A refugee from Transylvania and an apparent close relative of Dracula, the Count is mad about counting. He counts everything from black cats to cobwebs and from bats to belfries.

While most Muppets of the period are soft and rounded, the Count is hard and sharp-edged. As brought to life by Jerry Nelson—who became a full-time and vitally important member of the muppet performing troupe during the early years of *Sesame Street*—the Count has all the mannerisms of the Dracula family but has somehow managed to transform them into something wholesome—the medium of transformation being Jerry's strong comedic sense. The character also gains from Jerry's exceptional vocal talents, which not only supply the Count with the appropriate accent but also enable him to sing about the joys of numbers.

While the Count, Bert, Ernie, Kermit, Cookie, Grover, and other characters operate in cameo spots separate from the action on Sesame Street proper, Oscar the Grouch is a street regular, living in a garbage can at the side of a stoop and interacting on a daily basis with the program's human performers.

Despite his scruffy coat and permanent scowl, Oscar is one of *Sesame Street's* most popular characters. All kids are grouchy at times and have no difficulty in understanding Oscar's grumpiness. Their ability to identify with him prevents him from being the unsympathetic character he might have become. As performed by Caroll Spinney, Oscar is almost subtle, his apparently inflexible grouch stance occasionally subject to honorable compromise, though Jon Stone insists he is basically rotten through and through.

Caroll joined the Muppets at the launching of *Sesame Street*, specializing in puppet characters who perform with the show's humans. Curiously, neither of Caroll's most visible characters—Oscar and the wonderfully guileless Big Bird—were included in the original plans for the show.

"In the summer of 1969," Jon Stone explains, "we went down to Philadelphia and did five test shows on closed-circuit television to see what worked. We had been told by all our advisors that preschoolers have difficulty in differentiating between fantasy and reality. So the first idea was that you would have the street—a very real-looking set with real people on it—and then you would cut away to puppets, to animation, to all the things that make up the fantasy.

"We did the test shows that way—no Oscar, no Big Bird—and we realized right away that we had a problem because the people on the street couldn't compete with the puppets. We had children watching these shows and their attention span just went way down when we cut to the street....So the information we got from these test shows demonstrated that we needed a transition from the fantasy to the reality and puppets on the street seemed a good way to do it. Oscar was something we came up with together. Jim suggested Big Bird."

If Grover represents the child as Holy Fool, Big Bird portrays a typical preschooler (although according to *Sesame Street* tradition, he is actually six). He is especially valuable when there are difficult subjects to discuss: Maria's pregnancy, for example, or the death of Mr. Hooper—an original cast member who played the owner of the *Sesame Street* candy store.

SINCE ITS VERY first season, *Sesame Street* has attracted a wealth of human guest stars: a President's wife (Barbara Bush); a number of jazz greats (Ray Charles, Bobby McFerrin) and classical virtuosi (Itzhak Perlman, Yo-Yo Ma); talented comedians (Robin Williams, Whoopi Goldberg); and award-winning actresses (Susan Sarandon, Glenn Close).

None of these stars appeared on *Sesame Street* in order to further their careers. They sang with Grover and put up with Oscar's gripes because they believed in the program's aims and because nothing else in show business is quite as much fun as working with the Muppets.

When Will Lee, the actor who played Mr. Hooper, died, the producers of *Sesame Street* did not try to duck the issue. Rather, they had the writers confront it head on, making his death meaningful to their young audience by having the street's adults explain it to Big Bird. This seemed fitting, as Big Bird had a long and complex relationship with Mr. Hooper, often heightened by Big Bird's inability to master the store-owner's name:

("Oh—hi, Mister Looper."

"Hooper! Hooper! It's Hooper!"

"Sorry, Mister Dooper.")

Told that Mr. Hooper is dead, Big Bird appears to understand, then blithely asks, "When will he be back?" Only slowly does he grasp what death means and how it is appropriate to react.

Though Big Bird became the key Muppet in the street

segments of the show, in the early days, Kermit often functioned as the glue holding the entire show together. In his role as a roving reporter—complete with trench coat and snap-brimmed hat—Kermit appeared around *Sesame Street* posing the pressing questions of the day. Or, in a philosophic mood, he would sing Joe Raposo's "Bein' Green." Most memorably perhaps, Kermit has sometimes interacted with child visitors to the set.

The Kermit who emerged during the *Sesame Street* period was no longer a glib narrator or a two-dimensional vaudeville character. He had become a well-rounded personality with obvious star quality, as was quickly recognized by the media. He had taken on a life of his own, dependent on Jim's, perhaps, but also distinct from it. *Sesame Street* was the training ground that prepared Kermit for the rigors of *The Muppet Show*.

BOBBY McFERRIN · LILY TOMLIN · LINDA RONSTADT · YO-YO MA · TIM ROBBINS · SE JACKSON · CANDICE BERGEN · BO JACKSON · BARBARA BUSH · BILLY JOEL · SUSAN SARANDON · CARLY SIMON · GLENN CLOSE

Sesame Street was an overnight success. Big Bird was everywhere from the cover of *Time* magazine to the Emmy awards. *Muppet* had become a household word, and again the Henson team was forced to expand. The workshop on East 67th Street became busier than ever with new additions to Don Sahlin's staff, the most important being Caroly Wilcox, a highly talented puppet-builder who would become a mainstay of the Henson organization. More puppeteers were needed, and among those signed was Fran Brill, the first woman Muppet performer since Jane Henson.

Very early in the run of the show, a young actor named Richard Hunt auditioned and was hired for the show. Despite his lack of experience as a puppeteer, he would soon become a crucial addition to the troupe, creating such memorable characters as Don Music, a tin-eared tunesmith; Forgetful Jones, a cowboy whose memory is less than ade-

quate; the stagestruck Gladys the Cow; and the operatic superstar Placido Flamingo. Like Jerry Nelson, Richard Hunt possessed exceptional vocal talents. He could sing in almost any style and had a sure way with accents. In addition to being a natural performer, he displayed a spontaneous sense of humor that fit right in with the style established by Jim and Frank.

Valuable and versatile as he was as a puppet performer, Richard had as much to offer off camera, where his outgoing personality helped keep puppeteers and crew alike loose between takes. He soon became an indispensable member of the Muppet team, one of the people who would figure prominently in Jim's plans for the future.

If *Sesame Street* was designed primarily for preschoolers, the show as a whole makes itself available to both children and parents, siblings and baby-sitters. This is largely

due to the fact that its humor is multilayered. The name Placido Flamingo, for example, probably sounds very funny even to an average four-year-old who has never heard of opera star Placido Domingo. The pun is there to keep the preschooler's parents amused, too.

On occasion, a vivacious all-girl Muppet group has performed witty takeoffs on current hit songs. Madonna's "Material Girl" was transformed into "Cereal Girl"—the lead singer proclaiming her love for cornflakes and porridge as she bounced in and out of camera range. Similarly, the many parodies of television shows essayed over the years are designed to entertain adults as well as children. Certainly many preschoolers laughed at the title *Miami Mice*, but how many of them watch *Masterpiece Theatre*? Still, Cookie Monster appeared as Alistair Cookie to introduce *Monsterpiece Theatre*.

For adults, *Sesame Street* is a miracle because it allows them to reenter childhood without abandoning their adult dignity. This is possible because the show invests childhood with a dignity of its own; it accepts young children as com-

plex beings worthy of being treated with respect.

"Kids come to visit the studio," said Jon Stone, "and they and the puppets are old friends. Those puppets are in their living rooms every day. As soon as a puppet goes up on somebody's arm, the puppeteer ceases to exist. The child comes right up to talk to Grover or the Count. They don't look at the puppeteer. They don't look at the monitor.

"My stepfather is a pediatrician and he told me, a few months after *Sesame Street* went on the air, about these autistic children who were totally noncommunicative with parents and siblings and therapists but would suddenly open up to these puppets as they sat in front of a television set. They'd start conversing with Ernie and Bert to the point where doctors were beginning to use puppets in the therapy of autistic children. There's something that happens with puppets which doesn't happen in any other medium. There's a magic there that Jim understood.

"*Sesame Street* was like the perfect marriage. Out of five billion people in the world, somehow we came together with the right package, the right aim, the right motivation, the right job to be done, and everyone contributed a piece of the pie, and everything fit right together."

"I think there was a kind of collective genius about the core group that created *Sesame Street*," concurs Joan Ganz Cooney, "but there was only one real genius in our midst, and that was Jim."

THE CLASSIC CHARACTERS from the early days of *Sesame Street* are still very much part of the show, although they are often seen in clips shot ten or twenty years ago. In fact, reusing spots is the norm on *Sesame Street*; every successful spot is shown many times so that the lesson it embodies is reinforced by repetition.

But over the years, many new characters have been introduced to the show, and an almost entirely new team of puppeteers has taken over the responsibilities of performing them. These include Pam Arciero, Camille Bonora, Peter Linz, Rick Lyon, Noel MacNeal, Jim Martin, Joey Mazzerino, David Rudman, Judy Sladky, Bryant Young, and Carmen Osbahr—a Mexican performer who was brought in from the Mexican coproduction of *Sesame Street* to perform the bilingual character Rosita. It is the newer characters who keep the show fresh and enable *Sesame Street* to continue to evolve and grow.

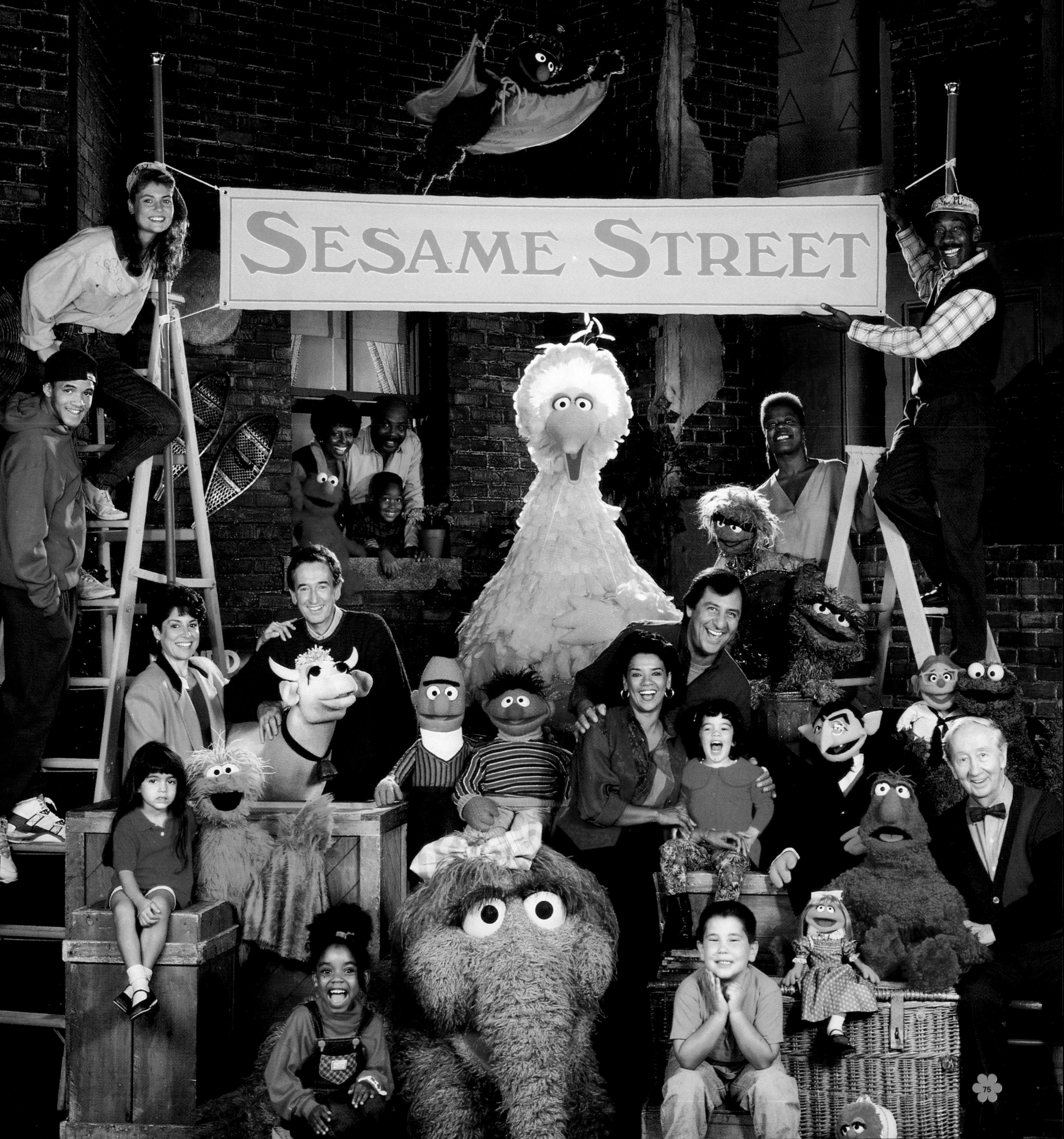
SESAME STREET

Left to right: Cheryl, Lisa and Brian Henson.

A family affair...

According to Jane Henson, one of the main reasons her husband wanted to be involved with *Sesame Street* was his realization that children could provide him with a very sophisticated audience. This realization grew out of the fact that he had five children whom he had been studying intently as they grew up. Lisa, Cheryl, Brian, John, and Heather were among the inspirations for *Sesame Street*, and also made occasional appearances on the show.

Heather, the youngest of the Henson children, in costume for a Halloween number.

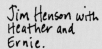

Jim Henson with Heather and Ernie.

Brian (left) and John ready for Halloween.

Jim and Jane Henson, in the late sixties, with (left to right) Cheryl, John, Brian and Lisa.

Always ready to entertain kids, Richard Hunt introduces visitors to the set to a monster.

...that welcomed all families

To the greatest extent practical, the *Sesame Street* set has always been open to kids. It is not uncommon to find preschoolers wandering around, making Muppet friends in real life. To a great extent, too, the show has featured real children on camera, making a virtue of their ability to interact unself-consciously with puppets, just as the puppets talk unself-consciously to the children at home.

Kermit interviews a young fan.

Jim Henson (behind stools) and Frank Oz are hard at work, but their guest is interested only in Kermit and Cookie.

The Count's young fans greet him with enthusiasm.

"Rubber Duckie"—a song heard round the world

Rubber Duckie, you're the one.
You make bath time lots of fun.
Rubber Duckie, I'm awfully fond
  of you.

Rubber Duckie, joy of joys,
When I squeeze you, you make
  noise.
Rubber Duckie, you're my best
  friend, it's true.

Oh, every day when I
Make my way to the tubby,
I find a little fellow
Who's cute and yellow and chubby.
Rub-A-Dub-Dub-By.

Rubber Duckie, you're so fine,
And I'm lucky that you're mine.
Rubber Duckie, I'm awfully fond
  of you.

Oh, every day when I
Make my way to the tubby,
I find a little fellow
Who's cute and yellow and chubby.
Rub-A-Dub-Dub-By.

Rubber Duckie, you're so fine,
And I'm lucky that you're mine.
Rubber Duckie, I'm awfully fond
  of you.

"RUBBER DUCKIE"—written by Jeff
Moss, one of *Sesame Street*'s talented
composers, in 1970—was a song sung
around the world. All in all, *Sesame Street*
has appeared in 120 countries.

CHAPTER FOUR

As far as Jim Henson was concerned, the success of *Sesame Street* had one major drawback. For all the show's sophistication and despite its proven appeal to adults, *Sesame Street* was a children's program. And inevitably, network executives began to think of the Muppets as kiddie entertainment. Thus, the early seventies was both a period of triumph and frustration for Jim—a time during which he was forced to contend with mistaken perceptions. In fact, Joan Cooney recalls a conversation in which Jim said to her, half-seriously, "Why did you have to be so successful?"

Meanwhile, Jim used his occasional specials both to demonstrate the Muppets' appeal to a family audience and to continue to develop the technical aspects of his work. Beginning with *The Frog Prince*, for example, all of Jim's productions, other than *Sesame Street*, were to some extent "platformed up." Platforming up means, quite simply, that the sets are built on top of platforms. This meant that the Muppet performers could be hidden under these platforms as well as among the props, operating their creatures through holes and "trenches" invisible to the camera. Muppets could thus move in a much more naturalistic way, and sets could be extensive and elaborate, allowing a cinematic flexibility that gave puppetry an entirely new dimension.

The arrival of platformed-up production was one of the crucial advances in the evolution of Muppet magic. Muppets were now almost as mobile on screen as humans and, with careful planning, many new kinds of illusions could be created.

ALTHOUGH HE WAS serious about getting *The Muppet Show* on the air, Jim Henson's hand-drawn cover for the proposal was anything but staid.

The Muppet Valentine Special—a 1974 production for ABC—introduced no major technical innovations but was important in that it anticipated some of the elements of the future *Muppet Show*. It teamed the Muppets with a single guest star—Mia Farrow—and interspersed elaborate and cinematic set pieces with a continuing narrative. The show demonstrated that the Muppets could achieve the kind of broad, cross-generational appeal that Jim was striving for. The networks, however, were looking for more.

Nineteen-seventy-five would prove to be a busy year for Jim Henson and his team. Bert and Ernie were installed at the Smithsonian Institution, and the Muppets made guest appearances on half a dozen series, as well as on specials starring Julie Andrews, Cher, and Andy Williams. In March, a series pilot—provocatively (and, of course, misleadingly) titled *The Muppet Show: Sex and Violence*—was aired on ABC. And in the fall, the Muppets began appearing in a series of weekly segments on the first season of the groundbreaking *Saturday Night Live* on NBC.

The *Sex and Violence* pilot anticipated the pacing of the eventual *Muppet Show*. It also featured a number of new characters who would become regulars on the series. The Swedish Chef was there, as was Sam the Eagle, Crazy Harry, Statler and Waldorf, Rowlf, and the eclectic members of the Electric Mayhem—Animal, Floyd Pepper, Janice, Zoot, and the irrepressible Dr. Teeth.

The show differed radically from *The Muppet Show*, however, in that there was no guest star. And even more significantly, except for a fleeting cameo appearance, Kermit was nowhere to be seen. His stand-in, Nigel—a mousy-looking humanoid puppet—was a wimp, totally lacking in spunk and charisma. As soon as the show was committed to tape, Jim realized that he had made a mistake in trying to

OF ALL the characters shown with Jim Henson in this spread from the proposal for *The Muppet Show*, only Rowlf and Kermit had significant roles to play in the eventual series. However, the text, also from the proposal, is an accurate enough description of the show that reached the screen.

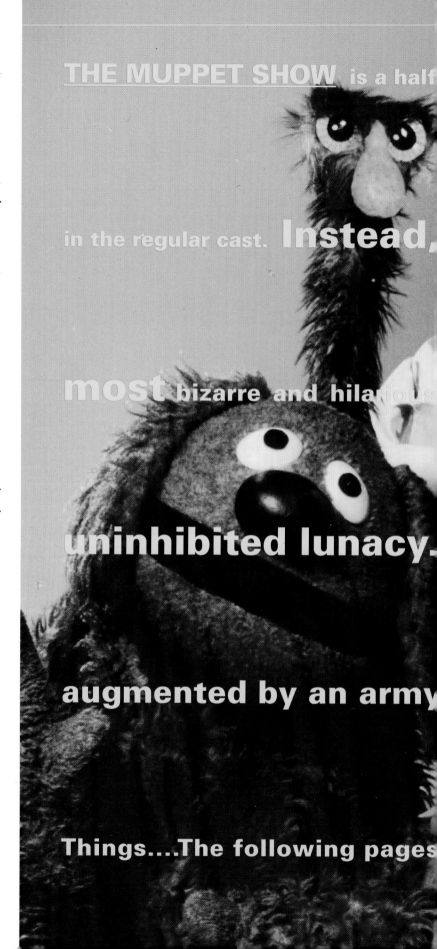

THE MUPPET SHOW is a half

in the regular cast. Instead,

most bizarre and hilarious

uninhibited lunacy.

augmented by an army

Things....The following pages

hour, prime-time entertainment program. There is not a single human being

we have Jim Henson's Muppets — among the

collection of puppets ever created—performing thirty minutes of

There is a cast of perhaps a dozen regular characters,

of creatures, animals, monsters, machines, and abstract

contain an outline of a typical edition of THE MUPPET SHOW.

BERNIE BRILLSTEIN, Jim Henson's longtime manager and career advisor, was a key figure in the selling of *The Muppet Show.*

"I first met Jim Henson in 1960. Burr Tillstrom had called me to meet with Jim when I was a young agent at the William Morris Agency. At this time, the last thing in the world I could understand or wanted to understand were puppets of any sort.

"My office was on the twenty-sixth floor at William Morris. Jim walked in carrying a black box that contained the original Muppets. He looked like a young Abe Lincoln in some kind of leather, and spoke in a voice that was hardly audible. When he opened the black box, the magic began."

LORD LEW GRADE'S involvement with *The Muppet Show* brought Jim Henson and company all the way to England, where the show was produced.

"The first time I saw Jim Henson was when he guested on one of my 'Julie Andrews' TV shows. I was so struck with his originality and humor that I arranged to meet him to see if he would do a TV series for me in England. He told me he had tried to get his own TV show in the States but without success. I there and then decided that we would make twenty-four half-hour shows in our Elstree Studios.

"The atmosphere and excitement during the making of these shows was electric, and in a very short while we had international celebrities clamoring to do the guest spot in his show.... The productions were such fun that it hardly seemed like the hard work it obviously was, because everybody enjoyed it so much.

"Jim and I became close friends and made several theatrical movies together; I shall never forget his quiet charm and total dedication to his work at all times."

elevate Nigel to the host's role, but by then it was too late.

Miss Piggy *was* present, but not by any means in her eventual, indelibly assertive form. One of the sketches in the *Sex and Violence* pilot was a spoof of *Planet of the Apes*, titled *Return to Beneath the Planet of the Pigs*, and it was in this parody that Piggy made her first brief appearance as one of a number of nondescript pigs. Despite her presence on the show, however, ABC decided to pass on it.

So far as design was concerned, Don Sahlin's influence was strongly felt, but Bonnie Erickson was coming to play an increasingly important role. So was Michael K. Frith, a former children's book illustrator and editor who had worked on *Sesame Street* books and had recently joined the company with the title of art director. When Don Sahlin died suddenly (in 1978), it would be Bonnie and Michael who would be asked to fill the vacuum he left. Bonnie would be Don's heir where the basic Muppet style was concerned, while Michael helped introduce the more complex look that characterized *The Muppet Show.*

Nineteen-seventy-five was a busy year elsewhere, too. During the latter half of that year NBC prepared to launch a variety program that would change the face of television. That program was *Saturday Night Live.*

The first season of *Saturday Night Live* provided a showcase for future stars and superstars such as John Belushi, Gilda Radner, Dan Aykroyd, Jane Curtin, and Chevy Chase. All were unknowns at the time, and Bernie Brillstein—at that time, the agent representing several of the key figures involved with the show, including Jim Henson—recalls that the network was counting on anchoring the show with more firmly established entities, namely Albert Brooks (who provided short, satirical films) and the Muppets.

For *Saturday Night Live,* Jim and his team created a group of completely new, deliberately grotesque, reptilian puppets—inhabitants of a planet of "bubbling tarpits" and "sulfurous wastelands" known as Gorch. These included the bullying King Ploobis (performed by Jim), his nagging wife Queen Peuta (Alice Tweedy), his spaced-out son Wisss (Richard Hunt), his craven sidekick Scred (brilliantly brought to life by Jerry Nelson), a dim-witted female named Vazh (Fran Brill), and, last but not least, the Mighty Favog.

Performed by Frank Oz, Favog was conceived as a "stone" likeness of the local deity (actually sculpted from latex foam), vaguely pre-Columbian in appearance. As a talking statue, Favog was something of a tour de force on the part of the Muppet workshop. But the reptilian puppets were perhaps even more remarkable. Elaborately formed from snipped and pieced foam and furnished with taxidermist's eyes (the first time Muppets had been given such naturalistic traits), these creatures were in part the products of Jim's still relatively new collaboration with Michael K. Frith.

Seen today on their own, the Gorch sketches are imaginative and funny, and Ploobis himself is a classic Jim Henson character. Within the context of the show, however, the sketches never quite worked. The young team of comics and writers recruited for the series quickly developed a chemistry of its own and a style of antiestablishment humor that was at odds with Jim's gentler anarchy. By all accounts, the *Saturday Night Live* writers never felt comfortable scripting the Ploobis episodes and, as a result, the Muppet contributions—though accomplished on their own terms—tended to interrupt the continuity of the show rather than sustain it.

The Muppets and *Saturday Night Live* were not made for one another, and they probably would have come to a parting of the ways even if it were not for the phone call Jim received one day that October from Bernie Brillstein.

Jim Henson—accompanied by Kermit—had first appeared in Bernie Brillstein's office back in the early sixties. Jim had recently moved to New York and Brillstein was an up-and-coming young talent agent with William Morris. At that meeting, Brillstein had been impressed with Jim's talent; but he was convinced that the last thing he needed was

Michael K. Frith had already had a successful career in publishing when he joined Henson Associates full-time in December of 1975, just weeks before the first episode of *The Muppet Show* was taped. Michael's association with the Muppets had begun some years earlier by way of *Sesame Street* publications, and Jim Henson soon realized that his talents as an art director could be directly applied to puppet design.

"Jim was a master of direction through indirection. When he gave me the great challenge of designing this new bunch [the characters from *Saturday Night Live*], about the only directions I remember were 'kind of mossy' and 'taxidermy eyes.' But just this departure from the 'usual' Muppet look spoke volumes.

MICHAEL K. FRITH

"Newcomers were often surprised by what Jim could communicate without seeming to say much — it was all rhythms, hints, expectations. For someone unused to it, it could be pretty baffling.

"In 1988, a few of us went to the then-Soviet Union to shoot a piece for an ABC special that featured a satellite link between some Moscow schoolchildren and a bunch of kids in New York. After interminable glitches and delays, the camera finally rolled for a take. Jim watched the playback, then raised Kermit back into position: 'I think it could be funnier,' he murmured mildly. We automatically readied to go again, but our Russian producer seemed taken aback. For a moment, his brow furrowed painfully. Then he brightened.

"'No,' he announced with great certainty. 'Is funny enough!'

"And with heretofore unhinted-at alacrity, the crew had lights and camera dismantled and out the door, leaving behind a profoundly puzzled puppeteer."

Queen Peuta

Scred

The Mighty Favog

Saturday Night Live

THE MUPPETS' association with *Saturday Night Live* lasted only one season. In retrospect, it was mostly important for its hints of things to come, though King Ploobis, Scred, the Mighty Favog, and the rest—denizens of a steaming, volcanic landscape—were characters of considerable inherent interest. *Muppet Show* producer David Lazer remembers Jim Henson sitting beside the pool at the Beverly Wilshire Hotel, planning the *Saturday Night Live* puppets. "He was laughing so much he was crying."

Back in New York, Jim handed responsibility for realizing the *Saturday Night* puppets over to Michael K. Frith, an artist who would contribute a good deal to the look of *The Muppet Show*. One of Jim's specifications for the characters was that they should be made with taxidermist's eyes, giving them a very naturalistic look. They would also be much more complex visually than the *Sesame Street* style of Muppet and this, too, had its impact on the characters designed for *The Muppet Show*.

King Ploobis

Wisss

Vazh

some puppet clients. As the meeting continued, however, he received a call from his boss.

"Have you heard of the Muppets?" his boss asked.

"Yes," said Brillstein tentatively.

"Have you seen them?" his boss continued.

"Yes," Brillstein said.

"Well, I think they're funny, and I think you ought to talk to this Jim Henson guy," his boss concluded.

Naturally, Brillstein was delighted to be able to tell his boss that "this Jim Henson guy" was sitting in his office at that very moment. Brillstein became Jim's agent, then his manager and a close friend.

Throughout the summer of 1975 and well into the fall, Brillstein had been aggressively trying to sell a Muppet series to the networks. After ABC dropped out of the picture, CBS seemed the best bet. But CBS programming executives were still doubtful of the Muppets' appeal to adult audiences.

Meanwhile, the head of ITC—the American division of Lord Lew Grade's British-based Associated Communications Corporation—had seen a reel of Muppet highlights and advised Lord Grade that the Muppets might be well suited for a series to be syndicated in the American market.

This made considerable sense at the time. The Federal Communications Commission had just created the programming concept known as prime-time access, taking the 7:30 to 8:00 P.M. time slot away from the networks and assigning it to local stations to use as they wished. It was the perfect position for a family show and hence for the Muppets.

The question was, would enough stations sign up to make the show viable?

This question was effectively answered when the five CBS-owned and -operated stations—each in a major market—indicated their intention to run *The Muppet Show* if it were made available to them. With their support assured,

(continued on page 94)

Rudolf Nureyev's
decision to
appear on the
show was a
great coup.

During the first
season, many
of the guest
stars were per-
sonal friends of
Jim Henson
or his manager,
Bernie Brillstein.

JULIET PROWSE

TWIGGY

HARVEY KORMAN

SANDY DUNCAN

LENA HORNE

BRUCE FORSYTH

CANDICE BERGEN

BEN VEREEN

JOEL GREY

FLORENCE
HENDERSON

AVERY SCHREIBER

KAYE BALLARD

PETER USTINOV

VALERIE HARPER

RITA MORENO

CHARLES AZNAVOUR

STEVE MARTIN

PHYLLIS DILLER

JIM NABORS

ETHEL MERMAN

RUTH BUZZI

ELTON JOHN

VINCENT PRICE

PAUL WILLIAMS

CONNIE STEVENS

MUMMENSCHANZ

MADELINE KAHN

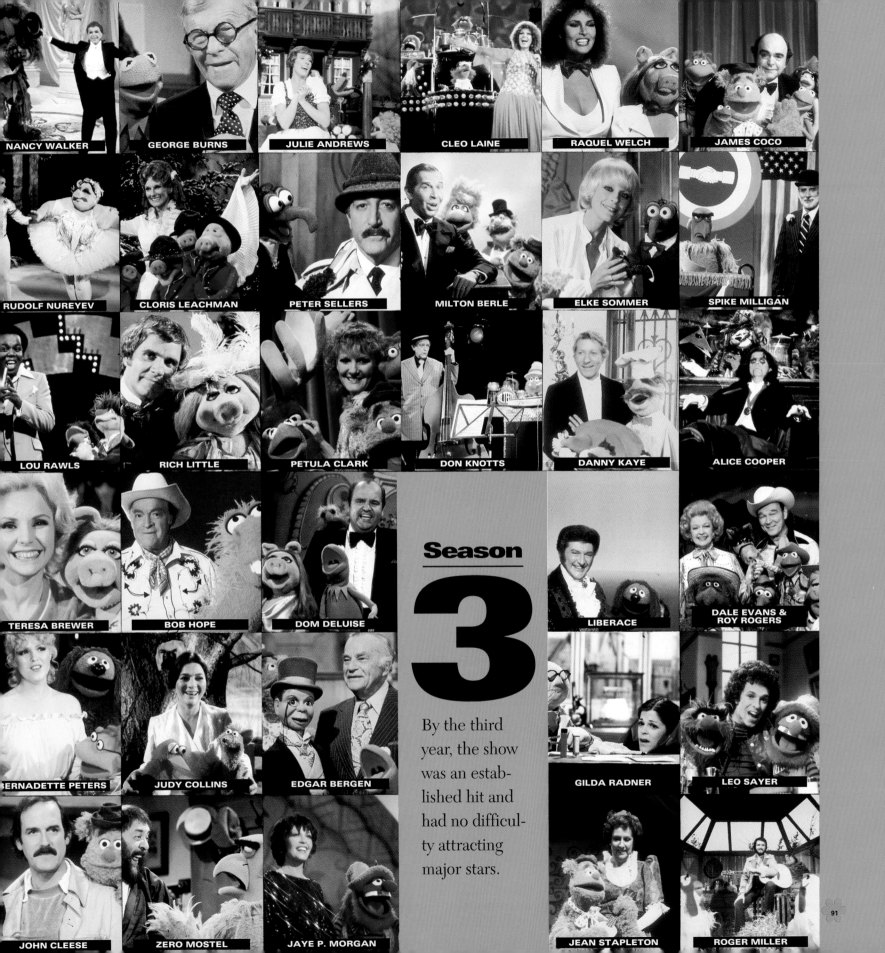

NANCY WALKER

GEORGE BURNS

JULIE ANDREWS

CLEO LAINE

RAQUEL WELCH

JAMES COCO

RUDOLF NUREYEV

CLORIS LEACHMAN

PETER SELLERS

MILTON BERLE

ELKE SOMMER

SPIKE MILLIGAN

LOU RAWLS

RICH LITTLE

PETULA CLARK

DON KNOTTS

DANNY KAYE

ALICE COOPER

TERESA BREWER

BOB HOPE

DOM DELUISE

LIBERACE

DALE EVANS & ROY ROGERS

BERNADETTE PETERS

JUDY COLLINS

EDGAR BERGEN

GILDA RADNER

LEO SAYER

JOHN CLEESE

ZERO MOSTEL

JAYE P. MORGAN

JEAN STAPLETON

ROGER MILLER

Season

3

By the third year, the show was an established hit and had no difficulty attracting major stars.

91

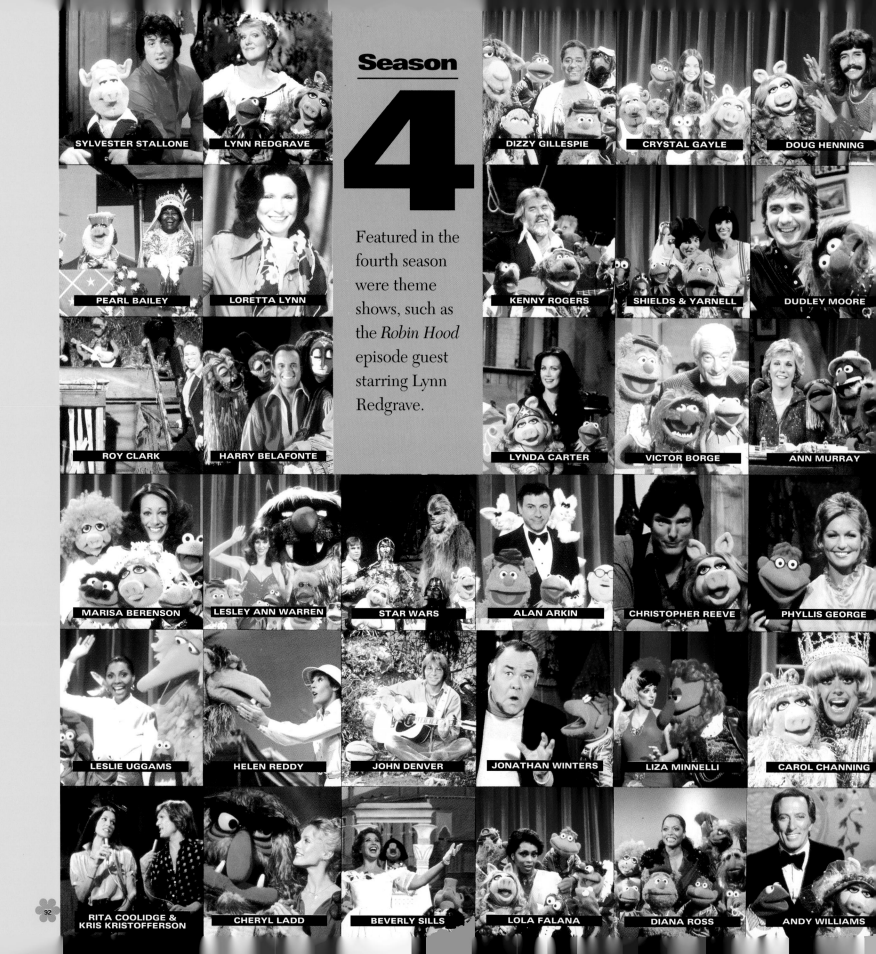

Season

4

Featured in the fourth season were theme shows, such as the *Robin Hood* episode guest starring Lynn Redgrave.

SYLVESTER STALLONE

LYNN REDGRAVE

DIZZY GILLESPIE

CRYSTAL GAYLE

DOUG HENNING

PEARL BAILEY

LORETTA LYNN

KENNY ROGERS

SHIELDS & YARNELL

DUDLEY MOORE

ROY CLARK

HARRY BELAFONTE

LYNDA CARTER

VICTOR BORGE

ANN MURRAY

MARISA BERENSON

LESLEY ANN WARREN

STAR WARS

ALAN ARKIN

CHRISTOPHER REEVE

PHYLLIS GEORGE

LESLIE UGGAMS

HELEN REDDY

JOHN DENVER

JONATHAN WINTERS

LIZA MINNELLI

CAROL CHANNING

RITA COOLIDGE & KRIS KRISTOFFERSON

CHERYL LADD

BEVERLY SILLS

LOLA FALANA

DIANA ROSS

ANDY WILLIAMS

LINDA LAVIN

DEBORAH HARRY

JAMES COBURN

ROGER MOORE

GENE KELLY

DYAN CANNON

JOHNNY CASH

GLADYS KNIGHT

MAC DAVIS

MARTY FELDMAN

ARLO GUTHRIE

LINDA RONSTADT

JOAN BAEZ

JEAN-PIERRE RAMPAL

BUDDY RICH

Season 5

In its final year, *The Muppet Show* featured a range of guest stars from Paul Simon to Glenda Jackson and from Gene Kelly to Jean-Pierre Rampal.

PAUL SIMON

TONY RANDALL

MELISSA MANCHESTER

CHRISTOPHER LANGHAM

WALLY BOAG

SEÑOR WENCES

LORETTA SWIT

CAROL BURNETT

SHIRLEY BASSEY

BROOKE SHIELDS

GLENDA JACKSON

HAL LINDEN

The Muppet *Show* ran for five years. At first, guest stars were hard to come by, but that soon changed. After all, guesting on *The Muppet Show* was like being featured in a special... with the additional advantage of having the support of a ready-made cast of gifted costars, dedicated to enhancing every guest's image.

Lord Grade gave his go-ahead to produce a full season of 24 shows, to be taped in England at his ATV studios.

Jim had always been suspicious of syndication, thinking that it represented a second-class way of getting a show on the air. But the international prestige of the Grade organization and the commitment of the CBS flagship stations made the deal acceptable. The arrangement even offered some definite advantages. Most important, Lord Grade promised to give Jim a free hand; network involvement would in all probability have meant attempts by programming executives to shape the series.

A deal was quickly hammered out. The show would be a coproduction of ITC and Henson Associates and would go before the cameras in January at ATV's state-of-the-art facility at Borehamwood, near London.

One early decision was to feature a guest star on each show. From Jim's point of view, this would help provide a bridge between the Muppet world and the audience. From ITC's point of view, it would make the show easier to promote.

By now it was already November, and the January start date meant that a production team had to be assembled without delay. The most urgent priority, perhaps, was to find a squad of writers who could provide enough Muppet material to sustain a full season.

One obvious choice—an essential one from Jim's point of view—was Jerry Juhl. Jerry had left New York in 1969 to return to California, but he had maintained an ongoing professional relationship with Jim and the Muppets at long distance. He had written many of the classic Bert and Ernie routines and had collaborated with Jim on the script for a proposed puppet stage show.

Jerry understood the Muppets as no other writer could, but he lacked network-style series experience. At Bernie Brillstein's suggestion, he was teamed with two experienced network writers, Jack Burns—formerly of the Burns and Schreiber comedy team—and Mark London. "We sat down in L.A.," Jerry remembers, "and in a matter of about eight weeks wrote twenty-four scripts. For some reason, we thought all the scripts should be in place before we went to England. That didn't work, of course, but it wasn't a complete waste of time because there were plenty of good bits in those scripts and we cannibalized them all season."

Meanwhile David Lazer—who had recently joined the company from IBM, where he had been involved with the Muppets in the production of a series of meeting-break films—was named executive producer for Henson Associates. His first task was to deal with the complex logistics of moving an American company of performers and craftspeople to London on decidedly short notice.

By January everything was in place for the taping of the first two shows—designated as pilots, though both would be aired as part of the first season—with Connie Stevens and Juliet Prowse as guest stars.

Finding celebrities was not easy at first. The old dictum that actors should avoid working with children and animals extended, it soon became apparent, to puppets. Bernie Brillstein recalls that he and Jim had to rely on professional friendships to keep the show supplied with guest hosts that first year. Luckily, they knew a lot of people.

As taping settled into a routine, the atmosphere was greatly buoyed by the positive reaction given to the Muppets by the British studio crew. The relaxed manner of the Muppet performers and their off-camera clowning enabled a rapport with cameramen, electricians, and grips to develop almost overnight.

"From the very first," David Lazer explains, "the crew thought that everything we did was hilariously funny...so that, of course, made everyone feel good."

Especially important among the British contingent were directors Peter Harris and Philip Casson and senior floor manager Richard Holloway. Another member of the crew, Martin Baker, would leave ATV for Henson Associates, where he became a key figure in the production team.

As Jim was the first to acknowledge, the first season of *The Muppet Show* was uneven. At their best, the shows were very funny—and even the weaker ones had hilarious moments—but the format was not yet polished enough to guarantee quality from week to week. Also, many of the characters were not yet fully developed.

One of the biggest problems was with Fozzie Bear. Fozzie was crucial to *The Muppet Show* because he was conceived as Frank Oz's main character, and the success of the show would depend to a significant degree on Frank having the opportunity to display the full range of his virtuoso performance and comedic skills.

It was logical to have a comedian as a primary character on *The Muppet Show*, particularly once the Muppet Theater had been established as its basic setting. And given the spirit of the Muppets, it was almost inevitable that he would be a bad comedian. The problem with Fozzie was that his bad jokes and failure to win over an audience provoked more embarrassment than sympathy.

Jerry Juhl and Frank Oz gradually transformed Fozzie by building up the positive aspects of his personality. They allowed his perpetual optimism to offset his onstage failures until he became a more rounded character. Fozzie's virtues ultimately made his ineptness acceptable—and even endearing. So successful was this metamorphosis that he became one of the most popular of all the Muppets.

Jerry's role in this was not lost on Jim Henson. As the first season progressed, he came to rely more and more on Jerry's deep-rooted understanding of the Muppets (their association, after all, went back almost fifteen years) and his gift for developing characters. By the second season, Jerry became head writer. The writing team was further enriched by the addition of Don Hinkley, formerly a mainstay of *The Carol Burnett Show* and many other network series. With Jerry, Don Hinkley would remain a stalwart of the Muppet

Dave Goelz came to the Henson organization as a puppet builder, but Jim Henson and Frank Oz felt sure that he had potential as a performer. *The Muppet Show* gave him the opportunity to realize that potential by developing The Great Gonzo and other key characters.

"Late one summer evening in 1985 while we were shooting *Labyrinth* in London, I met Jim and Frank Oz at CTS recording studios in Wembley to tape a series of Dial-a-Muppet messages.

"Each one had to time exactly fifty-five seconds, so we arranged ourselves in a circle with an oversized stopwatch facing upward in the center. It was late, we were all tired, and sure enough, as I began a solo segment I mispronounced a word and Jim and Frank began to giggle. It was impossible for me to continue. I asked them to leave. Frank obliged by going into the drum room behind me. Jim was sure it would be all right if he just crouched behind his music stand, which was directly in my line of sight.

"A music stand does not conceal much of a six-foot-three-inch man. True, I could not see his face, but his jacket, hands, and legs were wiggling as he wheezed and convulsed. Meanwhile, Frank's strangled laughter escaped from the sealed drum room as a whining, crying sound reminiscent of a tortured Miss Piggy. The engineers shifted in their seats. I was laughing so hard there was no way I could pull myself together.

"After the customary twenty minutes of reeling around the room gasping like morons, nature took its course and the three of us calmed down sufficiently to resume work."

(continued on page 100)

How things work

Visitors to Studio D in Borehamwood during the taping of *The Muppet Show* would have encountered sets that looked very much like this, except that they were generally more complex. Complex or simple, however, sets for Muppet productions are raised on stilts or platforms ⮞ to permit the Muppet performers to work standing, where possible, with their puppets held above their heads. To be on a level with the puppets and keep the performers' heads out of shot, the television camera ⇒ is elevated on a tripod or crane. One of the two performers here wears built-up ⮞ shoes to equalize their heights. Both wear headbands ⮌ from which are cantilevered microphones ⮞ into which they speak their lines. A script ⮞ has been placed where the performers can see it. They watch their performances on a monitor ⮞ *as* they perform, so that they see exactly what the audience will see at home. A speaker ⮞ is available for playbacks. The puppets seen in this picture are typical hand and rod Muppets. The rods ⮞ are used to control arm movements.

FRANK OZ, JIM HENSON

JIM HENSON, JOHN CLEESE

Muppet Reality

RICHARD HUNT

JIM HENSON, RICHARD HUNT

GILDA RADNER

FRANK OZ, EDGAR BERGEN

DAVE GOELZ, FRANK OZ,
AND STAGEHAND NIGEL LYTHGOE

RICHARD HUNT

FRANK OZ,
JERRY NELSON,
LOUISE GOLD

DAVE GOELZ

THERE HAS NEVER BEEN A PLACE quite like the set of *The Muppet Show*. If you had walked out onto Stage D while the show was in production, you might well have found a frog or a bear chatting to an Academy Award–winning actor or a world-renowned opera star—not for the benefit of the camera but just for the sake of making conversation. Or you might have overheard a pig chewing out a subordinate porker for having dared to stand in for her during rehearsals. Not that any script called for this behavior. It was just another example of the silliness that tended to set in once the line between everyday reality and Muppet reality had been crossed.

In the workshop, Richard Hunt would answer the telephone in Scooter's voice—"Elstree Studios here—home of the world-famous *Muppet Show*"—and there were times when the ad-libbing was funnier than the script. Sometimes this ad-libbing was used to keep the guest star loose. Mostly, though, it was the norm. The Muppet performers were having fun, and so the Muppets they controlled seemed to be having fun, too—on camera and off.

JIM HENSON, STEVE WHITMIRE,
FRANK OZ, RICHARD HUNT, DAVE GOELZ

99

Executive producer David Lazer was a key figure behind the scenes at *The Muppet Show.*

"Shortly after I joined Jim, the Sons of the Desert, a comedy club, wanted to present Jim with an award. We accepted and also agreed to do a guest spot on their program. It was to take place in the ballroom of a New York hotel.

"I was still spanking new to the Henson company and wanted everything to be perfect. Before getting there, I made sure every detail was covered: best spot on the program; best table while waiting to go on; and everything okay technically.

"When we arrived, my heart sank a little. It did not look like this was going to be a world-class event—in fact, it felt very homemade, almost bizarre. Anyway, I was taking my first gig most seriously—too seriously, because it apparently prompted Jim, Jane, and Frank to 'unstarch' me forever.

"Their conspiracy included pretending that Frank was drinking heavily. Soon, he could hardly speak without slurring, and then he got completely silly. By the time Jim and Frank were due onstage, I was looking for EXIT signs. What had I gotten myself into?

"Of course, Jim and Frank performed brilliantly. And from that time on, I never took myself quite so seriously again."

DAVID LAZER

LOUISE GOLD—the most versatile female puppeteer to work on *The Muppet Show*—was also the only British member of the cast. An experienced actress and an accomplished singer with a gift for vocal parody, she was often featured in musical numbers, though her most notable characterization was Annie Sue, Miss Piggy's sweet, young, and talented admirer who was not without her own streak of ambition.

writing corps, which eventually included David Odell, who contributed a strong sense of structure to the show, and Chris Langham, a British humorist responsible for some of the Muppets' wildest flights of fantasy.

Another important change was that David Lazer became sole executive producer for the series, a move that reflected his critical role in the success of *The Muppet Show* and the extent to which Jim had come to rely on him.

"The kind of comedy we do," Jim explained at the time, "depends on being able to work in a certain atmosphere—it's something we strive consciously to create. I've heard of other shows that thrive on the tension that exists between the stars, or between a star and the producers, but that wouldn't work for us. If we didn't manage to maintain a friendly atmosphere, we'd be in deep trouble....David Lazer is the person we rely on."

Lazer's responsibilities covered everything from overseeing *The Muppet Show*'s financial affairs to handling union disputes to making sure that the guest star was happy at all times. He carried out all of these tasks with flair, diplomacy, and the sense of fun that is so essential when working with the Muppets.

As the second season progressed, *The Muppet Show* began to take on a new vitality. The Muppet Theater format began to function flawlessly, and the on-set chemistry pushed performers to higher levels of achievement. And with all the other elements in place, the writers were able to turn out consistently funny scripts.

"About halfway through that second season," Jerry Juhl recalls, "I suddenly had the sense that everything was working—that we had reached a new plateau."

Among other things, it was becoming easier to develop storylines holding each show together. These were often demented variations on the old Busby Berkeley type of backstage movie plot crossbred with hilarious glosses on contemporary sitcoms. At the same time, the backstage format permitted the writers to slot musical numbers and other variety show elements seamlessly into the continuity, as well as glorious parodies of soap operas ("Veterinarians' Hospital"), space operas ("Pigs in Space"), and movie spoofs.

As the show picked up momentum, it also picked up in the ratings. People began to tune in regularly to see what stunt Kermit or Fozzie or Gonzo would pull next. Show business personalities and their agents noticed. Suddenly, Bernie Brillstein found that it was no longer difficult to engage guest stars to appear on the show.

A key moment in season two, and in the entire history of the Muppets, came when Rudolf Nureyev agreed to do the show. The news that the world's most famous ballet dancer—a cultural icon of monumental stature—would be appearing on the program generated unprecedented press coverage and audience curiosity. Fortunately, the show lived up to its advance billing, with Nureyev allowing himself to be the butt of outrageous gags, dancing at one point with a gargantuan pig dressed in tutu and toe shoes.

Nor was Nureyev by any means the only major star of the second season. Also featured were Steve Martin, Elton John, Bob Hope, George Burns, Zero Mostel, Lou Rawls, Julie Andrews, Peter Sellers, John Cleese, Bernadette Peters, Edgar Bergen (one of Jim's boyhood idols), and Milton Berle. And making guest stars feel at home became a key part of David Lazer's routine.

"When you book a guest star onto almost any other show," Lazer once explained, "the star gets into his car in Beverly Hills, drives twenty minutes to the studio, does his day's work, then drives home again. Here we're asking the guest to come to a foreign country and to spend several days working in what for him might be a completely unfamiliar environment. That makes him our guest in a very literal sense. It's one of my responsibilities to make sure he is comfortable, and not just in the physical sense, though that's part of it too, of course. I have to make sure he's comfortable

working with us—that when he sees the show he feels we made him look good."

It was during the second season, too, that a relatively minor character came to sudden prominence, electrifying the audience like Ruby Keeler in a Warner Bros. musical. For close to three dozen shows, Miss Piggy had remained in the background. She was little more than a featured player, most notable for her spots as Nurse Piggy in "Veterinarians' Hospital." During that second season, however, the writers gave her a scene that allowed Frank Oz a chance to raise her to the level of prominence *she* had always known she deserved.

"The script called for [Piggy] to slap [Kermit]," Frank once said. "Instead of a slap, I gave him a funny karate hit. Somehow that hit crystallized her character for me—the coyness hiding the aggression; the conflict of that love with her desire for a career; her hunger for a glamour image; her tremendous out-and-out ego...."

A superstar was born.

The original Piggy—sometimes performed by Frank, sometimes by Richard Hunt—had been a rather homely creature, though possessing a certain *chutzpah*. But she now became subject to a process of glamorization that involved the talents of the New York and London workshops.

One of the major tasks of the New York shop, under the direction of Caroly Wilcox, was the development of improved Piggy heads, both for practical reasons (Piggy was not an easy puppet to operate and maintain) and to make her more alluring, a process that involved many small but significant design changes. Simultaneously, the writers began to look for situations in which to feature the charismatic pig, and Frank Oz—now her sole performer—began to explore her psyche.

No Muppet benefited more from the presence of guest stars on the show than Miss Piggy, since, even as she became an authentic celebrity, she remained utterly starstruck. In her universe, showbiz success was all that mat-

Jim

PEOPLE tended to identify Jim Henson with Kermit, but Rowlf the Dog —laid back and down to earth—was perhaps the character who had the most in common with the real-life maestro of the Muppets.

SMART and unpretentious, Jim loved to perform dumb, pompous characters like Link Hogthrob. He gave them just the right pontificating voices and smug yet confused facial expressions.

JIM Henson avoided sarcasm, resorting instead to gentle teasing. However, when performing Waldorf —an incorrigible heckler—Jim was free to trade barbs about the best—or worst! —*The Muppet Show* could offer.

IF THE viewing audience were to forget everything else Jim Henson created, it would remember Kermit, the harassed master of the Muppet Theater and one of the most original inventions in the history of television.

Who's Who

BASED on the great New Orleans singer and pianist Doctor John, Dr. Teeth was something of a wish-fulfillment character for Jim, who was fascinated by the music world.

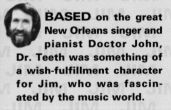

ALTHOUGH nominally one of Jim Henson's characters (Jim operated the head and provided the voice), the Swedish Chef was actually a collaboration between Jim and Frank Oz, who controlled both of the Chef's hands. Frank would deliberately do unexpected things—tossing chickens into the air, juggling meat cleavers—that Jim would have to go along with, winging it as only he could.

Frank O

A PUPPETRY virtuoso, Frank Oz was able to make something out of even the most unlikely material. But it was his work with Jim Henson —Bert and Ernie, Kermit and Piggy— that brought out the best in him. Able to inspire one another to ever-more-hilarious flights of lunacy, Frank and Jim created a body of work that was far more than the sum of its parts.

ALONG with Cookie Monster—also performed by Frank—Animal is the ultimate representative of a long line of Muppets who personify unbridled appetite.

A GIFTED puppeteer, Frank Oz has nonetheless known insecurity as a performer. This contributed enormously to his characterization of Fozzie Bear, a sweetly insecure and absolutely terrible comedian.

STIFF and censorious, Sam the Eagle is Frank Oz's interpretation of a bird whose feathers are ruffled all too easily.

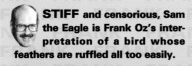

ONE of Frank's more unusual creations must have been Marvin Suggs, whose forte was banging on the heads of the hapless Muppephones—small, well-trained balls of fur—who would then dutifully yelp the melodies to such tunes as "Lady of Spain."

IF Jim Henson's name will always be linked to Kermit, Frank Oz will inevitably be remembered as the performer who brought Miss Piggy to life.

tered. So even though she regarded female guest stars as rivals, she never lost sight of the fact that they, too, had had to claw their way up the same ladder that she had. And as for male stars, she would pursue them inimitably: drooling on Roger Moore's immaculate lapels, snuggling against Christopher Reeve's supermanly chest, pumping Danny Kaye's ascot like a novice milkmaid nervously toying with the udder of a Guernsey cow.

For regular viewers of *The Muppet Show*, Piggy's rise to stardom was an enthralling weekly spectacle, rendered all the more so by the fact that the audience was privy to the vicissitudes of her personal life—namely, her pursuit of Kermit. It was like watching a hit series and reading *The National Enquirer* at the same time.

Within the context of the show, this did a lot for Kermit, too. He had played many parts during his two decades on the home screen, but never before had he been the love interest of a glamorous pig. That was bizarre even by Muppet standards, but it gave Jim a splendid opportunity to enrich Kermit's character. Piggy's clumsy advances provided Kermit with recurring opportunities to display the prickly aspect of his personality, and even to give notice of incipient paranoia.

With Miss Piggy's rise, Fozzie now became the third banana, which proved a boon because it was the role he had been born to play. And with *The Muppet Show* becoming such a hit, being third banana in the Muppet Theater was better than having the lead in most other shows. In a sense, too, Fozzie's role was emotionally as important as that of Kermit or Piggy; he was the embodiment of the basic sweetness that was at the core of the show.

As *The Muppet Show* crystallized, another star performer emerged in Dave Goelz. A California-born industrial designer, Dave began to build puppets and perform them in schools after discovering *Sesame Street*. He met Frank Oz in California, then visited the *Sesame Street* set in New York,

where he met Jerry Nelson, Richard Hunt, and others.

Soon after, Dave joined the Henson organization as a puppet builder, but displayed a flair for performance that was encouraged by Jim and Frank. In 1977, Dave became a full-time performer whose skills and quirky sense of humor made him—and his best-known character, The Great Gonzo—indispensable.

The original Gonzo had been built by Jim Henson himself, who liked to keep his hand in at the shop when he could find the time. The character was, in fact, a pure expression of Jim's visual imagination, having been made with no particular personality in mind.

When casting the show, Jack Burns had the notion of making this beaked mutant a hapless daredevil—a kind of overambitious hybrid of Harry Houdini and Evel Knievel. This was a natural concept for the Muppet Theater, but in the first season Gonzo suffered from a certain moroseness that was at odds with the absurdist enthusiasm behind his doomed feats of daring. This was in large part a consequence of his naturally gloomy expression. Besides, as with Fozzie in those early days, Gonzo's failures tended to provoke discomfort as much as sympathy. He was a downer.

Toward the end of that first season, though, during the taping of a backstage scene, Jim said, "We need more energy from Gonzo." Dave responded by having Gonzo overreact to the situation. He got a big laugh, and Dave began to have a sense of the character's full potential.

"Between seasons," Dave explains, "I built a new Gonzo with an eye mechanism that enabled him to look excited. That helped me develop the 'up' side of Gonzo's character, and Jerry Juhl and the other writers picked up on it. There was a moment during the second season when I had Gonzo ad-lib a line that was, I think, important for my understanding of his character. He'd been auditioning chickens for the show—dancing chickens—and they were all terrible. At the end of the scene I had him turn to the camera and say,

'Nice legs, though.' Something jelled right there. It told me something about him."

The fact that Gonzo had a healthy libido, even if it was directed primarily at poultry, helped make his character more intriguing. Beyond that, however, he possessed an immaculately perverse imagination, proving himself capable of devising epic stunts that could only result in the infliction of pain upon their perpetrator.

In fact Gonzo displayed many of the symptoms of a masochist. But it remained far from certain that he was one. He was a perfectionist, and perfection, as he would be the first to point out, sometimes involves overlooking personal comfort in favor of a greater goal.

Another character important to the continuity of the show was Scooter (Richard Hunt). Initially Scooter served largely as an irritant to Kermit, constantly reminding the beleaguered frog that the theater was owned by his (Scooter's) uncle. Later he became a good deal more sympathetic and was occasionally permitted to have an intimate moment with the guest star.

Even more central to the show's success, perhaps, were Statler (also Richard Hunt) and Waldorf (Jim Henson), those sardonic senior citizens who turned their Muppet Theater box into heckler's heaven. By criticizing everything, they permitted the television audience to take a more charitable view of the frequent onstage fiascoes.

Members of the Electric Mayhem, especially Zoot, generally gave the impression that they were too hip to be caught up in the backstage happenings. For them, *The Muppet Show* was just another gig (a good gig, certainly), though Floyd Pepper, as performed by Jerry Nelson, often got entangled in situations he would have preferred to avoid, as in the show where he was stuck with the task of looking after Miss Piggy's Fou-Fou, a one-pig dog. Most effectively used of the Mayhem members was Animal (Frank Oz), the latest in a long line of Muppets to be gov-

STEVE WHITMIRE

It was during the last season of *The Muppet Show* that Steve Whitmire—performer of such quirky characters as Rizzo the Rat—began to establish himself as a puppeteer of outstanding ability.

"In the winter of 1978, Jim flew me to New York to meet him and Frank Oz and to do an informal audition. I was nineteen years old and had been an obsessed Muppet fan for eight years.

"I got to the Henson offices at about 8:30 in the morning. I pressed the button. Suddenly, there was a rude buzzing noise. Now, I had never encountered a door with a remote locking mechanism, so I had no idea that when the buzzer sounded, I was supposed to pull the door open. In fact, I thought I had set off an alarm! The buzzing stopped. I thought for a beat, then pushed the button again. 'BUZZ!' came the sound.

"Suddenly, the door flew open. There was Jim Henson, squinting from his first dose of sunlight for the day. His hair was scruffy and his clothes were wrinkled. He had a broom in his hands. I smiled, offered my hand, and said, 'Hi! I'm Steve Whitmire from Atlanta.' He looked puzzled. 'The puppeteer...?' I said.

"'Oh, sure. Come in,' he said. 'Children sometimes play with the buzzer.'

"Inside, a wooden staircase went straight up three floors. Years later, I learned that Jim had worked late the night before and spent the night in the office. He had just woken up and was sweeping the stairs!"

(continued on page 114)

ONE OF JIM HENSON'S favorite episodes of *The Muppet Show* was the show from the third season that guest starred Harry Belafonte and featured his famous hit "Banana Boat Song." "Turn the World Around"—also featured in the show—allowed Belafonte to perform with Muppets from the regular cast and African masks specially created for the number.

TURN THE WORLD AROUND

We come from the water Living in the water Go back to the water Turn the world around We come from the fire Living in the fire Go back to the fire Turn the world around We come from the mountain Living on the mountain Go back to the mountain Turn the world around

Do you know who I am Do you know who you are See one another clearly So we know who we are

Water make the river River wash the mountain Fire make the sunlight Turn the world around

Heart is of the river Body is of the mountain Still it is the sunlight Turn the world around

Only can the spirit Truly of the spirit We are of the spirit Turn the world around

107

AS SOON AS A GUEST STAR had been booked for *The Muppet Show*, executive producer David Lazer would call and ask the crucial question: "Is there any particular Muppet that you'd like to work with?" Almost every guest star had a favorite, and the writers always tried to accommodate their requests. If there was a problem with this system, it was that too many people wanted to work with Kermit and Piggy, while the production team liked to feature as many different characters as possible.

Some guest stars had very clear ideas about what they wanted to do on the show. John Cleese helped write the script of the episode he starred in. Glenda Jackson, on the other hand, told the writers, "You people obviously know what you're doing. Write anything you like and I'll perform it."

For Jim Henson, working with the guest stars was one of the greatest rewards of the show and he kept notes of his experiences with them:

"We're working with Julie Andrews now, and I dearly love her. She's such a great person, always interested in people personally, and very professional about her work.... Loretta Lynn—wonderful, warm, real—an amazing story to her career—and she's like 'real folks' in North Carolina....Everybody has only the nicest things to say about Liberace. Surprisingly bad pianist, though...."

JOHN CLEESE

BROOKE SHIELDS

DOM DeLUISE

ZERO MOSTEL

GILDA RADNER

BEVERLY SILLS

ELTON JOHN

RUDOLF NUREYEV

RAQUEL WELCH

STEVE MARTIN

Miss Piggy

Like many superstars, Miss Piggy was in showbiz for a while before she was discovered. But once given the opportunity to shine, she was catapulted to international celebrity almost overnight.

The first version of the future *grande dame* was designed by Michael K. Frith in 1974 for the *Sex and Violence* pilot of *The Muppet Show*, which aired the following year. At that point, Piggy was just a bit player, used in a spoof of *Planet of the Apes*. But she hung on, becoming a supporting *artiste* in the first year of the series and even gaining featured status as Nurse Piggy in the "Veterinarians' Hospital" sketches.

It was during the second season, however, that the porcine seductress really came into her own. In a scene involving Piggy and Kermit, the script called upon Piggy to slap the frog. Instead of having her merely *slap* Kermit, Frank Oz, who was performing Piggy at that time (he and Richard Hunt had formerly shared the role), had her puff out her ample chest, assume that attitude of offended rage that would become so familiar, and deliver a vicious karate chop, accompanied by an appropriate, blood-curdling yell.

PIGGY (*above*) wears a hat in the image of her beloved. She and Kermit (*right*) show off their terpsichorean skills in *The Muppets Take Manhattan*.

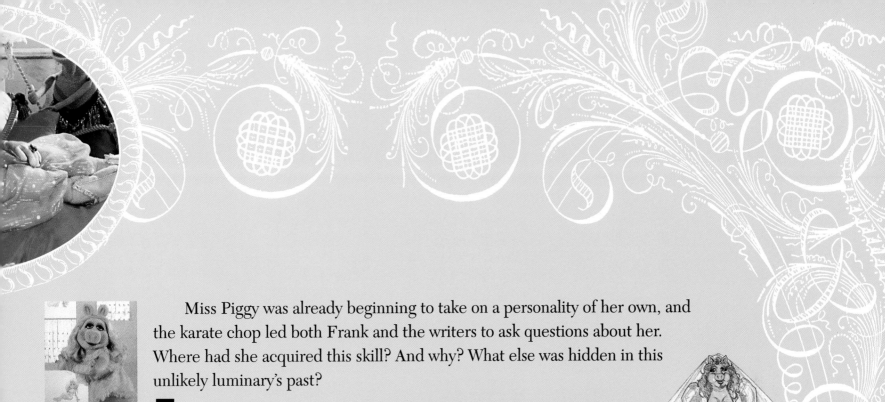

Miss Piggy was already beginning to take on a personality of her own, and the karate chop led both Frank and the writers to ask questions about her. Where had she acquired this skill? And why? What else was hidden in this unlikely luminary's past?

PIN-UP Piggy

Frank began to compile a profile—both biographical and psychological—of the pig. "Miss Piggy," he would tell visitors to the set, "grew up in a small town. Her father died young and her mother wasn't very nice to her. She had to enter beauty contests to survive. She has a lot of aggressiveness, but she needs a lot in order to survive—as many women do. She has a lot of vulnerability, which she has to hide because of her need to be a superstar."

He might have added that—as she once affirmed in a memorable duet with Raquel Welch—Miss Piggy, despite her difficult upbringing, enjoys being a girl. Indeed she perceives herself as the epitome of everything that is feminine. If others—notably Kermit—fail to share this perception, she has great faith in her ability to overcome this lapse in discrimination by means of patience and willpower. The latter she has by the trough-full, but patience unfortunately is not one of her strong suits. She is therefore still called upon, from time to time, to reinforce associates' recognition of her femininity by means of her trademark karate chops and very unpiglike snarls.

A HALSTON original design.

"It's time to play the music. It's time to light the lights. It's

ime to meet the Muppets on *The Muppet Show* tonight...."

"The Muppet Show Theme" by Jim Henson and Sam Pottle

A BIG PART OF THE FUN of tuning in to *The Muppet Show* was wondering what the Henson team would come up with next. One week it might be Miss Piggy in black leather riding with a gang of hogs on hogs, singing "I Get Around." Another week, it might be Kermit shut in a trunk with Gonzo's toxic fungi collection, or a mob of pigs dressed as Vikings setting sail in pursuit of villages to pillage while singing "In the Navy."

On *The Muppet Show*, tigers were apt to show up at the North Pole and penguins, protected by sunglasses, would put in appearances in tropical rainforests. There was the usual complement of zany vaudevil-lians, of course. Lew Zealand and his ever-popular boomerang fish act was a favorite, not to mention assorted jugglers and acrobats, the latter with unpronounceable Italian names. Musical acts included a choir of singing asparagus and a sort of living xylophone made up of tiny creatures (the Muppephones) that yelped in tune when hit on the head with a mallet by a character called Marvin Suggs.

Occasionally classic older routines—some going back to *Sam and Friends*—were revived, but for the most part *The Muppet Show* was sheer, unbridled invention. The miracle is that the writers and perform-ers were able to keep up this frantic pace for 120 shows.

Curiouser and Curiouser...

If Studio D at ATV's Borehamwood production facility was the nerve center of *The Muppet Show*—the place where the mayhem of the Muppet Theater actually unfolded—the large L-shaped room adjacent to it was equally crucial to the success of the series. This room housed the British edition of the Muppet workshop, though the accents heard there were mostly American. (At any given time, about half the puppetbuilders involved with the series were based in Borehamwood. The rest worked out of two shops in New York, and to some extent the crews rotated.)

The large L-shaped room was a wonderland, filled with familiar puppet characters waiting to be called on, and lined with cartons that bore hand-lettered labels reading, for example, "Chorus Costumes: Girls and Hens," "Odd and Large Eyes," "Wagnerian Hats," "Legs and Some Shoes." At any given time, a dozen or so men and women were likely to be working at benches, desks, and sewing machines, readying characters for the current show or creating new puppets for an upcoming sketch. Heads of lettuce (complete with eyes and mouth) were being assembled while nearby someone cut and sewed Japanese costumes that would fit a two-year-old.

"When I first got there," said Amy Van Gilder, who headed the London shop for four years, "there were just four of us and we were working till four in the morning every day. We were using a lot of live animals on the show at that time, and they always seemed to find their way into the shop, so you'd come in in the morning, after not much sleep, and find a piglet running round the floor, or a huge frog blinking at you from a workbench.

"And there was always something to be built in a hurry. Once we had to build a life-size moose in one day. That was fairly typical. I remember we made a grasshopper for one show. It was two or three inches tall and rigged to finger rings, and I brought it to the set when they were ready to begin shooting the scene. Jim said, 'That's just great. I need another one just like it, driving a car—in fifteen minutes.'

"Usually we had about three days to build something. The script might call for dancing cucumbers or singing corn-on-the-cob, or it might be something more enigmatic. One week we were asked to make a 'chill'—the sort that runs up your spine—and there was a character called 'the germ' who Sherry Amott constructed from cellophane and coat hangers.

"There were rigging situations to deal with, too. We had to rig puppets to drink, to swim, to wrestle, to row, to drive cars, to shoot arrows. We had to rig rats to hang from floating balloons. We had to rig Kermit and Piggy so that they could be catapulted into Statler and Waldorf's box. Once we had to rig a whole mob of Japanese pole vaulters so they could actually pole vault...."

---

erned entirely by their appetites.

Most other characters, although they would be seen backstage from time to time, were primarily used in sketches and running features. The Swedish Chef was built and performed (with Frank Oz's assistance) by Jim Henson. Because of his elaborate hand movements, the chef was perhaps the most impressive example of a two-man puppet operation in the Muppet repertoire. Only perfect coordination between the two performers could permit the chef to wrestle with a chicken that had no intention of ending up in the pot, or gesticulate at a talking chocolate cake.

"At times," Frank recalls, "we didn't know what the hell we were doing with the Swedish Chef. A lot of it was made up on the spot, and it depended on the special rapport that Jim and I had when we were working together. The Chef was special. It was one of those situations—like Ernie and Bert—where we just knew what the other was going to do next and there was no need to talk about it."

Link Hogthrob (Jim Henson) found a home on both "Bear on Patrol," where he costarred with Fozzie, and "Pigs in Space," where he was joined by Dr. Julius Strangepork (Jerry Nelson) and Miss Piggy. The mad scientist Bunsen Honeydew (Dave Goelz) and his hapless assistant Beaker (Richard Hunt) were used primarily in a series of sketches

THE MUPPET SHOW WORKSHOP contained whole galaxies of eyes, noses, and wigs.

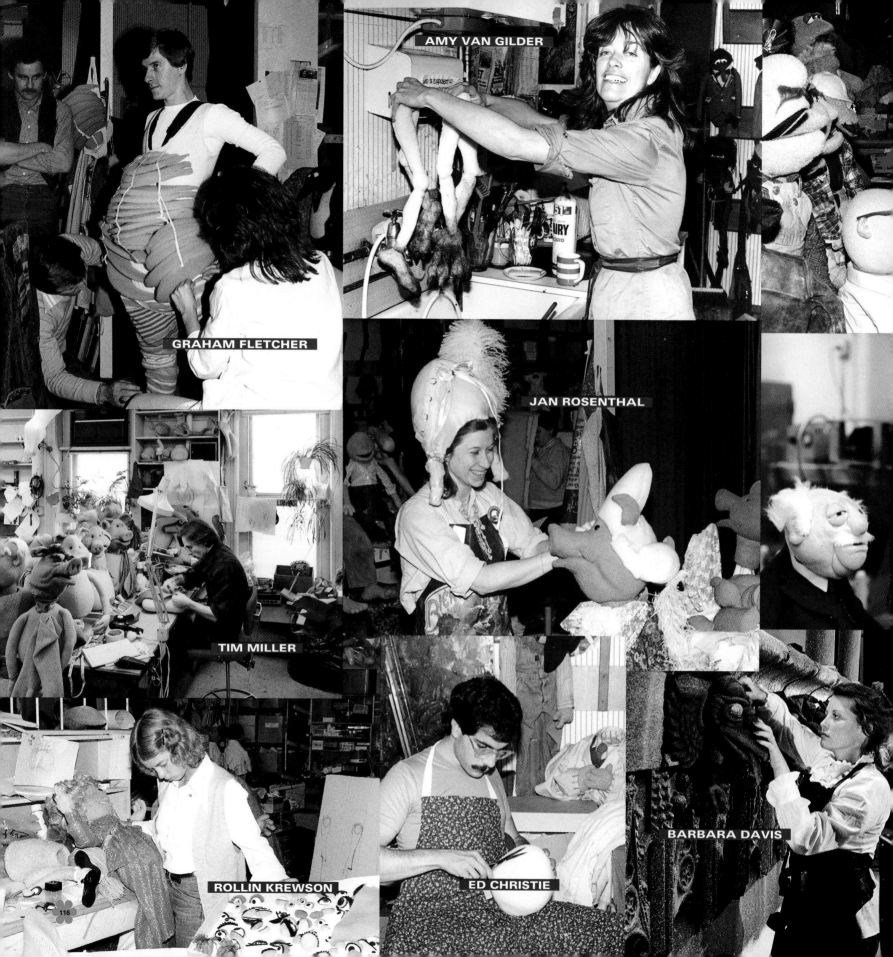

AMY VAN GILDER

GRAHAM FLETCHER

JAN ROSENTHAL

TIM MILLER

ROLLIN KREWSON

ED CHRISTIE

BARBARA DAVIS

116

DAVE GOELZ AND BOB McCORMACK

BOBBY PAYNE

CALISTA HENDRICKSON

BONNIE ERICKSON

CHERYL HENSON

POLLY SMITH

NO TWO DAYS were alike in the *Muppet Show* workshop.

As Miss Piggy's fame grew, her wardrobe alone demanded the full-time attention of one designer—Calista Hendrickson. Eventually it occupied almost an entire wall of the Elstree shop and became one of the highlights of the studio tour that was given to guest stars and other visitors. Many other costumes were needed for the show, of course, and Polly Smith proved to be a gifted costume designer, able to adapt her skills to the challenging vagaries of the typical *Muppet Show* script.

Some of the Muppet performers began their careers as puppet builders, so it was not unusual to find Dave Goelz, for example, in the shop, working on one of his own characters. Similarly, some of the Muppet builders—such as Bobby Payne and Rollin Krewson—doubled as performers when extra hands were needed in front of the cameras.

In the early days of *The Muppet Show*, almost everything was built and maintained in the London shop, but later—even though the London staff doubled, then tripled—much of the puppet manufacturing was done in New York, where art director Michael K. Frith and designer Bonnie Erickson were able to keep day-to-day tabs on the development of new characters and on experiments with new materials and techniques.

Among those who labored in the workshops in England and America, in addition to those already mentioned, were Sherry Amott, Leslee Asch, Cheryl Blalock, Ed Christie, Lyle Conway, Barbara Davis, Sal Denara, Faz Fazakas, Nomi Fredrick, Jane Gootnick, Joanne Green, Marianne Harms, Cheryl Henson, Larry Jameson, Mari Kaestle, Janet Kuhl, Kermit Love, John Lovelady, Bob McCormack, Tom McLaughlin, Wendy Midener, Tim Miller, Sara Paul, Tim Rose, Jan Rosenthal, Debbie Schneider, Ann Keeba Tenenbaum, Amy Van Gilder, and Caroly Wilcox. Some of them are shown at work on these pages. All made valuable contributions to the success of *The Muppet Show*.

Richard Hunt

JANICE

ONE OF the key performers on *The Muppet Show*, Richard Hunt created the laid-back guitarist Janice, Sweetums, Wayne of Wayne and Wanda, the irrepressible Scooter, the unfortunate Beaker, and Statler, master of the hackle-raising heckle.

SWEETUMS

WANDA AND WAYNE

SCOOTER

BEAKER

STATLER

Dave Goelz

BEAUREGARD

GONZO

DAVE GOELZ'S characters are the products of an imagination that is quirky even by Muppet standards. Most famous (certainly in his own eyes) is The Great Gonzo, while others include Beauregard—the Muppet Theater's slow-witted janitor—Zoot, and Dr. Bunsen Honeydew.

ZOOT

DR. BUNSEN HONEYDEW

Jerry Nelson

FLOYD PEPPER

CRAZY HARRY

ROBIN

JERRY NELSON'S many characters for *The Muppet Show* **include Floyd Pepper, Crazy Harry, Kermit's nephew Robin, Pops the stage doorman, Lew Zealand, and Muppet Theater owner J. P. Gross.**

POPS

LEW ZEALAND

J. P. GROSS

in which Beaker would be the victim of Bunsen's bizarre experiments. "Veterinarians' Hospital" starred Piggy, Nurse Janice (Richard Hunt), and, of course, Dr. Bob, alias Rowlf the Dog. Rowlf, in fact, popped up all over the show but was seldom used backstage as a continuity character.

"I have no doubt," says Jerry Juhl, "that Rowlf could have been one of the stars of the show if only we could have had him interacting on a regular basis with Kermit and Piggy....But, from a practical point of view, it just wasn't possible."

The practical problem Jerry Juhl refers to is that Kermit and Rowlf were both performed by Jim Henson. Except with the help of elaborate cutting, they could not appear together. For exactly the same reason, it was impractical for Frank to perform both Piggy and Fozzie in the same take, so the writers had to avoid such situations.

When *The Muppet Show* began, Jane Henson recalls, nobody thought that it could run for more than about three seasons. Everyone assumed that it would be impossible to come up with fresh Muppet material for any longer than that. In reality, it turned out that the characters generated more material than anyone had dared to hope for.

On top of that, guest stars as varied as Liberace and Dizzy Gillespie were lining up to do the show, and each new guest suggested fertile areas to explore. In any case, the growing success of the show dictated that the third season was followed by a fourth, then a fifth. Nor was this success just in the English-speaking world. By the fourth season, *The Muppet Show* was the greatest international television hit of all time, being aired in more than 100 countries.

In the fifth and final season, the show was as popular as ever, but a variety of factors combined to persuade Jim Henson that it was time to bring down the curtain. Jim felt he and his associates had done all that they could within the thirty-minute TV format, at least for the time being. Once again, he was anxious to move on to new challenges.

CHAPTER FIVE

"There are many images of Jim that linger," says Dave Goelz, "but one of the strongest is of him standing in front of a big studio monitor with his arms folded in front of him and one hand on his chin, laughing out loud at a playback of another puppeteer's work. Jim Henson was an incredibly generous performer who was able to complement his comrades so that everyone could shine. He always gave due credit."

This is not to say that Jim did not indulge in a little friendly competition from time to time, but he was able to compete without things becoming too serious.

"Jim loved upstaging," Dave Goelz explains. "He pursued it with a religious fervor and encouraged everyone else to do it. There were limits to what was appropriate, but within those limits upstaging was one of the hallmarks of his work. Everything he did was on many levels, and there were performance elements that would not be seen on first, second, or even third viewings. The upstaging element was one of the things that allowed our work to seem fresh viewing after viewing. There was always more than you could take in at one time.

"This made it fun for us. We reveled in finding ways of upstaging that would be outrageous but would not be noticed till it was too late. On one occasion, Jim and I were relegated to a position high on a balcony, far in the background of a Spanish town set with working pig musicians. Far below, Piggy was seducing the camera with a spirited musical rendition. During the instrumental break, Piggy began dancing. Meanwhile, my pig leaned backwards over the balcony for an upside-down trumpet solo, and that broke Jim up. He loved that kind of thing.

"Another time we were shooting the song 'In the Navy' as performed by pig Vikings who pillaged a peasant village by the ocean. Between takes I put a little bead of Styrofoam in each nostril of Steve

THE MUPPETS made the leap from television to the movies in 1979. This led to Kermit being asked, by *Time* magazine, to pose in a director's chair.

Whitmire's pig. After the take, he discovered and removed them. We did more takes, but it turned out that the take with the Styrofoam beads was the one we used. Jim cracked up when I pointed it out to him."

If Jim encouraged upstaging as a way of enriching performances, he also worked hard at upstaging himself in terms of pushing forward to new career goals. So it was that the period associated with the global success of *The Muppet Show*—1976 to 1981—also saw the launching of the Muppets on a movie career. And that was preceded by one of Jim's most important and ambitious television specials—*Emmet Otter's Jug-Band Christmas*—taped in Toronto in March of 1977. *Emmet Otter* was a very elaborate production, involving mechanical devices such as a boat that can be rowed on an artificial river, and naturalistic, platformed-up sets of the sort that could be used for a full-scale, theatrical movie.

The Muppet Movie was a natural outgrowth of both the commercial success of *The Muppet Show* and the technical advances of *Emmet Otter*. Lord Grade agreed to back the movie after the second season of the television series, by which time it was evident that the show was a solid hit.

Jim and Jack Burns sketched out the story. Then, as the third season of *The Muppet Show* went into production, Jim began to work on the final script with Jerry Juhl. That summer, the Muppet performers and a sizable crew of Muppet builders temporarily relocated to Los Angeles, where, on July 5, the first scene went before the cameras at the CBS/MTM studios in the San Fernando Valley.

Coproduced by Jim Henson and David Lazer and directed by James Frawley, *The Muppet Movie* opens at World Wide Studios in Hollywood (actually the CBS/MTM lot), where the whole Muppet gang is gathered to watch a preview of the movie. Kermit introduces the film to the audience. Then, as he sits down to watch, he is asked by his nephew Robin if this is the real story of how the Muppets came into existence. After a moment's hesitation, Kermit explains that "it's approximately how it happened."

At that point, the movie within the movie begins with a long helicopter shot, the camera starting out high above a cypress swamp. It swoops down through the trees to discover Kermit, seated on a log, strumming a banjo and singing "Rainbow Connection." Immediately, the audience has been given a signal that this is not just *The Muppet Show* on a big screen. The setup would have been far too complex and expensive for any television show, and it works all the better because it follows the World Wide Studios opening and Kermit's throwaway line to Robin.

Jim Henson is upstaging himself again.

It is typical of Jim's approach to puppetry, as well as to film and television, that he starts by telling the audience, "This is an illusion you're watching." Paradoxically, this has the effect of making it easier to accept the illusion, perhaps because members of the audience have been let in on the secret and thus can enjoy the role of co-conspirator.

In *The Muppet Movie*, however, this does not preclude the idea that the audience can still be foxed by the expensive technical magic that is apparent from the outset. In the swamp, Kermit—surrounded by water—is seen in full-length shots that cause the inquisitive viewer to wonder where the puppeteer can possibly be hidden. Soon after comes a scene—probably the one that astonished audiences more than any other—that presents Kermit riding a bicycle!

The Muppet Movie is full of such magic, and in a sense the entertainment value of the film comes, in part at least, from the sheer exhilaration of seeing the Muppets brought so convincingly to the big screen. They walk down city streets, drive cars, and in general interact with the full-scale human world in a totally believable way. If *The Muppet Show* proved how well Muppets could consort with guest hosts, *The Muppet Movie* demonstrated that Kermit, Fozzie, and all of the rest could perform equally convincingly in a bustling saloon or at a crowded county fair.

To say that this is a tour de force of puppetry is an understatement. *The Muppet Movie* represents a marriage of film and puppetry that is simply astonishing. From a purely technical point of view, it goes far beyond anything anyone else had even dreamed of. And it is a measure of Jim Henson's achievement that just about everything up there on screen—every trick, every technique, every illusion—was devised either by Jim alone or in conjunction with members of the team he had assembled so carefully.

Yet, at the same time, those are just puppets up there on screen—not essentially different from the simple hand puppets the teenage Jim Henson had built for *Sam and Friends*. And one of the most amazing things about Jim's accomplishment in *The Muppet Movie* (and in later films) was that he was able to introduce an enormous amount of technical sophistication into the creative mix without losing sight of the fundamentals he had exploited so skillfully in his earlier and more basic performances.

Brian Henson notes that his father always believed that the key to a project's success lay with the performers. In the end, everything came down to having a team of skilled puppeteers, like Frank Oz, Dave Goelz, Jerry Nelson, Richard Hunt, Steve Whitmire, and Kevin Clash, not to mention Jim himself. The puppets themselves might be more or less simple or complex, but they were, after all, only puppets.

"Jim had a lot of respect for puppetry, but not much for the puppet as a physical object," says Frank Oz. "It was just a means to an end. If he was giving a live demonstration, he didn't care if people saw him put his hand in the puppet, and he didn't try to sustain the illusion once the performance was over.

"A typical puppeteer will end his show by having his puppet say something like, 'I must try to sleep now so I'm going off to my own little house.' Jim approached the problem differently. He'd just take the puppet off his arm and toss it in a box. It was as if he wanted the puppets to accept that they were puppets…'I know I'm a puppet. I know I have no legs—but so what? I have my limitations, but look at what I *can* do.'

"To me it's still fascinating that people accept the characters we perform and talk about them as if they were alive. Without brilliant performers like Dave and Jerry and Richard and Stevie and Kevin, all you'd have is a dead piece of cloth. There's something very charming and pure about the way the audience believes in the characters so much, but as a performer I have to be able to separate myself from them, and that's something I learned from Jim. I love Muppets with all my heart, but I don't think about them when I get home. And Jim was the same way.

"People say that Jim was like Kermit. Well, I suppose Kermit was inside him somewhere, but there's no way you could say Jim *was* Kermit. Kermit could not have run this company. When Jim took Kermit off his arm, he had no difficulty leaving him behind and going on to something else."

Jim Henson was the most effortless of puppet performers—Kermit in particular came to seem like an extension of his being—but he was also much more. In *The Muppet Movie,* he exhibited some of his many talents, orchestrating characters, story, and special effects into a delightful whole that, despite all the planning and effort involved, seemed as light as a perfect omelette.

The plot of the film is well suited to the Muppets' needs. It gently parodies Hollywood clichés and conventions while providing the chief Muppet characters with plenty of opportunities to display the foibles and eccentricities that had already become familiar via the television series. There are good guys and bad guys and many guest stars—from Mel Brooks to Orson Welles. There are car chases and comic set pieces and a *High Noon*–style climax.

On screen, it all looks very simple and lots of fun. But

(continued on page 128)

WHY ARE THERE SO MANY SONGS ABOUT RAINBOWS

FIND IT. THE RAINBOW CONNECTION...THE LOVERS, THE DREAMERS, AND ME.

SOME CHOOSE TO BELIEVE IT. I KNOW THEY'RE WRONG, WAIT AND SEE...SOMEDAY WE'LL

RAINBOWS ARE VISIONS, BUT ONLY ILLUSIONS, AND RAINBOWS HAVE NOTHING TO HIDE...SO WE'VE BEEN TOLD AND

The success of *The Muppet Show* made it logical that Kermit, Piggy, and the rest of the gang would star in a movie of their own. At the same time, however, many in the industry predicted that *The Muppet Movie* would fail. How could puppets be expected to work convincingly on the big screen, people asked, let alone sustain a feature-length motion picture? It was a revival of the skepticism that had greeted Walt Disney when he announced that he was producing a full-length animated film version of *Snow White.*

Like Walt Disney, Jim Henson knew exactly what he was doing and paid no attention to the skeptics. So far as genre was concerned, he wisely went with the kind of gentle satire and parody that was already a trademark of the Muppets. The movie was made in Los Angeles, and so the idea of the Muppets

coming to Hollywood to find fame and fortune was a logical hook on which to hang the story. Thus it happens that Kermit and Fozzie set off for Tinseltown in a vintage Studebaker, encountering many old friends, a dozen or so guest stars, and a dastardly scheme to have Kermit become the spokesfrog for a chain of fast-food frog's-leg restaurants.

The movie was great fun, but beyond that it was a technical tour de force, taking puppets where none had dared venture before—bringing them convincingly into the real world by means of clever special effects, skillful editing, and sheer performance magic.

PERHAPS THE MOST MAGICAL moment in *The Muppet Movie* comes near the beginning when—after a helicopter approach shot—Kermit is discovered in a bayou, seated on a log, strumming a banjo and singing "Rainbow Connection" (written by Paul Williams and Kenny Ascher). This was not an easy scene to put on film. Among other things, it involved Jim Henson working long hours in a cramped underwater chamber in order to bring Kermit to life. But the results were well worth it, as this scene set the standard of cinematic illusion for the entire movie.

THE MUPPET MOVIE in 11 easy steps...

In a scene that amazed his fans, Kermit sets off in search of fame and fortune—astride a bicycle!

Then Kermit and Fozzie run into the Electric Mayhem...

Headed for Hollywood, Kermit and Fozzie encounter Big Bird on his way to New York to break into public television.

...and meet Charlie McCarthy and Edgar Bergen.

126

Kermit and Piggy enjoy a romantic interlude.

Kermit faces the villains of the piece...

They are interrupted by Mel Brooks as a mad scientist.

...in a *High Noon*-style showdown in a western ghost town.

Kermit and the gang regroup under the stars.

All ends happily in Tinseltown.

127

what went on behind the scenes was anything but simple. For example, the staging of each scene was critical because "coverage" of the puppets had to be thought out in advance, down to the last detail, so that the characters could move through the human world without seeming out of place. In order to achieve this feat, all the edits had to be planned before shooting, just as would be the case with an animated film.

In a conventional live-action film, the director will generally shoot a master shot of each scene—a shot that includes all of the key players, almost as if he/she were filming a piece of live theater. Then the director shoots close-ups

have to be planned in advance by means of storyboards so that only what is finally seen on screen is actually animated.

A puppet film calls for an approach that falls somewhere between animation and conventional live action. It is economically viable to have more than one take. But it is almost impossible to have a master shot that lasts for any significant length of time, so the cuts still have to be planned in advance.

In Jim Henson's words, "We can't do it [the live action] way.…We will shoot a master as long as we can, but that

FRANK OZ, Jim Henson, Dave Goelz, and Jerry Nelson (*left to right*) watch a playback on location.

KEEPING THE characters at the right heights in relation to an automobile requires some lying down on the job.

ing a piece of live theater. Then the director shoots close-ups or medium shots of the individual players performing the same scene, or perhaps asks for "two-shots" in which two key players are isolated on camera. This gives the director plenty of coverage—allowing the scene to be reconstructed in any of several different ways. Later, in the cutting room, snippets of these shots will be pieced together to create the montage that the audience sees on screen.

With animation, this would be hopelessly expensive— every foot of film costs a great deal to produce. The cuts

usually means maybe twenty seconds because the limitations of the puppetry dictate the edits. The way we shoot is very technical. Often there is no choice. We have to go to a given shot because that's the only way you can get from the first shot to the third shot." In short, every take, however brief, has to be planned down to the last detail.

In the case of *The Muppet Movie*, this meticulous planning paid off handsomely. Audiences loved *The Muppet Movie*, and its success guaranteed that there would be another Muppet film.

There was no wholesale move to Hollywood this time, however. Instead, at the end of the fifth and final season of *The Muppet Show*, the performers and workshop personnel simply moved across the street from ATV Studios to Elstree Studios—also located in Borehamwood and home base for the *Star Wars* movies. Since most of the new movie, eventually titled *The Great Muppet Caper*, would be set in London, this was a logical choice.

Produced by David Lazer and Frank Oz and directed by Jim Henson, *The Great Muppet Caper* begins with a

indicates the area of the screen where the title is being spelled out against the clouds.

You have to have credits, says Kermit, but Fozzie disagrees, insisting that nobody reads them anyway. Kermit defends the need for credits. "These people have families," he says. For a moment Fozzie forgets his situation and takes an interest in the proceedings. "What does A.S.C. stand for?" he asks when the director of photography's name appears. Soon, though, Fozzie is loudly voicing the wish that this be over as soon as possible. Trying to calm him,

JIM HENSON and Frank Oz relax on location with their most famous alter egos, Kermit the Frog and Miss Piggy.

PUPPETEERS occupy the spaces between platforms to bring their characters right into the middle of each set.

witty credit sequence that encapsulates much of Jim's gently irreverent attitude toward both filmmaking and puppetry and once again quickly sets the tone.

Kermit, Fozzie, and Gonzo are discovered aloft in the gondola of a hot air balloon. Gonzo, of course, loves it and wonders if it might not be fun to try flying *without* a balloon. Fozzie, on the other hand, would rather be back on solid ground. "How long are we going to have to stay up here?" he wants to know. Just long enough for the credits, Kermit explains. "What credits?" Fozzie demands. Kermit

Kermit points out that at least these opening credits don't last as long as those at the end of the picture. Finally, the credit sequence over, the trio inadvertently cause the balloon to land on the street set that is the location for the beginning of the movie proper.

The story line casts Kermit and Fozzie as ace reporters who, for unexplained and inexplicable reasons, are described as identical twins. Gonzo is the photographer who completes the team, and they soon find themselves investigating a series of jewel robberies. The victim is Lady Holiday

Produced in England with Jim Henson as director, *The Great Muppet Caper* is more lavish than *The Muppet Movie.* The plot centers on the attempt by Kermit, Fozzie, and Gonzo to restore their sullied journalistic reputations by identifying the thief who has been stealing gems from fashion designer Lady Holiday (Diana Rigg).

To a large extent, though, this film belongs to Miss Piggy. As an aspiring fashion model, Piggy arrives at Lady Holiday's door and simpers her way into a job as a receptionist, soon attracting the wandering eye of Lady Holiday's caddish brother (Charles Grodin). The scene is set for moments of high drama and spectacular production numbers that display Piggy's histrionic range and terpsichorean talents to their fullest.

Among the former must be counted the scene in which Piggy —mounted astride a motorcycle, suitably coiffed and coutured —smashes through a stained-glass window to rescue her frog. Among the latter is the Busby Berkeley–like number seen in production here, in which her charm and grace transmogrify London's upper crust.

Never has Miss Piggy's scene-stealing ability been more in evidence, and steal scenes she does, till the audience wonders who is the greater thief: the jewel robber or the porcine superstar.

IN THIS scene from *The Great Muppet Caper*, Fozzie, Kermit, and Gonzo (in the box labeled "Whatever") have just landed smack in the middle of an English village pond after being thrown from the freight hold of an airliner.

THE SOLO bike-riding sequence in *The Muppet Movie* had been such a hit that it was decided to top it in *The Great Muppet Caper* by having an extended group bike-riding sequence, to be shot in London's Battersea Park, in which first Kermit and Piggy and then a whole gang of cyclists would participate. Faz Fazakas devised an elaborate marionetting rig to do the job, but nobody in the Henson organization had the experience to operate it. Luckily Brian Henson (seen at left in the picture to the *right*) was on vacation from high school. He had learned a great deal about marionetting from Don Sahlin—a master of the art—and was able to make the rig work, rescuing one of the film's most spectacular sequences.

(Diana Rigg), a celebrated London fashion designer. The thief's ultimate aim is to relieve Lady Holiday of her prize gem—the world-famous Baseball Diamond.

Miss Piggy, meanwhile—in search of a high-fashion career—finds employment with Lady Holiday as first a receptionist and eventually a star model. There she attracts the amorous attention of her employer's ne'er-do-well brother Nicky (Charles Grodin), arousing Kermit's jealousy. Kermit, Fozzie, and Gonzo find the rest of the Muppet gang ensconced in a dilapidated structure known as the Happiness Hotel and are thereby assured that they will have plenty of willing help when it comes to tracking down the jewel thief.

To nobody's surprise, this turns out to be the caddish Nicky, assisted by three of his sister's top models. There is a showdown in an art gallery, with Piggy—in motorcycle leathers—coming to the rescue as she crashes through a stained-glass window on her hog.

Considered simply as a spoof of the caper movie genre, *The Great Muppet Caper* (written by Jay Tarses & Tom Patchett and Jerry Juhl & Jack Burns) succeeds admirably and contains many scenes that are hilarious simply because of the way the script exploits situation and character. One very funny extended sequence, for example, presents John Cleese as a stuffy Englishman who is far too well bred to be distracted from his dinner by the sight of an overdressed pig crawling through his dining room. Again, however—as with *The Muppet Movie*—many of the delights of the film depend upon the technical virtuosity Jim Henson and his team brought to the production.

Kermit's bike-riding scene in the previous movie is

topped when Kermit and Piggy ride bicycles together—eventually joined by a whole crowd of Muppet and human cyclists. Another astonishing sequence in *The Great Muppet Caper* is an Esther Williams–style water ballet in which Miss Piggy performs underwater feats that would make any frog proud.

The technical prowess of the Henson team had now advanced to the point where almost nothing seemed impossible. Much of this was due to Faz Fazakas, Jim's resident technical wizard, whose expertise created everything from elaborate marionette rigs—such as the one that permitted Kermit to ride a bike—to fully remote-controlled figures.

Faz's experiments with radio control had once been limited to relatively simple supplementary functions such as eye movements. Now they had advanced to the point where he and his assistants were able to provide performers with the opportunity to convincingly operate entire puppets from a distance. This meant that situations could be devised in which characters could be placed out in the open with no need to hide the puppeteer from the camera—because the puppeteer was, in fact, standing behind the camera, twenty or thirty feet from the actual puppet.

Both as entertainment and as a technical tour de force, *The Great Muppet Caper* provided a very satisfying experience for Muppet fans. It was followed in 1983 by a third Muppet film. Shot on New York's Empire City Stages and on location in and around New York City, *The Muppets Take Manhattan* was produced by Jim Henson and crisply directed by Frank Oz.

Frank, who has since proven himself to be one of Hollywood's best comedy directors, took on a plot that was

ANOTHER SPECTACULAR sequence in *The Great Muppet Caper* was the aqua ballet performed by Miss Piggy and a bevy of aqua maidens in a giant studio tank. Inspired by Busby Berkeley's "By a Waterfall" number in *Footlight Parade* and by water ballets in later Esther Williams spectaculars, this sequence came complete with volcanic fountains and underwater shots of Piggy delighting any watching frog with expert scissor kicks as she wove her way through elaborate submerged formations. At one point she even dived into the pool—a feat difficult for an ordinary puppet to achieve. This aqua ballet provided the first occasion for the use of a full-body version of Miss Piggy, a puppet with a person inside. Calista Hendrickson's design for Piggy's costume (sketch by Michael Frith, *left*) shows that, although Miss Piggy is proud of her figure, she leaves nothing to chance.

(continued on page 139)

133

THE SHOW brought to Broadway by the Muppets is called *Manhattan Melodies.*

Directed by Frank Oz, *The Muppets Take Manhattan* is a retelling of that old story in which a group of talented youngsters put on a show and, against all the odds, conquer Broadway. In other words, it was just the kind of well-worn material with which the Muppets have always been most at home.

In a sense, almost everything Jim Henson did with the Muppets went back to those early *Sam and Friends* skits in which Yorick and Mushmellon and the rest —including the proto-Kermit—lip-synched to familiar novelty songs and performed spoofs of current television hits. The Muppets have always used the familiar as a springboard to the fantastic, and *The Muppets Take Manhattan* is no exception to this rule. The plot is one of the hoariest of Hollywood clichés. Jim, Frank, and the entire Muppet team take this cliché, turn it inside out, and discover

a multicolored lining that nobody had noticed before.

The plot gave the Muppet gang the opportunity to exploit New York situations they had not explored before—despite the company's being New York–based. There is a wonderful little cameo in which Piggy joins Joan Rivers in the cosmetics department of a department store modeled after Bergdorf Goodman. But mostly *The Muppets Take Manhattan* provides the Muppets with the opportunity to perform some classic production numbers.

THIS FRAME FROM the final production number in *Manhattan Melodies*—the show within the movie—presents a grouping of characters that would seldom be encountered backstage at the Muppet Theater. Kermit is flanked by Miss Piggy and Fozzie Bear, two Frank Oz characters. Behind Fozzie is Rowlf, who, like Kermit, is a Jim Henson character. For obvious reasons, these characters are seldom asked to interact on camera, but back-up puppeteers can be used to make the conjunction possible in a prerecorded musical number like this.

ONE OF THE MOST memorable scenes in *The Muppets Take Manhattan*—and the only one in the movie that was actually staged by Jim himself—is the sequence in which five rats prepare breakfast in the New York coffee shop where Kermit and the gang gather. This is an enormously satisfying sequence thanks to a combination of careful planning (illustrated by these storyboard sketches by John Davis), creative rigging and mechanics (thanks in large part to the skills of Faz Fazakas), and brilliant performances by Steve Whitmire and other puppeteers. To illustrate the difficulties involved, at one point the shop was given the task of sewing a rat to a fried egg! This proved impossible, so the rat was attached to a piece of toast instead by sewing through the toast and into a small piece of fabric beneath it. *Above* is one of Jim's early sketches of the scene. *Below*, puppeteers surround the kitchen set.

Faz Fazakas helping to rig the rat who will skate on a pat of butter.

To whip the pancake batter, the rat's feet are attached to the eggbeater, which is driven from underneath using a waterproof bearing.

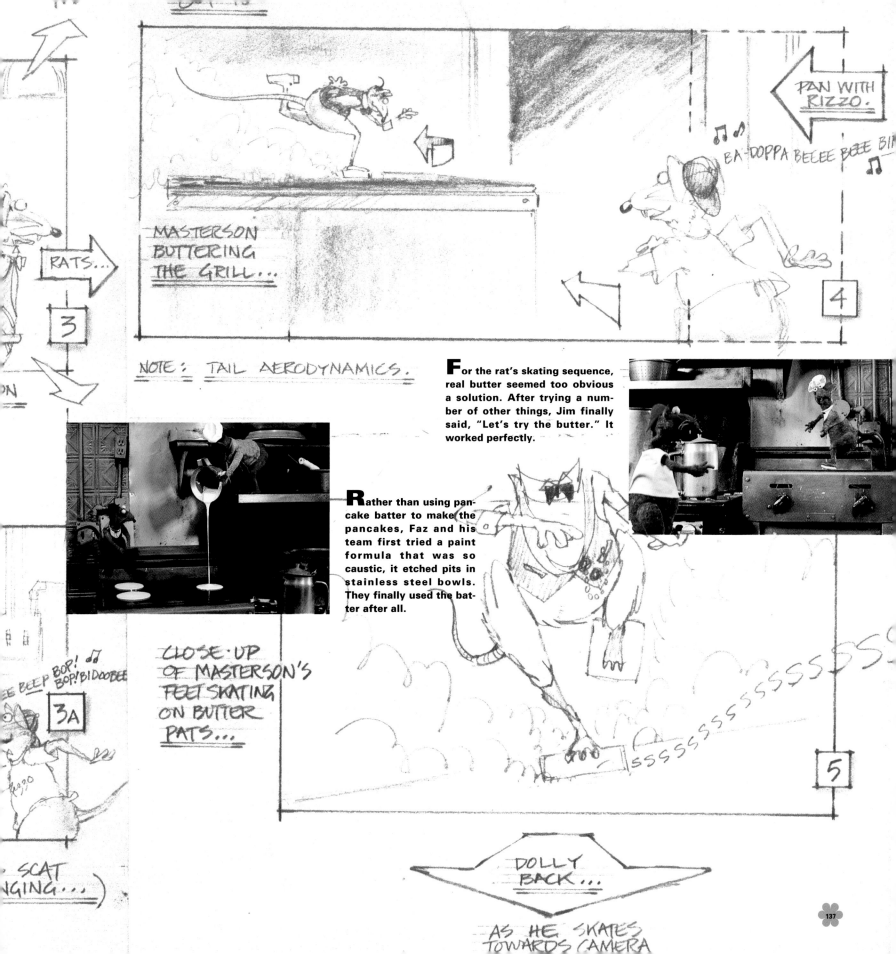

For the rat's skating sequence, real butter seemed too obvious a solution. After trying a number of other things, Jim finally said, "Let's try the butter." It worked perfectly.

Rather than using pancake batter to make the pancakes, Faz and his team first tried a paint formula that was so caustic, it etched pits in stainless steel bowls. They finally used the batter after all.

THE MUPPETS TAKE MANHATTAN is a joyous romp through

show-business conventions.

well worn when Judy Garland and Mickey Rooney were cast in several variants of it four decades earlier. It was, in fact, the old saw about a troupe of gifted amateurs who put on a show and, against all odds, take Broadway by storm. Luckily for Frank (and, in large part, thanks to Frank) the Muppets are masters of mild-mannered parody and were perfectly equipped to take on this cliché-ridden theme.

Beyond gentle parody, however, *The Muppets Take Manhattan* has many imaginative and hilarious moments that make it mandatory viewing for any Muppet fan. There is a technically amazing set piece involving a squad of energetic rats, and an amusing musical number in which the chief Muppet characters appear as babies—a puppet forerunner of the animated television show *Jim Henson's Muppet Babies*. There is also a strong twist at the end when the onstage marriage of Kermit and Piggy—supposedly just part of the show—turns out to be for real. Maybe.

Taken together, the first three Muppet films must be seen as one of the high points of Jim Henson's career. By the time *The Muppets Take Manhattan* was made, Jim had been reinventing the world of puppet drama for almost three decades, and everything he had learned during those years—the performance skills and technical innovations—can be found in these three lovingly prepared packages.

In a very real sense, they are the summation of the kind of screen magic he began to explore with *Sam and Friends*, and they provide an invaluable permanent record of both Jim's imagination and the diverse talents of the extraordinary team of performers, designers, and fabricators he had assembled to realize his dreams.

LIKE MOST HENSON PRODUCTIONS, *The Muppets Take Manhattan* offered a satisfying blend of the expected and the unexpected. The plot clearly called for stylized production numbers (*top left*) and favorable reviews in *Variety* (*bottom right*), but it also provided a framework for the introduction of the Muppet Babies (*top right*) and for the long anticipated marriage of Kermit and Piggy (*bottom left*). The latter was staged as part of the show within the movie, but much to Kermit's consternation, the man who played the minister in the movie was actually a minister in real life.

ha! hi!
he!
hep! hop!
hum!

CHAPTER SIX

Jim Henson was very successful. From the day when, as a teenager, he took Pierre the French Rat to audition at WTOP in Washington, financial rewards and critical acclaim came almost simultaneously. From then on, both grew steadily.

Critical acclaim—especially the approval of his peers—was important to Jim, but he was not shy about enjoying the fruits of his earnings as well. There were lovely houses and a variety of high-performance cars. More important, there was security for his family and the freedom to experiment. Because of his early triumphs, he was able to develop his artistry largely outside of the show-business mainstream, which permitted his own originality, and that of his collaborators, to come to the fore.

Jim would have been the first to admit there was an element of serendipity in all this. At the same time, though, a large dose of downright hard work was involved. This was allied to a strong streak of pragmatism and backed up by a grasp of the business world that often surprised people who saw him as a laid-back, almost bohemian artist—a long-haired, bearded man who preferred floral patterned shirts to pin-striped suits.

An early sign of Jim's realistic attitude was his willingness to plunge so enthusiastically into the business of making commercials. This activity was crucial to the health of his company in its Washington years and for a decade or more after its move to New York.

Henson Associates was tiny back then, and Jim could afford to run it informally, trusting to his own instincts and judgments to make sound decisions. When the company consisted of himself, Frank Oz, Jerry Juhl, and Don Sahlin, little structure was necessary; everyone knew what everyone else was doing.

JIM HENSON chose these eye-catching logos for the various divisions of his company. "Ha!" stood for Henson Associates, the parent organization (now known as Jim Henson Productions). "Hi!" was Henson International, Inc., a production subsidiary based in New York. "He!" stood for Henson Enterprises (the international licensing division), "hep!" was Henson Electronic Products, "hop!" was Henson Organization Publishing, and "hum!" was Henson Universal Music.

A Shrine to the Almighty Dollar

WHEN JIM HENSON converted an antique sideboard into a shrine to the Almighty Dollar, he did so, of course, with tongue in cheek. Similarly, when he replaced George Washington with Rowlf on a one-dollar bill (*above*), it was a typical Henson joke. Throughout his life, Jim was first and foremost an artist and entertainer, but he was also a shrewd businessman, understanding that the only way he would have the power to do what he wanted was by having access to the necessary financing.

Well before he had graduated from college he had discovered that he could supplement his income as an entertainer by producing commercials, and the financial security provided by this activity gave him the freedom to be more selective as an artist than might otherwise have been the case. Especially during the period between his move to New York and the launching of *Sesame Street* (the 1970 business card

seen *below* dates from the period immediately afterward), the production of commercials was vital to the health of his company. It was these commercials that made *Timepiece*, for example, possible, and gave him the leisure to explore the possibility of an ambitious project like Cyclia.

Rowlf's success on *The Jimmy Dean Show* had led to Rowlf hand puppets being marketed, but it was with the success of *Sesame Street* that Jim was first introduced on a significant scale to the financial possibilities of character licensing. With *The Muppet Show*, he became ever more deeply involved in licensing and other peripheral activities. The end result was that his formerly tiny company was transformed into a sizable business empire that brought him both new rewards and new responsibilities.

JIM HENSON

Even the success of *Sesame Street* did not change things too drastically. There were a few more puppeteers on the payroll now, a few more workshop personnel, but it was still a small company. The licensing of *Sesame Street* characters, of course, became big business, and as owner of the puppet characters, Jim was involved in policy decisions and benefited from the profits. However, he was essentially content with Joan Ganz Cooney's supervision, although he continued to play an important role in negotiations, especially during the early years.

But with *The Muppet Show*, Henson Associates began to grow astronomically. Till then, the Muppet business entity was something Jim could almost take for granted. Now, overnight, it became something that threatened to become quite distinct from the Muppet *creative* entity.

To begin with, the company was suddenly scattered between two continents, with some people left behind in New York and some newly installed in London—though nobody knew for how long. (As it turns out, the London office is still active.) With other key personnel, like Frank Oz and David Lazer, Jim became a transatlantic commuter. Half the year now was spent in England where *The Muppet Show* was taped. But the series spawned a successful business, and that was based in Manhattan.

Al Gottesman joined the company in 1972 as chief counsel and head of business affairs. Until the launching of *The Muppet Show*, he handled almost all business and legal matters himself, with the assistance of a network of outside attorneys. In 1976, all that changed.

"The first thing that happened," he recalls, "was that we began to make licensing deals in the UK, because the show aired there first and it was a hit right away. Then, in the second season, the show took off in America and we started to get hundreds of applications for licenses over here.

"Jim was very concerned about quality control. That had started with *Sesame Street*. . . . It was very important to

Muppet Meeting Films

A major showcase for the Muppets in the sixties and early seventies was one that was never broadcast on television or seen by the general public. This was the series of "meeting films"—also known as "coffee break films"—that were commissioned from Jim by the computer giant IBM. Work on these witty little productions was inaugurated in 1965, and the concept was developed by Jim in partnership with David Lazer, who was then employed by IBM and still a decade away from becoming executive producer of *The Muppet Show*.

The idea was to make mini-films for use at IBM business seminars—mini-films that taught lessons in salesmanship and corporate creativity, but taught these lessons with humor and even a touch of craziness rather than with solemn admonitions. In this respect, they were very much in the style of the commercials with which Jim had made his reputation, except that—because they did not have to be so brief—they gave him and his collaborators an opportunity to stretch a little. The fact that these meeting films are still in use indicates that they are successful teaching tools, and probably nobody learned more from them than Jim Henson himself.

(continued on page 153)

With the worldwide success of *Sesame Street, The Muppet Show, Fraggle Rock,* and the various Muppet movies, *Muppets* became a household word from Juneau to Jakarta. This was reflected in articles on the Muppets and their creator in dozens of languages and in magazines as varied as *People, Der Spiegel,* and *Macworld.* Miss Piggy alone was featured in scores of periodicals, making herself equally at home on the cover of *Tatler* or *TV Guide.*

PUBLISHING at Henson Associates began with *The Miss Piggy Calendar 1980*. This had been conceived the previous year as Piggy began to emerge as a superstar, and it featured photography by Nancy Moran and Donal Holway. It was followed by others, including *Miss Piggy's Cover Girl Fantasy Calendar* (also photographed by Moran and Holway) and *The Miss Piggy Calendar 1982: Great Lovers of the Silver Screen* (photographed by John E. Barrett), in which she imagined herself as the star of various classic movies. The former included the fanciful *Time*, *Life*, and *Cosmo* covers reproduced here, and the latter daydreams such as Piggy and Kermit in *Annie Hall* (*top*) and Piggy helpless in the grip of King Kong (*opposite, bottom right*).

"There were no personality calendars back then," Michael Frith points out, ". . . no Cindy Crawford, no guys from Chippendales. Piggy's calendar was something completely new. She was the Cindy Crawford of her day."

LIFE

USO Welcomes MISS P

. . AT THE U.S.O.! MISS PIGGY!

MAY 1942

YEARLY SUBSCR

TIME
THE WEEKLY NEWSMAGAZINE

COSMOPOLITAN

THOMAS GAINSBOROUGH
Green Boy

HENRI DE TOULOUSE-LAUTREC
La Belle Epigue

EDGAR DEGAS
The La Danseur

The Kermitage

The Kermitage Collection was Michael K. Frith's attempt to carry the idea that had originated with the Piggy calendars to its logical conclusion. He would take well-known Muppet characters—Fozzie, Gonzo, and even Zoot as well as Kermit and Piggy—and insert them into famous paintings by great masters from Vermeer to Picasso. It was a concept that Jim Henson loved and encouraged, and it was carried out with such care and attention to detail that the results were eventually exhibited at the Berry-Hill Galleries in New York and published as a book, *Miss Piggy's Art Masterpieces from the Kermitage Collection*, with text by Henry Beard. The book's conceit was that Piggy, of course, believed totally in the authenticity of her "priced-less artworks"; and she happily reported in her introduction that "various critiques have been kind enough to call [the collection] 'unbelievable,' 'indescribable,' and 'simply staggering.'"

AUGUSTE RODIN
The Smooch

HENRI ROUSSEAU
The Sleepy Zootsy

GRANT WOOD
American Gothique

ABLO PICASSO

g Before a Mirror

LEONARDO DA VINCI

Mona Moi

JAN VAN EYCK

The Marriage of Froggo Amphibini and Giopiggi Porculini

JAMES A. McNEILL WHISTLER

Arrangement in Gray and Black with Creep (Whistler's Weirdo)

HANS HOLBEIN

Jester at the Court of Henry VIII

SANDRO BOTTICELLI

The Birth of You Know Who

REMBRANDT VAN RIJN

Arisfroggle Contemplating the Bust of a Twerp

JAN VERMEER

Young Lady Adorning Herself with Pearls (and Why Not?)

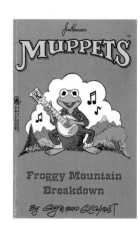

Onstage with Moidonna and Kermit Springsteen

THE SUCCESS OF the first Miss Piggy calendar led to a consultant from the publishing industry, Jane Leventhal, being called in to coordinate the next calendar. Jim Henson had been toying with the idea of getting the Muppets into the book business and was so pleased with the way the second calendar turned out that he asked Jane to stay on to run a newly organized publishing division, which soon moved on to developing books—especially children's books, which Jim loved—a magazine, and even a newspaper comic strip (*top left*).

JIM HENSON'S entry into publishing enabled him to connect with people—especially children—in new ways. Since the beginning of his involvement with *Sesame Street*, he had taken a keen interest in early education, and especially in the importance of reading. His publishing division gave him an opportunity to reach out to young readers by means of the characters he had already made familiar on television.

But publishing also meant having fun, as was the case with any Henson enterprise. *Muppet Magazine* was an opportunity for everyone to have a good time. Miss Piggy could continue her fantasy life, imagining herself as Madonna (*opposite, right*), Janice could picture herself as Tina Turner (*above*), and even Kermit could let his guard down once in a while and indulge himself by pretending to be Bruce Springsteen (*left*), Pee-wee Herman (*opposite, center*), or Luke Skywalker (*opposite, left*).

In the early days of the first Piggy calendar, staged still shots like these had been made with whatever backup puppets were available. By the time *Muppet Magazine* was launched, in 1982, special still photography figures had been built that made it possible to place characters in almost any pose imaginable.

JIM HENSON loved music, although he certainly did not possess the kind of singing voice that would have encouraged him to think about taking up opera. By the time he performed Rowlf on *The Jimmy Dean Show*, however, he had progressed from miming to records to occasionally singing along with the show's star. *Sesame Street* called for a great deal more singing, and soon Jim—as Ernie—had his first hit song, "Rubber Duckie." This was followed by Kermit's immortal "Bein' Green." Later *The Muppet Movie* provided Kermit with another megahit in the form of "Rainbow Connection." (The first of these songs was written by Jeff Moss, the second by Joe Raposo, and the third by Paul Williams and Kenny Ascher.)

Over the years, a total of six Muppet performances earned gold and platinum records, while four were honored with Academy Award nominations and nine won Grammys.

him that his characters looked right, no matter where they were being used, and he'd veto anything he didn't like. When we started to license *Muppet Show* characters, he wanted to approve everything himself, and that got crazy. We'd have a courier on the plane to London almost every day with a bag full of prototypes for him to look at. It wasn't that Jim couldn't delegate responsibility. I think it was just that he'd been used to running a very small company where that was part of his job, but he soon came to realize that he had to trust other people with some of those decisions."

Jim may have taken a short while to adjust to some aspects of the company's rapid expansion, but he never lost touch with the underlying issues. On the one hand, the company would have to become more orderly. On the other, he saw no reason why this should change its essential character. He would have to hire more business people and lawyers to take care of the expansion, but he would not fall into the trap of creating a company that broke down into two parts—the creative personnel on one side and the business people on the other.

To avoid that schism, he tried to hire business people who would fit comfortably into the creative family that was already in place. Henson Associates became a place where accountants and attorneys felt comfortable hanging out in the workshop or on the studio floor. More unusual, it became a place where performers and puppet-builders felt at home hanging out in the offices of accountants and attorneys.

Helping maintain the harmony was the fact that Jim was on a first-name basis with everyone in the organization, down to the newest secretary. And no matter how many new peripheral projects came up, Jim, with his remarkable ability to concentrate, seemed able to stay on top of all of them.

One factor that made things easier was the success of the show and the movies, which generated business in a quite remarkable way. Jim's team did not have to go out to sell; everyone came to them. Numerous deals were struck with outside licensors. But the most exciting business activities were generated from within. The classic example, perhaps, is the evolution of Miss Piggy in print, which began in earnest with four Miss Piggy calendars and continued with the bestselling *Miss Piggy's Guide to Life*.

"One of the *Sesame Street* calendars I had done earlier used *Sesame Street* characters posed in comical situations," Michael Frith recalls, "and I thought that it would be fun to do something like that with Miss Piggy. We did some setups using whatever bits and pieces of back-up puppets we could find around the New York shop. They were incredibly crude by our later standards, but they worked, and when I showed the Polaroids to Jim and Frank, they were astonished. There was one in particular, of Piggy on an art deco bed with satin sheets. Frank looked at it and said, 'My God, she's sexy!' That led to the first Piggy calendar, and it was an enormous success."

Another area in which the Muppets have had great commercial success is in the marketing of recorded music. Although musical, Jim did not by any means possess an outstanding singing voice. Yet he found himself performing hit *Sesame Street* songs like "Rubber Duckie" and "Bein' Green." Frank Oz is even less of a singer, but even he was able to make a bestseller out of the likes of "C is for Cookie." Other Muppet performers, like Jerry Nelson and Richard Hunt, had excellent voices and did much to enhance some of the *Sesame Street* albums. *The Muppet Show* brought more successful albums, and another major hit came along with the release of *The Muppet Movie,* for which Paul Williams and Kenny Ascher wrote "Rainbow Connection."

Even as Henson Associates continued to expand—

AS EARLY AS *The Jimmy Dean Show* period, a Rowlf hand puppet was produced under license. Muppet character merchandising began in earnest, however, with *Sesame Street* and continued unabated with *The Muppet Show,* the movies, and *Jim Henson's Muppet Babies.*

 (continued on page 163)

Home Sweet Headquarters

Perhaps the best place to observe the special family feeling that characterizes the company to this day is the town house near Central Park that supplies Jim Henson Productions with its New York headquarters. This building was purchased in 1977, when the success of *The Muppet Show* made a physical expansion necessary. Jim had not planned to buy anything quite as grand—he had been thinking, rather, of something like an old industrial building, and he briefly considered a disused schoolhouse and an old fire station. But he fell in love with this gracious structure in the middle of New York's diplomatic district—with the grand staircase that spiraled up from the lobby to the third floor, and with the elegant second-floor library that would make an ideal boardroom.

It took more than a year to renovate the building,

AS *The Muppet Show* became a major hit, Jim Henson realized he would need more working space and a new headquarters. After looking at a number of interesting New York buildings, he finally settled on an elegant 1920s town house on Manhattan's Upper East Side (*above*). The building had formerly belonged to the New York Pharmaceutical Society, whose members can hardly have dreamed of the day when it would be home to stained-glass windows such as this one (*left*), a gift to Jim from Jerry Juhl. The Ernie and Bert portion was actually constructed first; it wasn't until a year later that the likenesses of Jim and Frank were added.

ONE THING that convinced Jim to buy the town house was the circular staircase that runs from the ground floor to the third floor (*opposite right*). Along with extensive structural modifications, the building was enlivened with artwork such as Coulter Watt's mural of the Muppet Theater in the lobby (*above*).

THE BASEMENT of the building was opened up and extended, with the help of a huge skylight, to form a spacious area that, during the era of *The Muppet Show,* became a busy workshop (*left*). One of the few rooms that was unaltered structurally was Jim Henson's office (*above*), though the art and artifacts with which he filled it totally transformed the space so that it took on the imprint of his personality.

but when it was finished it was a magnificent sight. Murals and stained-glass windows portrayed the characters who had made ownership of this building possible, and restrooms were papered with Muppet wallpaper. At the same time, though, the building had been restored (by architect Peter Strauss) with great respect for its period charm, making it a graceful blend of two worlds. Helping to integrate the two were the masses of carefully tended flowers and plants with which the building was (and is) always filled.

What made the building especially pleasurable to visit in the late seventies and early eighties was the fact that for a few years it contained a significant part of the New York workshop, installed in a bright, airy basement area that opened onto a sunny courtyard and was illuminated by an enormous skylight

projecting from the rear of the main building. It was there that you would find Calista Hendrickson decorating a gown for Miss Piggy with bugle beads. It was there that you would come across Leslee Asch restoring classic Muppet figures for a traveling museum show. It was there that you would encounter Faz Fazakas tinkering with electrodes and transistors.

Today, although the workshop has moved a few blocks away, feelings of creativity and camaraderie still permeate the building. Visitors to the office get a chance to sit in red velvet theater seats in front of Coulter Watt's mural of the Muppet Theater—as close to the "original" experience as you can get. The atmosphere is relaxed, with an air of cheerfulness that is catching.

The office is one of those rare places where people enjoy coming to work in the morning.

The score: Frog, 101; Chaos, 100.

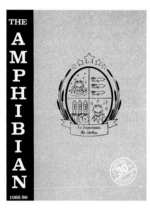

ANYONE who showed up at Central Park during one of the Henson Associates spring picnics would have had a hard time picking out the president of the company—or any of the other senior officers—from among the happy, raucous softball players. (An indication of how good a time everyone had at company events is the fact that, as editorial director Louise Gikow reports, the victorious-looking softball team (*top*) actually *lost* the game that year.) Despite the fact that Jim always felt himself to be terrible at sports—he was often the last to be chosen for any teams when he was in school—he was always out there on the mound or in the field in his khakis and brightly colored shirt, having a great time along with everyone else. The company at these times resembled nothing more than a large family on an outing, with Jim as its avuncular head.

Working at Henson Associates wasn't quite like working anywhere else. The company yearbook (*above*) looked like a parody of a high school yearbook. Annual company-wide business meetings often fea-

tured anything-but-businesslike presentations (one contained, among other things, a silent-film parody complete with an acquisitive, mustachioed villain played by chief financial officer Bob Bromberg.) And the New York masquerade balls, first held in 1984, brought out the creative in everyone. The balls also attracted their share of celebrities who wanted to join in the fun. Andy Warhol (shown *above* with Jim) was one.

IN 1984, Jim Henson began to hold spectacular masked balls in New York as a way of celebrating the creativity of all the people in the company.

The first masked ball was held in a small town house off Fourteenth Street; the second was at a loft on lower Fifth Avenue; the last two were at the Waldorf-Astoria. The balls were, in a way, Jim's gift to the people who worked for him. And Jim, who delighted in fantasy and loved costumes, enjoyed every one of them. He invariably wore a tuxedo and a magnificent mask of some sort —made of feathers, fake jewels, glitter, and other materials.

Everyone in the company— from the building staff to the accountants to the most creative shop personnel—spent weeks creating the most spectacular (or silly) costumes they could. (Often, their goal was to try to prevent Jim from guessing who they were...a goal that was occasionally met.) The remarkable thing was not how magnificent many of the workshop costumes were—that, in a way, was to be expected—but how well the rest of the company did. The clever and disconcerting two-faced mask (*inset, above*) was created by shop member Bruce Morozco. But it was editor Joanne Barkan from publishing who, with her husband, Jon Friedman, came as a beech tree (*left*); and publishing's art director Lauren Attinello who, with her husband, Dan Schneider, showed up as "Surf and Turf" (*inset, left*).

159

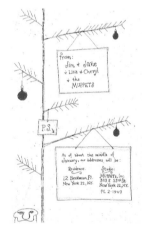

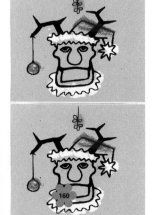

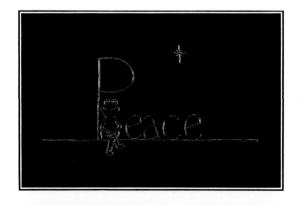

became more elaborate but always reflected the corporate family spirit that Jim valued.

ANOTHER EXAMPLE OF FAMILY SPIRIT within the Henson organization is the tradition of presenting beautiful handmade quilts on

special occasions such as births. Many people contribute individual squares to these quilts. The work of putting them together is coordinated by

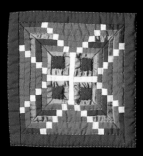

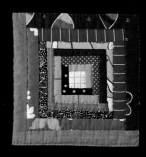

Stephen Rotondaro, who came up with the idea. This particular example was given to Caroly Wilcox when she left the company after twenty years.

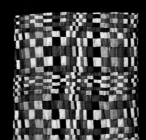

between 1975 and 1980, the company went from having 30 people on the payroll to employing over 130—the sense of family somehow concurrently grew. This made for a good deal of socializing, including spectacular Christmas parties, gala masked balls, picnics, and baseball games in Central Park.

It also encouraged a series of elaborate practical jokes.

One day, during the filming of *Labyrinth*, Jim informed Duncan Kenworthy—now a senior vice president of production, who works out of London—that a Dutch producer named Kees was interested in using the Jim Henson Creature Shop for a film. (The Creature Shop is the name that the London workshop adopted after the filming of *The Dark Crystal*, in honor of the complicated, realistically animated creatures for which it is known.) Duncan at the time was in charge of negotiating new projects for the Creature Shop, but Jim offered to help by meeting the Dutch producer with him. During the meeting, while Jim was away taking a call, Duncan realized that the Dutch producer wanted the Shop to create realistic animals for a sex film.

"I couldn't wait for Jim to come back," Duncan reports ruefully. "When he did, I was completely taken aback, because he didn't seem at all shocked or amused by the idea, discussing it with Kees as if it were a pretty normal request. At that point, Kees left the room to go to the bathroom and things got even more surreal, because even in private—when I expected we'd share the joke and work out how to let the guy down as quickly as possible—Jim supported the idea of doing the film. He thought we shouldn't be turning down work at a time when the Creature Shop needed money, and in any case the puppeteers would really get a kick out of this sort of challenge. When Kees came back, my head was spinning.

"The discussion plunged along until shortly afterwards," Duncan continues, "when Jim idly opened a drawer and I saw a tiny TV monitor with my face on it. Then he

KERMIT made his debut in the Macy's Thanksgiving Day Parade in 1978. Company members in frog costumes guided the Kermit balloon along Central Park and into Herald Square.

shouted, 'Come on out, guys,' and three people emerged from behind drapes up on the mezzanine. The whole thing was revealed as an enormous practical joke. In fact, it had taken them all the best part of a day to set the stage!"

Jerry Nelson tells a story of a fiddler he knew as a way to illustrate Jim's working style...the style that would carry over into every corner of his company.

"It's time to go to work," Jerry once casually remarked to the musician just prior to a performance they were giving.

"Hell," the man had replied. "We're not going to *work*. We're going to *play*!"

No matter how much serious business went on at the Henson offices, working there was always serious fun.

CHAPTER SEVEN

As the eighties began, Jim Henson began to focus on an ambitious project that had been on his mind even prior to the filming of *The Muppet Movie*.

In August of 1977, he had entered into an agreement with a young British illustrator, Brian Froud, whose book *The World of Froud* evoked gnomes, trolls, and fairies out of the mists of Celtic myth and Nordic legend. Although he owed a debt to earlier British artists and illustrators like Richard Dadd and Arthur Rackham, Brian brought a fresh eye to this subject matter and—most important, from Jim's point of view—rendered his vision with a precision and sense of detail that made it viable to consider translating it into cinematic terms.

Jim's interest in the illustrations led him to pay a visit to Froud at his home on the edge of Dartmoor—the wild region of southwest England immortalized in Sir Arthur Conan Doyle's *The Hound of the Baskervilles*. Cheryl Henson, who accompanied her father on that occasion, recalls how the visit fired his imagination.

"My father already loved Brian's drawings, but seeing them there, in conjunction with the landscape of Dartmoor, made them that much more exciting. Dartmoor itself began to suggest a world where those drawings could come to life. It's such a world of contrasts—so lush and rich in some parts, so bleak and windswept elsewhere."

Among the things Jim Henson saw on this visit were little sculptures of fantastic characters made by Brian, and these made him all the more convinced that Brian's world could be brought to the screen. Jim had no story in mind. It was his idea that he and Brian would begin by evolving an imaginary world—landscape, weather, flora, fauna—creating a visual entity from which the characters and story could develop. The result of their collaboration was Jim's first fantasy film, *The Dark Crystal*.

AUGHRA, an ancient seer and the guardian of traditional wisdom, is one of the central characters in the world of *The Dark Crystal*.

This drawing of skekZok (*left*), the Ritual Master, hints at the ornateness of the robes favored by the decadent Skeksis hierarchy.

The Pod People (*above*)—peasants of this strange world.

WHEN JIM HENSON set out to make the fantasy movie that became *The Dark Crystal*, it was his idea from early on that the world to be recorded on film would be based entirely on the visual imaginings of Brian Froud, some of whose drawings for the movie are seen on these pages. This was not a question of Brian being asked to design a film around a script or even a story idea. Rather it was a matter of him being invited to set down visual ideas and being given the opportunity to imagine a fantastic world that, when a small creative team had had time to become immersed in it, would provide the setting for a story about characters who had been conjured up in pencil, ink, and watercolor before they had ever been described in words.

A Skeksis portrayed in a moment of fury (*below*).

Creating *The Dark Crystal*

SkekNa, the
Slave Master (*above*), is perhaps the most purely sadistic of the Skeksis.

Kira and Jen (*left*)
are the Gelfling he-
roes of the movie.

Wise and gentle,
the Mystics (*left*)
are alter egos
of the Skeksis.

BRIAN FROUD was contacted by Jim Henson after Jim saw the British illustrator's work in a collection titled *The World of Froud*.

"The first time I saw Jim, I didn't know it. The Muppets had so much individual personality that I thought little about who might be bringing them to life. The next time, I didn't see him either, but saw little fragments of him in the frenzy of fur, glue, and fabric that was the Muppet workshop at ATV studios.

"The next time I saw Jim was in a dark and cavernous TV studio. Way in the distance was a glowing patch of brilliant color and movement—Jim looking into a TV monitor with a green and vibrant Kermit held aloft. Suddenly, there was laughter. There was always a lot of laughter.

"But when I really first met Jim was that evening over dinner. Dinners and food were destined to become important in our working relationship.... In sharing food with Jim, in his beguiling company, you somehow shared in his dream. Dinner with Jim was a magical space where food turned into movies, talk became vision, and a wineglass, the Holy Grail."

EVEN AFTER a script was written, there was still work for Brian Froud. He had imagined the world that inspired the story; now he began to use his knowledge of that world to help develop the characters. Seldom before in the history of the movies have characters been expressed so fully in visual terms, and Brian oversaw every detail of this, from general appearance down to details of costume. He produced thousands of drawings, as well as three-dimensional maquettes. He then worked closely with the puppet-builders and other craftspeople who were to take what he had set down on paper and begin to translate it into terms that would permit his world to be reconstructed on film.

THE SETS built for *The Dark Crystal* were enormously complex. At *left*, filming is under way for a scene set in Mystic Valley as the Mystics perform final rites for their dead Master. (Jim is in the lower left foreground, wearing a hat.) This was the first sequence in the movie to be shot and its successful completion did much to set the minds of performers and crew at rest. *Above*, Gary Kurtz (coproducer), Jim Henson (producer-director), and Frank Oz (codirector) are seen on the Crystal Chamber set.

"After a while," Jim said in 1982, "*The Muppet Show* had gotten into such a mixture of styles that I found the idea of going to an extremely unified style [with Brian Froud] really refreshing. To put all of those design decisions into one person's mind—one person's sense of judgment— I loved that idea."

In January of 1977, Brian arrived in New York to join a small team that Jim had assembled to develop the project. Brian began to turn out hundreds of paintings, drawings, and sketches while puppetmakers set to work translating some of them into working prototypes. In dozens of meetings, ideas were batted about until gradually a world began to take shape—a pantheistic world in which storms and conjunctions of heavenly bodies had meaning and all matter had the potential of becoming animate. As its cosmography began to evolve in the minds of the core group, possible creatures and characters began to populate the fantastic landscapes.

Later that winter, Jim and Cheryl Henson were stranded

at Kennedy Airport during a blizzard. They managed to reach the sanctuary of a nearby motel and took advantage of the unexpected free time to make notes about the projected movie. At first this involved defining the character groups that had been extensively discussed with Brian Froud and other members of the creative team at the New York shop. From this, Jim and his daughter moved on to talking about how the different characters might interact.

By the time they were able to continue their trip, a plot was taking shape. Names would later be changed and the story would be altered in detail and emphasis, but in all essentials the material sketched out during the blizzard became the basis for the screenplay of *The Dark Crystal*.

For a few months more, development of the project was centered in New York, where mysterious creatures called Mystics, Skeksis, Garthim, and Pod People began to take shape, both on paper and in the form of three-dimensional maquettes and prototypes. Sherry Amott, who had come to Henson Associates from a background in theatrical costuming, was named creative coordinator and began to expand the team that would be needed to bring this ambitious project to fulfillment.

Wendy Midener—a young dollmaker from Detroit who was a key member of that original team and would later marry Brian Froud—sculpted a number of versions of the humanoid characters who would become Jen and Kira, the movie's hero and heroine. Lyle Conway—a sculptor and toy designer who became one of the most important members of the team—sculpted all of the Skeksis and Aughra (another of the principal characters in the film). Conway also designed and built the mechanisms that operated their heads. These mechanisms included remarkably sophisticated balloonlike devices that held small pockets of air. The "balloons," connected via some rubber tubing to rubber bulbs, were placed in the characters' cheeks. When performers squeezed the bulbs, a very subtle, life-like "breath" animated the characters' faces.

In October 1978, a short test sequence was shot in upstate New York. Satisfied that he was on the right track, Jim moved the project to the next phase. The following year, he bought an old postal sorting station on Downshire Hill in the Hampstead section of North London, a short walk from the home he had bought during the run of *The Muppet Show*. Part of this sorting station became the new workshop that eventually would become known as the Creature Shop. There, in strict secrecy, Brian and the members of the team continued their experiments, joined now by young British artists and craftspeople recruited by Sherry Amott, many of them straight out of art school.

Progress might well have been faster if the success of *The Muppet Show* hadn't dictated that the first two Muppet movies be produced before *The Dark Crystal*. However, these delays actually benefited *The Dark Crystal*, because they permitted a longer preproduction period—critical because of the many technical problems that arose during the creation of the naturalistic characters required by the film.

These technical challenges would have been apparent to anyone visiting the Downshire Hill workshop during the summer of 1980. At times, it resembled nothing less than a modern-day alchemist's laboratory, as people in coveralls and masks experimented with the new kinds of materials—plastic foams and such—that would be needed for the project.

By then, well-developed examples of all the character groups had been built. Most startling, perhaps, were the Skeksis. Evil members of a decadent aristocracy, the Skeksis were human-sized creatures who resembled both reptiles and birds of prey, with their bony beaks, menacing teeth, and anxious, predatory eyes. In the movie these creatures

JEN, hero of *The Dark Crystal*, rests amid the exotic fauna of his home, meticulously constructed to look—and behave—in an otherworldly manner.

(continued on page 176)

KATHY MULLEN was chosen to perform the key role of Kira in *The Dark Crystal*.

"It was 1981, and we were about to start shooting *The Dark Crystal*. This was going to be the big one, the art piece, the 'real' thing. In line with that idea we, of course, had to do 'real' acting with our puppet characters. To that end, Jim Henson, Frank Oz, and I assembled in the living room of Jim's house in London one Saturday afternoon. Frank, who was officially co-directing with Jim on this project, was intent on getting 'real' acting from Jim's and my puppet characters via us doing the acting ourselves.

"This may not seem so odd to anyone who does not know the people involved, but it was intensely uncomfortable. Jim, who never 'acted' without a wacky foam-and-fleece substitute on his arm, was to actually try to do a fairly soppy, sentimental scene with me—an actual nonfoam, nonfleece actress. Frank thought it would be a really good way to get to the core of the scene and discover our true characters. So we tried to improvise around the scene. We tried—and failed.

"In retrospect, as intensely embarrassing as it was at the time, it was probably one of the funniest moments of my Muppet life. Had any of our colleagues been flies on the wall, they would have fallen on the floor clutching their stomachs in helpless laughter. As it was, we kept our awkward dignity to the end, when Jim graciously bid us good-bye, saying he felt we had accomplished a great deal. He was kind that way."

CREATING A WORLD from scratch is no small feat. In the case of *The Dark Crystal*, this involved relatively straightforward tasks, such as imagining a bedchamber for a dying Skeksis (*opposite, top left*), and more unusual challenges, such as bringing vegetation to life (*above*). Most challenging was the creation of the different character groups, such as the Skeksis (*opposite, right*) and the Landstriders (*left*), who serve as steeds for Jen and Kira during one of the movie's more exciting scenes.

The Landstriders evolved as they did largely because choreographer and mime trainer Jean-Pierre Amiel discovered that one of his recruits was an expert stilt walker. After several performers had shown their ability to move easily on special stilt rigs, the Landstriders were constructed using these rigs in combination with plastic body molds of the performers.

The basic skeleton had a flexible spine, a movable rib cage, and a fully articulated pelvis. Artificial tendons were stretched from the pelvis to the leg molds at the top of each carbon fiber stilt. Thin but strong fabric was then stretched over this armature so that, when the Landstrider moved, muscles seemed to ripple beneath its skin. The illusion of life was reinforced by means of the movable, radio-controlled eyes with which each creature was equipped.

Kira and Jen, along with Kira's pet, Fizzgig, set off on their quest.

As the three suns converge, Jen sits astride the Crystal, about to replace the missing shard.

Scenes from *The Dark Crystal,* a tale of heroes and villains

In their grotesque castle, the Skeksis sit down to a decadent banquet.

The gentle Mystics have raised Jen after the slaughter of the Gelfling race.

The Pod People share a simple meal.

Inside her observatory, Aughra contemplates events to come.

Inside the castle, the Ritual Master works himself into a self-righteous rage.

Riding friendly Landstriders, Jen and Kira head for the Crystal Chamber.

The Mystics understand that the conjunction of the three suns will transform their world.

IN *THE DARK CRYSTAL*, the cinematic imagination of Jim Henson, the personal vision of Brian Froud, and the superlative performance skills of the Henson puppeteers are blended with the talents of hundreds of other artists and craftspeople to create a world that is original and bizarre, yet has obvious parallels with our own.

We are presented with familiar emotions—love, the lust for power—but they are embodied in beings as strange as any we might encounter in our most outrageous dreams. Still, for all its otherworldy sophistication, the film depends upon the same basic skills, the same powers of suggestion, the same essential magic that puppeteers have relied on for thousands of years.

Above all, it is a film that relies upon visual impact rather than upon dialogue and narrative devices.

"I've always felt," said Jim Henson, soon after the movie was completed, "that music and image work on one level, and the spoken word and dialogue work on another, much shallower one. That's one of the reasons why in *The Dark Crystal* I started off trying to do a film with as little dialogue as possible. I think that if you're working with images and music, you're really doing a much more interesting thing, and you're talking to people on more of a gut level."

As for Brian Froud, he has described how he despaired of things ever coming out as he wanted them to. "There were so many differences of opinion and so many compromises had to be made to accommodate the characters to the physical limitations of the human body. But everything did turn out all right in the end. Somehow the exchange between artist and builder and performer took us through a full circle and brought us back to what we had been trying to do in the first place."

175

would be asked to walk and fight (with scepters and swords), eat food, and generally interact with one another in a variety of elaborate ways. They therefore required extremities that, if not quite as mobile as those of humans, were at least fully convincing.

To this end, workshop technicians—notably Leigh Donaldson—had devised what were in effect sophisticated artificial limbs, operated by cable and articulated so precisely that they could be used to pick up objects as small as a pencil. Flexible rods—inserted through tubes and controlled by a remote trigger device—regulated the motor functions of each joint, each finger. The system worked well and was adapted to the needs of many of the characters.

In the case of the Skeksis, these cable controls could be hidden beneath the voluminous robes each character would wear, robes that also served to conceal the principal puppeteer and members of his cable crew, since it took up to five people to operate one Skeksis.

Rod and cable mechanisms also controlled facial movements, so that each Skeksis was capable of a variety of expressions. Latex mouths could be stretched into smiles or pulled down into sneers. Most important, the taxidermist's eyes—custom-made for the project—were fully mobile in articulated sockets operated by cable or, in some cases, by radio control.

One fundamental consideration was that a Skeksis should not look like an actor in costume. So a special lightweight metal harness was devised, enabling the armature of each Skeksis to be cantilevered off the principal performer's hips (the hips being the most efficient load-bearing point). The character, in effect, would "float" above the principal puppeteer. The puppeteer could control the creature's gross body movements, but those movements would have a decidedly nonhuman peculiarity about them.

The difficulty of wresting a convincing performance from such an assemblage of mechanical devices can easily be imagined. Luckily, however, some members of the Henson team had just had some experience with another technically sophisticated puppet because of the George Lucas *Star Wars* movies.

As *The Dark Crystal* was beginning to take shape, Gary Kurtz, the line producer of *Star Wars*, had approached Jim with a request for assistance in the creation of the character Yoda, who would be featured in *The Empire Strikes Back*. Stuart Freeborn, a special-effects artist associated with the *Star Wars* series, was planning to realize Yoda by means quite similar to those being planned by Henson technicians for *The Dark Crystal*. Freeborn would remain responsible for the overall design of Yoda, but the Henson shop's experience would be of enormous value in articulating the character effectively. Jim showed Kurtz what was evolving in the Downshire Hill studio and said that he'd be glad to help with realizing Yoda so long as there was no conflict of interest involved. In addition, Kurtz accepted Jim's suggestion that Frank Oz be enlisted to perform Yoda.

The collaboration worked for both Lucas and the Hensons. Yoda became one of the most popular characters spawned by the *Star Wars* saga. And from the point of view of Jim and his associates, the Yoda experience provided valuable insights into the difficulties they could expect to face when producing an entire movie peopled with naturalistic, cable-controlled puppets. (From a purely physical point of view, Yoda had proved extremely difficult to work with.) It also led to Jim asking Gary Kurtz to coproduce *The Dark Crystal*.

Kurtz joined a production team that came to include cinematographer Ossie Morris (*Beat the Devil*, *Oliver*, *Fiddler on the Roof*), film editor Ralph Kemplen (*The African Queen*, *Moulin Rouge*, *A Man for All Seasons*), and production designer Harry Lange (*2001: A Space Odyssey*). David Lazer would be executive producer, while Jim himself would share directing duties with Frank Oz.

Principal photography was set to start at Elstree in April of 1981, just two months after the completion of *The Great Muppet Caper*, which had employed largely the same production crew. Months earlier, however, workshop personnel had begun moving from Downshire Hill to Elstree, and by the end of 1980 everyone was ensconced in various facilities adjacent to the soundstages where the movie would be shot.

By this time, most of the technical problems had been solved, but there was still a great deal of work to be done in each character group. It was Jen and Kira, hero and heroine of the film, who presented the greatest challenge. Even their basic appearance was difficult to determine, and Wendy Midener had sculpted literally dozens of heads before the final elfin yet decidedly human versions were arrived at.

Like the Skeksis, Jen and Kira required cable-controlled prehensile hands and fully articulated limbs, but their body movements had to be much more subtle—more human—than those of the Skeksis, and the controls had to be squeezed into a much smaller volume. And beyond these technical problems, there was the all-important question of performance. If these two characters were not convincing, the entire movie would fail.

The role of Kira had been awarded to Kathy Mullen. Kathy was then a relatively inexperienced puppeteer, though she had made some valuable contributions to *The Muppet Show* and had had the important experience of working with Frank Oz on Yoda, so that she was familiar with cable-control technique. She had several months to rehearse with Kira, but even so, as the start date approached, she was still uncomfortable with her character. The cable controls passing up through the puppet's neck hampered her wrist and hand movements, and she found it disconcerting to have the cable crew hovering close to her as she worked.

Jim Henson had reserved Jen for himself. He encoun-tered the same technical problems as Kathy, and in addition was so involved with supervising preproduction and with other projects that he had had very little time to practice with Jen. As the first day of shooting approached, the movie's two principal characters were still, to a large extent, unknown quantities.

There were other problems as well. A successful proto-type of a Mystic—one of the kindly characters who serve as Jen's teachers—had been built, but the movie required ten of these saintly, lumbering creatures and each of them had to be carefully differentiated from all the others according to Brian Froud's drawings. Also, people had to be trained to work inside the cumbersome Mystic rigs, which required the per-formers to remain in uncomfortable crouching positions for extended periods of time.

The Mystics—like another character group, the Garthim (crablike warriors who were the minions of the Skeksis)—would be dependent on mime rather than pup-petry skills. To assist in this area, Jim had hired a gifted French mime, Jean-Pierre Amiel, who would both perform and coach other performers, some of whom were dancers, circus acrobats, or athletes.

Because of his knowledge of what the body could be asked to do, Amiel was able to make valuable contributions to character design. This was particularly important in the case of the Landstriders, sympathetic creatures with vestigal wings and giraffelike legs. A key moment in their evolution took place when Amiel discovered that one of the men he had hired was an expert stilt walker. This led to the develop-ment of a special stilt rig around which the characters could be built.

Most Muppetlike of the puppets employed in *The Dark Crystal* were the peasantlike Pod People. These were classic puppets of the sort Jim had employed for years, but even they were considerably more naturalistic than anything seen on, say, *Sesame Street*. Much the same is true of the

Jim Henson Presents the World of Puppetry

many forest creatures who would enliven various scenes. Fizzgig, on the other hand—Kira's puppylike pet—would have been comfortably at home in the Muppet Theater.

Mystic Valley was the first set to be built, and the Mystics were the first character group to go before the cameras. Instead of looking at this early footage in a studio screening room, Jim arranged for it to be shown, late at night, to a select group drawn from the *Dark Crystal* team at the Leicester Square Cinema—a huge motion-picture palace in London's West End—so that the results could be judged under optimum circumstances.

A collective sigh of relief was almost audible as the Mystics lumbered on, fabulous creatures in an otherworldly landscape. Brian Froud's drawings had come to life, and even on this giant screen the Mystics were totally convincing, all that had been hoped for. Perhaps for the first time, everyone involved began to believe that *The Dark Crystal* was more than just a dream.

Visiting the soundstages at Elstree that spring and summer was always a fascinating experience. The sets themselves were magnificent and structurally sophisticated. As with the earlier Muppet movies, they were totally platformed-up. The floors consisted of interlocking modules, any of which could be removed to accommodate puppet performers, permitting wide establishing shots. The modules often corresponded to design elements in, for example, the stonework of the Skeksis's castle, and Harry Lange had

extended the modular concept to the vertical architectural elements in some of the sets. (Skeksis architecture was based on the triangle, giving it an otherworldly feeling.) Thus, parts of the Crystal Chamber could be reassembled to represent other rooms inhabited by the Skeksis.

If the sets were unusual, so was the whole style of performing and directing the movie. Although the puppet performers spoke their lines during scenes—a necessity for lip-synchronization—the actual voices heard in the theater would be dubbed in by actors during postproduction. (For obvious reasons, Jim did not want Jen's voice to be in any way reminiscent of Kermit, nor did he want the Skeksis Chamberlain, performed by Frank Oz, to sound like Grover or Miss Piggy.) This meant there was no need for absolute quiet on the floor during shooting—a situation that was reminiscent of the *Sam and Friends* days, when the Muppets lip-synched to recordings.

Given the technical problems confronted in almost every scene, this had the benefit of reducing tension—it was one less thing to worry about—and also permitted the directors to make adjustments during takes. In the middle of a take, Jim might call out suggestions to a performer, or the assistant director might warn a prop man to move because he was too close to a camera crane. It was a lot like being on the set of a silent movie.

Unlike silent-movie sets, however, the soundstages at Elstree were dotted with high-tech equipment, notably the dozens of monitors that enabled the performers and their crews to see what they were doing.

Any movie is dependent for its success upon convincing performances in the lead roles, which, in the case of *The Dark Crystal*, meant Jen and Kira. Even though Kathy Mullen had been practicing with Kira, she still did not feel comfortable with the cable-control system. A few weeks before production began, she went to Faz Fazakas for help, knowing of his work with radio control.

Faz told her there was no reason why the functions of Jen and Kira that were now controlled by cable could not be controlled by radio signals instead.

Some radio control had been used in *The Great Muppet Caper*, but there it was applied to characters far less naturalistic than Jen and Kira. Even so, Jim and Frank—who had been coaching Kathy—thought it was worth a try and asked Faz to build prototypes. For his part, Faz was convinced that remote control would enable the puppeteers to coax far more convincing performances from the Gelflings.

"Actually," he explains, "remote control applies well to characters of that sort. The cable-control system is inefficient. Because it is an engineering system with no fulcrum, it involves a lot of work to create very little effect. People tend to be too strong and use too much force for the effects they're after. Radio-controlled servo-mechanisms, on the other hand, can be very expressive and subtle."

In the New York workshop, Faz quickly built radio controls into two substitute heads and brought them to London. They were relatively crude, but Jim and Frank were delighted with what Faz showed them and asked him to build two robot heads with full controls for ears, eyelids—everything.

"We did the work in three and a half weeks," says Faz, "and it turned out very well—perhaps because we had to keep things simple."

"Having a remote-control Kira made my performance," adds Kathy. "I did a couple of scenes with the cable-controlled version and the difference was like night and day."

LABYRINTH

WHILE *Labyrinth* **has many things in common with** *The Dark Crystal*, **it differs from the earlier film in that it starts and ends in the everyday world and features human performers alongside the creations of Jim Henson's Creature Shop—even in the fantasy sequences that make up most of the movie. Seen here in a climactic scene is David Bowie, who played the goblin king in the film. He poses on a set that is a three-dimensional representation of an M. C. Escher illusionary maze—one of the many variations on the labyrinth theme featured throughout the movie.**

180

What radio control did for Jen and Kira was allow the performers to concentrate on acting, free of encumbrance. While each Skeksis was followed about by a swarm of assistant operators, Kathy and Jim were unhampered on the set. As Jim put Jen through his paces, Wendy Midener would sit a few feet away with a control box, about the size of a shoe box, in front of her. While Jim controlled the basic head and body movements, giving the performance its breadth, Midener—with a little gentle pressure on this lever or that—added the inflections that brought the hero of *The Dark Crystal* to life. The last of the major technical problems had been overcome.

Shooting was accomplished without major delays or cost overruns. Then the project moved to a postproduction phase that was more complex than most. This was largely due to the fact that the entire sound track, including dialogue, had to be created after principal photography was complete.

While shooting was still in progress, associate producer Duncan Kenworthy had begun to audition voice talent. It had been decided in advance what kinds of voices would be needed—deep and warm for the Mystics, brittle and abrasive for the Skeksis—and each voice was matched as closely as possible to a given character. In addition, a device known as a harmonizer was used to electronically alter the voices and make them sound stranger and more otherworldly. Among its various unusual features, the harmonizer can make a voice higher or lower without changing its speed of delivery.

At one point, Jim even considered the idea of having the different character groups speaking in different languages, with subtitles appearing on the screen. This idea was eventually abandoned as being too farfetched, but it gives some notion of just how seriously Jim took *The Dark Crystal* and how determined he was to create a world that was internally consistent.

SEPTIMUS

GURTIE

MUSKUL

WEECH

As recorded by the London Symphony Orchestra supplemented by synthesizer and a variety of unconventional instruments, Trevor Jones's score further added to the otherworldly character of the sound track. Jones, who had written music for half a dozen feature films, including John Boorman's *Excalibur*, had been chosen to work on *The Dark Crystal* because of his familiarity with both conventional orchestral scoring and the latest electronic technology and his willingness to work closely with the filmmakers in a flexible and experimental way. As recorded, his score was a combination of the innovative and the archival, featuring instruments as unusual as an eleventh-century double flageolet, which was used to represent Jen's double flute.

Finally, months after principal photography had ended, *The Dark Crystal* was completed.

Even in a period that brought other elaborate fantasies (such as the *Star Wars* cycle) to the screen, *The Dark Crystal* was a unique film because no human was ever seen on screen. The vision of Brian Froud, the cinematic imagination of Jim Henson, and the superlative performing skills of Jim, Frank Oz, Dave Goelz, Steve Whitmire, Kathy Mullen, and the other puppeteers were blended with the talents of hundreds of other artists and craftspeople to create an extraordinary cinematic experience. It is a film that

TRYING TO DESCRIBE *Labyrinth*, Jim Henson asked the rhetorical question, "Is it all a dream, like *Alice's Adventures in Wonderland* or *The Wizard of Oz*? In my mind it is. But it's all rather ambiguous—dream or reality? Fantasy or fact? It's whatever you like to make it."

One thing he was certain of was that *Labyrinth* "is about a person at the point of changing from being a child to being a woman. Times of transition are always magic. Twilight is a magic time and dawn is magic—the times during which it's not day and it's not night but something in between. Also the time between sleeping and dreaming. There are a lot of mystical qualities related to that, and to me this is what the film is about."

Certainly much of *Labyrinth* has a dreamlike quality, and its atmosphere also relates (as Jim pointed out) to the books that the movie's heroine, Sarah, reads: books like *Alice's Adventures in Wonderland* and *The Wizard of Oz*. And, as with *The Dark Crystal*, Jim called on Brian Froud to help imagine the world to be conjured up (drawings *top* and *opposite*). Appropriately, Toby—the baby kidnapped by Jareth (David Bowie)—was played in the movie by the son of Brian and Wendy Midener Froud.

Jim Henson and executive producer George Lucas stare intently at a monitor as one of *Labyrinth*'s scenes unfolds (*above*). In addition to his ability to produce fabulous special effects, Lucas brought his knowledge of story structure to the project.

Labyrinth was chosen as the occasion for a Royal Command Performance, and before the screening the Princess of Wales was given the opportunity to meet Ludo, one of the movie's most sympathetic characters (*left*).

WITH GEORGE LUCAS as executive producer and Jim Henson as director, it could almost be taken for granted that *Labyrinth* would feature amazing creatures and astonishing special effects. Lucas's Industrial Light and Magic effects shop was responsible for the many optical effects—camera tricks—such as the matte paintings that were used to extend the mazes built as sets (*below*) so that they seemed to extend to the horizon (artist's study, *above*).

Meanwhile craftspeople at Jim Henson's Creature Shop (*right*) built on the experience that had been gained creating the protagonists of *The Dark Crystal*. Among other fantastic beings, the new movie called for the construction of a knightly terrier, his sheepdog steed, a host of vicious goblins, a talking junk pile, articulate door knockers, and a giant gate that guarded the goblin king's castle by turning into a monstrous mechanical foe.

"It was at the time of *Labyrinth*," says Brian Henson, "that the idea of the Creature Shop really became settled in my father's mind. During the making of *The Dark Crystal*, he began to realize that he had put a remarkable group of people together and he wanted to hold it together somehow. With Lyle Conway running it, the Downshire Hill shop had stayed in business by doing work for *Dreamchild*. [*Dreamchild* is director Gavin Miller's film about Lewis Carroll's *Alice's Adventures in Wonderland*.] But it was with *Labyrinth*, I think, that the Creature Shop really developed into a self-contained entity that would be able to go out and generate its own business."

"The creatures in *Labyrinth* are the most sophisticated characters we've ever built," Jim said at the time. "We use a lot of remote-controlled radio techniques and teams of puppeteers, who each operate various parts of the characters. I think that some effects we've achieved look so real that people won't even realize we've done anything special."

TWO YOUNGER members of the Henson family made significant contributions to *Labyrinth*, both as performers and behind the scenes. Along with Shari Weiser, who inhabited the costume, and a number of other assistants, Brian Henson (seen *above* with Jim) performed Hoggle, one of the film's major puppet characters, and also served as the production's puppet coordinator. Cheryl Henson was one of the puppet-builders who helped design and develop the characters known as Alph and Ralph, and was also a member (*below*) of the team that performed one of the "fierys"— aggressively hyperactive creatures who were capable of literally losing their heads.

THE FEATHERY, bright red fierys (*above*)—who perform an extraordinary dance to a musical number by David Bowie—are just one example of the kinds of astonishing creatures to be found in *Labyrinth*. Among others shown on this spread are the goblins (*right, above*), seen here surrounding baby Toby (Toby Froud), who seems rather to enjoy his captivity in Jareth's castle; Humongous (*right, below*), an armored, axe-wielding monster who comes alive when two huge metal gates are slammed shut; the Wiseman (*opposite, left*), a doddering oracle with a bird on his head, performed by Frank Oz with his usual brilliance; and Hoggle (*opposite, lower right*), a denizen of the maze who at first wants nothing to do with Sarah (Jennifer Connelly), the story's human heroine. Hoggle eventually helps Sarah reach Jareth's castle, where she finally confronts Toby's captor, played by David Bowie, who has previously romanced her in a glittering ballroom scene (*opposite, upper right*).

Although the creatures in this production relied heavily on modern technology to bring them to life, the world evoked is one of fairy tale and traditional fantasy. "Puppetry is an ancient tradition that draws heavily on myth and legend," Jim explained at the time, "but I enjoy converting [that tradition] to the worlds of film and television."

carried the art of puppetry to a point of technical sophistication that would have been almost unthinkable just a few years earlier.

So radical were the advances that the word *puppetry* seemed insufficient to describe how many characters were brought into being. To characterize the blend of cable control and radio control used to bring Jen and Kira to life, Jim used the word *animatronics*. Though there had been other pioneers of this technology, it was *The Dark Crystal* that really proved the viability of animatronics on a massive scale, and it is the Henson Creature Shop that has dominated the field ever since.

In 1983, Jim Henson began to plan a new fantasy movie, *Labyrinth*. As with *The Dark Crystal*, Brian Froud was to be the conceptual designer. But this time, the development process would be somewhat different.

To begin with, *Labyrinth* would include human characters and take place partly in the everyday world. This was not a case of inventing everything from scratch, even though much of the film would take place in a make-believe setting and involve many animatronic creatures created in the Downshire Hill Creature Shop.

Labyrinth would keep the Creature Shop busy devising everything from talking door knockers to a walking junk pile. It's impossible to come up with a "typical" *Labyrinth* character, but the kind of complexities involved can be understood by taking the case of Hoggle—a major figure in the movie who reluctantly befriends the film's heroine.

On one level, Hoggle was simply an evolution of the "humans with Muppet heads" concept that had begun with *Hey Cinderella!* Inside the basic Hoggle suit was an actress provided with a concealed view hole and a television monitor that showed her what the camera saw. But Hoggle's enormous head went way beyond anything imagined at the time of *Hey Cinderella!* This was a remote-controlled, animatronic device requiring several people to operate it, one

performing the lips, one the eyes, one the brows, and so on—all supervised by Brian Henson.

Coexisting with Hoggle would be characters like Sir Didymus—a courtly terrier who speaks Elizabethan English and rides a sheepdog named Ambrosius. Other inventions included Ludo (a gentle, lumbering giant with matted red fur), and the manic "fierys," who could cause flames to leap up from the ground and separate their heads and limbs from their bodies. In fact, *Labyrinth* would contain the full gamut of puppet styles and animatronic innovations Jim had introduced over the years.

Labyrinth was directed by Jim Henson with all the technical flair he had brought to his early film projects. And while he did not perform any major characters, several

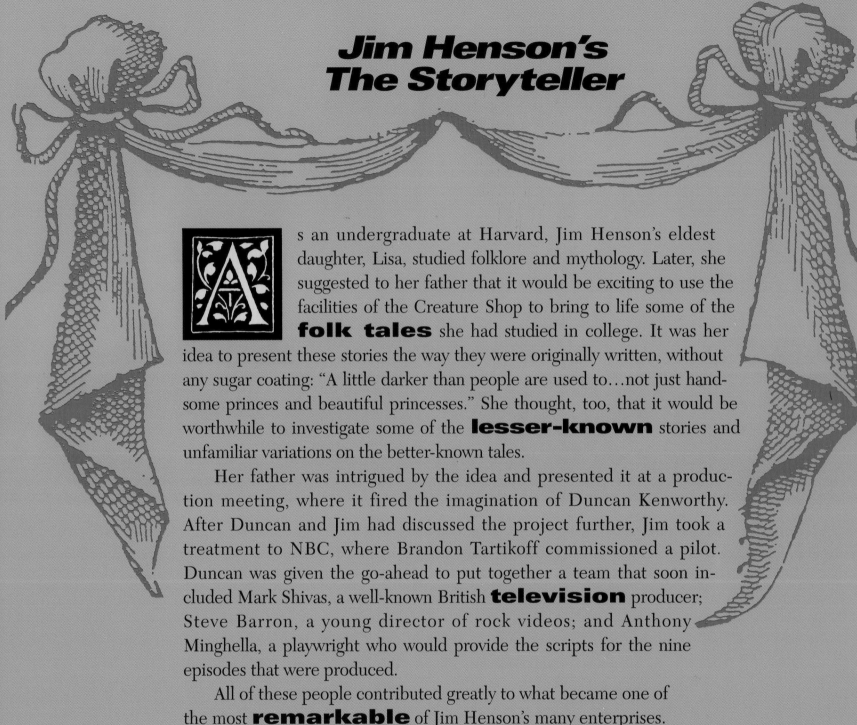

Jim Henson's The Storyteller

As an undergraduate at Harvard, Jim Henson's eldest daughter, Lisa, studied folklore and mythology. Later, she suggested to her father that it would be exciting to use the facilities of the Creature Shop to bring to life some of the **folk tales** she had studied in college. It was her idea to present these stories the way they were originally written, without any sugar coating: "A little darker than people are used to…not just handsome princes and beautiful princesses." She thought, too, that it would be worthwhile to investigate some of the **lesser-known** stories and unfamiliar variations on the better-known tales.

Her father was intrigued by the idea and presented it at a production meeting, where it fired the imagination of Duncan Kenworthy. After Duncan and Jim had discussed the project further, Jim took a treatment to NBC, where Brandon Tartikoff commissioned a pilot. Duncan was given the go-ahead to put together a team that soon included Mark Shivas, a well-known British **television** producer; Steve Barron, a young director of rock videos; and Anthony Minghella, a playwright who would provide the scripts for the nine episodes that were produced.

All of these people contributed greatly to what became one of the most **remarkable** of Jim Henson's many enterprises. *Jim Henson's The Storyteller* may not be as well known as some of Jim's other productions, but the quality of the nine shows that make up the series is indisputable, and Jim himself told associates that he thought it was one of the best things he had ever done.

THE SOLDIER AND DEATH

A group of remarkably lifelike devils play cards in *The Soldier and Death*.

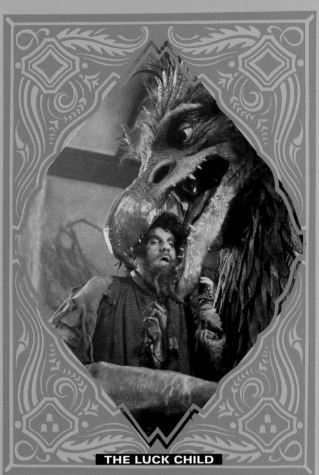

THE LUCK CHILD

The Little Man displeases his master, a giant, threatening Griffin, in *The Luck Child*.

THE STORYTELLER

Each episode of *The Storyteller* is introduced by a master storyteller (John Hurt), who tells the story of the day to his dog. As the narrative proceeds, the viewer begins to see the story—much as he or she might imagine it—performed by humans and Creature Shop inventions.

HANS MY HEDGEHOG

Hans rides a rooster.

The storyteller himself plays cards with a beggar in *A Story Short.*

A STORY SHORT

SAPSORROW

Sapsorrow (a variant of *Cinderella*) and her prince.

The Oral Tradition

ALTHOUGH THE SERIES remains faithful to oral traditions, each episode of *Jim Henson's The Storyteller* is highly cinematic. The presence of the storyteller himself is always felt, but the stories are fully realized in visual terms, text and imagery being blended in novel and inventive ways. The effect of watching these shows is a little like listening—eyes closed, feeling a little drowsy—to a story told on the radio and letting the imagination bring characters and situations to life. It is almost as if the visuals are unfolding inside the viewer's head. But in fact they derive from beautifully designed sets, clever video effects, and the wonderfully convincing creations of the Creature Shop. The way the stories have been visualized is all the more effective because they are never entirely naturalistic. The continuity often has a dreamlike quality, sustained with the help of unexpected visual transitions, such as paintings that come to life, while individual scenes have an almost surreal clarity.

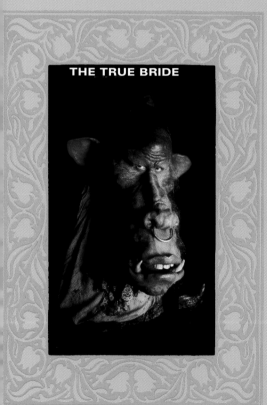

THE TRUE BRIDE

The evil Troll who keeps Anya prisoner in *The True Bride.*

The Storyteller conveyed viewers into the magical world of fairy tales.

A STORY SHORT

THE THREE RAVENS

A wicked queen casts a magic spell in *The Three Ravens.*

A spoiled young prince and his mother, the queen, from *A Story Short.*

Muppet Show and *Sesame Street* veterans did, including Dave Goelz, Steve Whitmire, and Kevin Clash, along with Brian Henson and *Dark Crystal* alumni like Dave Greenaway.

Labyrinth is a film that combines traditional fairy-tale elements with a story line that at times recalls books such as *The Wizard of Oz* and *Through the Looking Glass*. The heroine, Sarah, is a somewhat self-absorbed teenager who resents her baby half-brother, Toby. In a reckless moment, she wishes aloud that the King of the Goblins would kidnap the child. Jareth obliges, and Sarah spends the balance of the movie trying to retrieve her sibling by penetrating a maze—the labyrinth of the title—that surrounds Goblin City and Jareth's castle, where Toby is hidden. She is assisted in her quest by Hoggle, Ludo, and Sir Didymus, but eventually must confront Jareth on her own and, in doing so, vanquishes her adolescent demons, bringing herself and the baby safely back to the everyday reality of her home.

The pleasures of the tale, however, are in the telling and—as is so often the case in Jim Henson's projects—the telling is essentially visual. In a sense, the labyrinth itself is the film's central character, and it is splendidly realized in all its manifestations. In places it is made up of damp, high walls, from which an exotic form of creeping plant watches with beady eyes. Elsewhere, it is like a topiary maze, such as can be found at Hampton Court Palace and in formal gardens throughout the world. Sometimes, it is just a rocky landscape, or a forest where the path winds back on itself, presenting innumerable confusing intersections. There are doors that open and close by themselves and hidden trap-doors that lead to an infernal bog or—in one case—to a chute lined with talking hands. Finally, inside Jareth's castle, the labyrinth becomes a complicated Escher-like puzzle that dislocates space and time. Always, though, the maze is achieved so convincingly that it seems to draw the heroine onward, and the viewer with her.

Some critics have seen films like *The Dark Crystal* and *Labyrinth* as having little to do with Jim's previous work, and certainly they did represent a departure from his Muppet style. But they were very much the products of the same sensibility that had produced, for example, the *Saturday Night Live* puppets. If Jim had not tackled fantasy subjects in earnest till the eighties, it was not for lack of interest, but rather because he had been occupied with other things and had not yet attained the technical means of realizing his visions. In fact, the fantasy films were just a beginning for Jim, and he returned to this vein again with the brilliant television series called *Jim Henson's The Storyteller*, which made its debut not long after *Labyrinth*'s release.

The genesis of this powerful series of folktales dated back to the early eighties, when Jim's eldest daughter, Lisa, was a student at Harvard.

"My main field was classical Greek mythology," she recalls, "but one class I had was a general folklore course. I did a good deal of reading and discovered these wonderful old tales. I began to think that it would be great fun to do a show using the Creature Shop to tell these folktales the way they were really written. Not violent, necessarily, but not sugar-coated, not glamorized, and not just handsome princes and beautiful princesses. A little darker than people are used to."

After graduating from Harvard, Lisa took a job at Warner Bros. in Hollywood. "It was that period when the networks were programming series like *Tales From the Dark Side* and *Amazing Stories*," she recalls, "and I figured that this was a time when Dad could sell an anthology series. He came out to Los Angeles on one of his business trips and we spent a weekend brainstorming the idea."

Shortly after this, Jim Henson went to London for a project development meeting. *The Storyteller* was one of the ideas he brought up, and it immediately caught the imagination of Duncan Kenworthy, who had been associate producer of *The Dark Crystal* and was by now an important member of the Henson production team.

THE WHITE LION who rescues Anya in *The True Bride*.

a yes to a pilot with the possibility of an order for twenty-six episodes."

Eventually, it was decided to produce nine episodes of *The Storyteller* (it was impossible to do more because of time constraints imposed by the series's high production values). Anthony Minghella, a British playwright known for his extremely original and emotionally charged work, was hired to write the scripts.

The format called for the folktales to be told by an unnamed storyteller (John Hurt). He would sit in his favorite chair, a fire burning in a large, gothic fireplace behind him. His audience would consist of a big, floppy hound dog (performed by Brian Henson) given to uttering sardonic asides.

As the storyteller told the story, characters would come alive in the flames in the hearth or in the room itself. Television viewers would then be permitted to follow the characters—as if in their own imaginations—into the world of the story, sometimes accompanied by the voice of the now-unseen storyteller, sometimes left to overhear the dialogue of the protagonists.

Individual scenes were dramatized in conventional fashion, but took place in settings that were usually rather simple and slightly stylized, helping to sustain the feeling of a fairy-tale world. Clever transitions helped move the narrative along in ways that were very different from normal cinematic practice. And always the storyteller's voice was ready to pick up the narrative—whether he was on screen or off—maintaining the viewer's contact with the oral tradition.

Brilliantly written and sensitively performed, the nine episodes that were produced can justifiably be called miniature masterpieces. Not only do they translate the folk tale into the electronic age with great fidelity, they also demonstrate what the television medium is capable of when it is placed in the hands of gifted men and women who care about what they are doing.

The use of the video effects that helped define the

"Nobody had ever really done anything like that before," he says, "taking a fairy story and bringing it to television while staying true to the oral tradition. Usually fairy stories are dramatized, but this would be totally different. It would be a matter of hearing the story and creating images to match it—making metaphors real. That was the challenge.

"We sat down for about an hour and talked about the idea. Then Jim took a treatment back to New York and pitched it to Brandon Tartikoff at NBC, and Brandon gave

GREEK MYTHS

look of the series can be attributed largely to the influence of Steve Barron, a leading producer of rock videos at the time. Jim had been extremely impressed with Barron's direction of a *Labyrinth* music video, and was determined to work with him on the *Storyteller* project. Barron ended up directing three episodes, including the first in the series, "Hans My Hedgehog."

Barron was acknowledged as an innovator in the use of the type of special effects that had seldom if ever been used in the context of television drama. Electronic matting tech-

JIM HENSON'S The Storyteller: Greek Myths **was planned as a sequel to** *The Storyteller. Greek Myths* **again featured the idea of stories told by a narrator—this time, a roguish character (Michael Gambon) who has taken shelter in the ruined Labyrinth of Knossos. Like the storyteller of the original series, this narrator has a canine companion; in fact, the dog that appeared in** *The Storyteller* **"plays" this role as well. Shown above are the Gorgon (***left***) and the Minotaur.**

niques and digitally controlled transitions made all kinds of magical transformations possible. Human characters could be metamorphosed into animals. Scenes painted on pieces of pottery could be brought to life.

If some members of the production team were initially

nervous about employing such "untraditional" methods in the telling of folktales, Jim Henson was enormously enthusiastic about applying new technology to these stories, and his enthusiasm was borne out by the results. The special effects were just that—special—permitting the producers to achieve a close visual equivalent of the narrative devices found in folktales and fairy stories.

For its part, the Creature Shop contributed many innovative characters. In *Fearnot*, for example, there is a water monster with luminous whiskers and a demon capable of splitting itself into several parts. For *The Soldier and Death*—of which Jim, who directed it, was especially proud—the Creature Shop created a hoard of devils that might have flown out of a painting by Hieronymus Bosch.

The Creature Shop was particularly successful in devising the simplified controls of the storyteller's dog. Previously, such a character would have required several people and a combination of cable control and radio control to operate. By using a computer to enhance the remote-control devices already in use, the dog could be performed by a single puppeteer—in this case, Brian Henson.

This was an important development because, obviously, the more complicated the control system, the more difficult any character is to perform. In films like *The Dark Crystal* and *Labyrinth*, elaborate control systems had taken some of the characters about as far away from the simple Muppet-style hand puppet as could be imagined. Now, with the storyteller's dog, there was the beginning of a move toward resimplification that would permit future characters—however naturalistic in appearance—to be performed in a relatively straightforward way. A single puppeteer could have as much control over his character as he would if performing Kermit or Fozzie or Gonzo.

Artistically, the nine episodes of *The Storyteller* are as satisfying as anything Jim Henson ever achieved. In Europe, and in countries such as Japan and Australia, *The Storyteller* proved to be a considerable hit. In America, the series suffered from the fact that it was impossible to produce episodes fast enough to make up a conventional network series. NBC did broadcast the shows, but they were so scattered in their airings that, although they received laudatory reviews and the pilot won an Emmy,

DREAMCHILD is writer Dennis Potter and director Gavin Miller's meditation upon *Alice's Adventures in Wonderland*; it is a fascinating film that moves back and forth in time and in and out of fantasy and reality. Many of the key scenes were realized with the help of Jim Henson's Creature Shop, whose craftspeople brought to life characters such as the Caterpillar, the Mad Hatter, and the Dormouse.

they never found their audience. There are, however, plans to repackage the nine tales for showing as a coherent group, and also to release *The Storyteller* in videocassette form.

Among Jim's last completed projects was the fantasy film *The Witches*, for which he served as executive producer. Though the movie was very much his conception—he had read the Roald Dahl novel and thought it ideal for adaptation—it never became a full-fledged Henson project (in the sense of being indelibly marked by his sensibility), largely because Nicholas Roeg was chosen to direct it.

A former cinematographer (*Far from the Madding Crowd, Fahrenheit 451*), Roeg is best known as the director of offbeat cult favorites such as *Performance, Walkabout,* and *The Man Who Fell to Earth.* Jim, who selected him, had no intention of attempting to shape the director's quirky vision. He therefore functioned as a conventional executive producer rather than as a creative supervisor, leaving the crucial aesthetic decisions to Roeg.

The Creature Shop, however, had a major role in bringing *The Witches* to the screen, since the plot required turning children into small rodents. It was necessary to produce mice that could "act" while appearing totally naturalistic, even when set alongside the many real mice that were also employed.

"We had three different sizes of mice," explains John Stephenson, Creature Shop supervisor. "There was a life-size version, which was very limited because of its small size. Then there was a medium version, three times larger, which made it possible to get all the mechanics we wanted into it. Finally there was one nine times bigger than life size, which was a hand puppet, so we could do lots of expressions and facial movements for close-up photography."

Most of the mouse animation was done with the aid of cable-control systems, though computer-assisted radio control was also used extensively. As always, Jim had stayed abreast of these new technical advances. He constantly sought out technological innovations that could provide his audience with novel experiences.

But he also never lost sight of the fact that it took a gifted performer to bring any kind of puppet to life—no matter how sophisticated the animatronics involved.

THE WITCHES

—for which Jim Henson functioned as executive producer, with Mark Shivas producing and Nicholas Roeg directing—is another film that benefits greatly from the contributions of the Creature Shop. Based on a story by Roald Dahl, the movie stars Anjelica Huston as the Grand High Witch (*far left*), who plans to rid the world of children with the aid of a magic potion that turns them into mice. After Skeksis and goblins, mice might seem to be an easy build for the Creature Shop. But this was far from the case; the puppet mice had to be completely realistic so they could be matched with the real mice also used in the movie. The shop also provided the witches with realistic prosthetics (*left* and *right*).

CHAPTER EIGHT

Despite the fact that Jim Henson was producing Muppet programming for adults as well as for children, children continued to rank among the most ardent admirers of his creations. Whether it was the kindergarten-and-under set watching *Sesame Street* or savvy eight-year-olds laughing at *The Muppet Show*, kids often made up the lion's share of the Henson audience.

It was for these young fans that in March 1977 Jim Henson created one of his most successful television specials—*Emmet Otter's Jug-Band Christmas*, based on the charming and award-winning book by Russell and Lillian Hoban.

One of the more important aspects of *Emmet Otter* was the fact that the book's somewhat naturalistic illustrations gave the Muppet workshop personnel a chance to work on animals that were more realistic-looking than the anthropomorphic Kermit, Piggy, and the rest. This would prove critical to the development of Jim's fantasy films.

In the beginning, Muppets were almost "abstract" puppets. It was impossible to be sure if Mushmellon, say—or even the earliest incarnation of Kermit—represented a human or an animal or something completely different. They were basically plain puppets. "There's something about the very pure form of abstraction," Jim said once. "It's a purer form of puppetry, and I enjoy it very much."

Even when *Sesame Street* came along, many of the characters remained just "plain puppets" in the best sense of that phrase. Cookie, Oscar, and Grover, for example, are as abstract as any of the regulars on *Sam and Friends*. But some of their fellow Muppets—Guy Smiley, for example—were definitely humanoid, while others—like Big Bird—were anthropomorphized animals. This was a trend that had started with Rowlf and with the evolution of just plain Kermit into Kermit the Frog.

With *The Muppet Show*, anthropomorphized animals were everywhere. There was Kermit, of

IN *EMMET OTTER'S Jug-Band Christmas*, Jim Henson experimented with puppets and settings more naturalistic than any he had employed before.

Innovative in its realism, *Emmet Otter's Jug-Band*

***Christmas*—with its lifelike animals and detailed**

sets—explored new technical approaches to puppetry

that made the Henson movies of the eighties possible.

course, but in addition there were Miss Piggy and other porkers like Link Hogthrob; Fozzie, the fun-loving bear; mischievous rats; and singing penguins. These animals were recognizable in terms of species, but they were simplified and caricatured, not unlike Mickey Mouse or Bugs Bunny.

The characters that began to take shape for *Emmet Otter's Jug-Band Christmas*, however, were almost like a new species of puppet—far more naturalistic than anything that had come before.

"We looked," Jim Henson said a few years after *Emmet Otter* was made, "for rather realistic movement and animals that looked like animals. They still had somewhat cartoon-like features and so on, but we were looking for fully dimensional animals out in the real world."

Taped in Toronto, *Emmet Otter's Jug-Band Christmas* presented Emmet and his friends—an assortment of woodchucks, beavers, possums, and porcupines—as denizens of an unspecified northern landscape where a river flowed between low banks dotted with cabins, farms, and little clusters of clapboard houses. All this was re-created with great attention to detail, as if the art director were planning full-sized sets for a live-action film.

The plot concerns the good guys' successful attempt to undermine the nefarious plans of a sleazy pack of villains known as the Riverbottom Gang. These villains—including a lizard, a snake, and a pop-eyed catfish—resemble conventional Muppets in that they are somewhat simplified caricatures of types rather than fully rounded portraits. But Emmet and his friends are presented in a decidedly naturalistic way. Although they do not escape anthropomorphism entirely—nor should they—and are dressed in clothes, they closely resemble real animals and were performed in a restrained way distinct from the sometimes frenetic and always animated style of performance that was the norm on *The Muppet Show*. Adding to the naturalistic feel were the clever props built by Faz Fazakas. These included,

"FAZ" FAZAKAS, a veteran puppet-builder, is also the technical innovator who devised rigs that could allow Emmet to row a boat and who drew on his extensive knowledge of servo-mechanisms and electronics to permit the use of remote-controlled puppets.

"Jim had wanted to do a heavy production number on a river, since rivers are where otters live. Bill Beeton, the set designer, prepared a tank the full width of the studio. The river set was the focus of the entire show. The script called for Emmet and his mother to row down the river in a boat while singing a song.

"At a production meeting, it came out that the special effects people intended to achieve this by rigging heavy chains along the bottom of the tank. I suggested to Jim that we could render the boat entirely independent by controlling it with radios. 'How,' said he, 'could a puppet row a boat?' Each oar had its own little reversible electric motor, controlled by radio from a remote location. Emmet's body was sprung so that it leaned over backward. His arms pulled his body into the natural rowing positions. The only difference between Emmet and a real rower is the source of the motive power.

"The other person in the boat was, of course, Emmet's mother. I made the bodies myself but Don Sahlin made the heads, and he had not yet finished with Mama. That is why her head looks more like a block of wood!"

most notably, a boat in which Emmet could row convincingly downstream while singing a duet with his mother, and Kermit's first bicycle.

Another notable feature of *Emmet Otter* was its extensively platformed-up sets. "*Emmet Otter* was the first time we had gotten into those kind of elaborate sets," Jim explained, "where we had floors in the interiors and we would take a wide-angle shot with characters coming up through holes in the floor. Or we'd cut into the set and remove the floor and have the characters moving through space in waist shots. That was the most elaborate production we'd gotten into at that point. *Frog Prince* had been platformed-up and *The Muppet Show* was always platformed-up, but in *Emmet Otter*...we'd go right *into* a

Down at Fraggle Rock

On April 3, 1983, Jim Henson took the Concorde from Heathrow Airport in London to John F. Kennedy Airport in New York. During the flight he filled a notebook with a number of ideas about the show as they had been formulated during a previous series of meetings.

At this point in the show's development, the future Fraggles were temporarily dubbed "Woozles"—"this name will very likely be changed," Jim remarked in his notes—but otherwise his description of what he hoped to see on screen was very much what the audience did see when the series was finally aired. The different levels of reality—represented by Fraggles, Doozers, and Gorgs—were already sketched out with some specificity (if with different names), as were the peculiarities of the basic character groups and the essential theme of peace and harmony.

The overall concept of the show was clearly set out in these preliminary notes:

"Our first job," Jim wrote, "is to make this world a lot of fun to visit. It is a high-energy, raucous musical romp. It's a lot of silliness. It's wonderful.

"However, the second thing that we're doing with this show is saying something. The show has a direction and a point of view. This will be beneath the surface, and if anybody becomes very aware of it, we will have missed.

"What the show is really about is people getting along with other people, and understanding the delicate balance of the natural world. These are topics that can be dealt with in a symbolic way, which is what puppets basically do all the time."

In a later insert, he added:

"The world of the Woozle will have its own natural balances, although these will be rather insane. But still we will make the point that everything affects everything else, and that there is a beauty and harmony of life to be appreciated."

At *left* is an early Michael Frith drawing of a Doozer family.

FRAGGLE WORLD

Fraggles average about eighteen inches in height, come in all shapes, colors, and ages, and have an endless supply of energy. Fraggles like to sing, dance, wear silly hats, eat Doozer sticks, and swim.

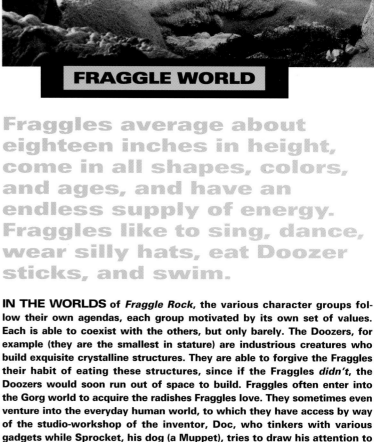

IN THE WORLDS of *Fraggle Rock*, the various character groups follow their own agendas, each group motivated by its own set of values. Each is able to coexist with the others, but only barely. The Doozers, for example (they are the smallest in stature) are industrious creatures who build exquisite crystalline structures. They are able to forgive the Fraggles their habit of eating these structures, since if the Fraggles *didn't*, the Doozers would soon run out of space to build. Fraggles often enter into the Gorg world to acquire the radishes Fraggles love. They sometimes even venture into the everyday human world, to which they have access by way of the studio-workshop of the inventor, Doc, who tinkers with various gadgets while Sprocket, his dog (a Muppet), tries to draw his attention to the invading strangers from the underground caverns. The efforts of the inhabitants of these worlds to get along together form the core of *Fraggle Rock*.

200

GORG WORLD

Gorgs are huge
—ten times
the size of a
Fraggle. There
are only three
Gorgs that we
know about—
Ma, Pa, and
Junior. Pa claims
that at one time,
their clan ruled
this universe.

DOOZER WORLD

Doozers are six
inches tall, or
knee high to a
Fraggle. Doozers
are methodical,
thorough, plodding,
and single-minded.
They spend most
of their waking
hours building.
Often their building
is accompanied by
marching songs and
various Doozer chants.

DUNCAN KENWORTHY came to Henson Associates from the Children's Television Workshop and was one of the principal contributors to the development of *Fraggle Rock*.

"Jim was single-minded about the real reason for doing this series [*Fraggle Rock*]. It was for the world, for the audience in all those different countries that had been joined together by *The Muppet Show*. 'We're not doing this to make money or just to be back on television,' he insisted. 'It's got to have an idea.' He was talking a lot at that time about the arms race and how crazy it was. By the time, later on, when it came down to five of us cre-

ating the series, he knew exactly what the idea was. He sat us down in his front room in Hampstead and said our task was to create a series that was going to stop war in the world.

"When everyone had stopped laughing, picked themselves up off the floor, and saw that Jim was serious, we started to talk about what it meant. Obviously, if you were going to change the world's ideas about how to resolve conflict, you had to start with children. And so we began."

JOCELYN STEVENSON, like Duncan Kenworthy, was involved from the beginning in the project that became *Fraggle Rock*, and she did much to shape the series.

"Jim, Jerry Juhl, Duncan Kenworthy, Michael Frith, and I had spent most of the day trying to come up with names for the characters for the project we were calling 'The International Children's Show.' At that point, it was definitely on its way to becoming *Fraggle Rock*, but it wasn't there yet. And we hadn't been able to

think of a good name for the little guys who worked all the time. Workalots? Too obvious. Drudgies? Too much attitude. Rgllmzaxpoops? Too hard to spell.

"It was a lovely day, so we decided to clear our minds with a walk on Hampstead Heath. Jim and I walked together, deep in thought. He occasionally said, 'Hmmm...,' but that was about it until we reached the bench which Jim had dedicated to Don Sahlin, a Heath-lover like himself.

"'Want to sit on Don's bench?' asked Jim. So we did. At the same time. And the minute we both touched wood, we said, out loud, simultaneously—*Doozers*! Perfect name! 'I knew Don would figure out a way to work on this show.' said Jim. So we thanked him and went back to work."

---

scene. We'd have the whole set in three dimensions... rigged so we could pop parts and come out through the openings, which is really time-consuming...." All in all, *Emmet Otter* was a ground-breaking production, opening up possibilities that Jim and his team would explore over the next decade and more.

Another ground-breaking television production began to surface a few years later, during the filming of *The Dark Crystal*. It was then that discussions began about the TV series that would eventually become *Fraggle Rock*.

In its development phase, *Fraggle Rock* was first known as "The International Children's Show," and one of the main points of the project was that it was to be custom-designed for international coproduction. This concept grew out of Duncan Kenworthy's experience in helping adapt *Sesame Street* to the requirements of foreign markets.

The fact that *Sesame Street* had not been planned for coproduction created a variety of problems in different parts of the world. To give a single example, the character of Mumford the Magician could not be used in Arab countries because the Muslim religion forbids depictions of magic.

When Kenworthy and writer Jocelyn Stevenson presented Jim with the notion of an internationally adaptable show, Jim was enthusiastic, but he asked the obvious questions: "What will the show be about? What will make it special?" Shortly after, he answered those questions himself. Coming across a newspaper headline describing some new atrocity of man against man, he decided on the show's theme: world peace.

Needless to say, Jim did not delude himself into thinking he could create a television show that could actually prevent wars, but he did sincerely believe that he could produce a program that would help sow the seeds of pacifism in the minds of the world's children.

A couple of meetings in London led to a core group—Jim, Duncan, Jocelyn, Jerry Juhl, and Michael Frith—

brainstorming in Jim's house in Hampstead during the summer of 1981. "We had already decided that there were going to be five main characters, and they'd be living in this underground world but would leave it sometimes for our world," Duncan recalls. "It was during this time that we came up with the names. Jerry Juhl, for example, named Wembley because he was reading in a newspaper about some event at Wembley Stadium."

At first, the characters were called the Woozles, which no one liked much. Michael reports that Jerry kept coming back to an old name for a bunch of Muppet monsters from the 1960s called Frackles; when the "ck" was softened to "gg," it won the vote. Later, Michael suggested Fraggle Hill as a name for the show. Too wimpy, said Jocelyn. How about Fraggle *Rock*?

Busy with other projects, Jim gave the *Fraggle Rock* team more autonomy than any previous group involved with a major production. At the same time, however, he remained as involved with the show as he possibly could. He directed a number of episodes, performed Cantus the Minstrel (a musical Fraggle sage) and Convincing John (a Fraggle who could convince anyone of anything), and continued to monitor *Fraggle Rock*'s philosophy.

That philosophy can be summed up by saying that, while each episode would provide plenty of entertainment, it would also teach a meaningful lesson—the value of cooperation, for example—without being too heavy-handed. And these lessons would always be related to the central theme of promoting the idea of peace.

Fraggle Rock is a complex of underground caverns perceived by its inhabitants as the center of the universe. (Michael Frith based the setting in part on the limestone caves of his native Bermuda.) Fraggle mythologists glorify the Fraggles as a noble race that has reached the pinnacle of civilization. Music is said to be the Fraggles' most elevated art form, and Fraggles are reported to be superb

Faces Behind *Fraggle Rock*

The puppeteers who created the Fraggle Five were (*left to right, from top row*) Dave Goelz, Steve Whitmire, Jerry Nelson, Kathy Mullen, and Karen Prell. The Gorgs each required two performers, who included (*lower right picture, clockwise from upper right*) Richard Hunt, Rob Mills, Trish Leeper, Myra Fried, Gordon Robertson, and Jerry Nelson (*not shown*). One performer wore the full-body Gorg costume; the second operated the Gorg's mouth and eye movements via remote control and also performed that Gorg's voice.

physical specimens, possessed of great athletic prowess combined with the grace of dancers.

That's what the mythologists say. The truth is that the Fraggles' subterranean world is in fact inhabited by cute little Muppet creatures who sing in squeaky voices and frequently bump their heads as they make their way through the stone corridors of their homeland.

Sharing the Fraggle domain are Doozers—tiny, hard-hatted construction workers who are perpetually and purposefully on the go, like an army of ants, building an interconnecting network of crystalline towers constructed primarily of radish dust. The Fraggles are completely nonplussed by the Doozers, but the two species manage to coexist without friction, even when Fraggles eat Doozer architecture. (In fact, the Doozers rely on the Fraggles' appetites. If Fraggles didn't eat Doozer towers, the Doozers would soon run out of room to build.)

The Fraggles' known world extends to a neighboring garden inhabited by three giant Gorgs—Pa (who considers himself king of the Gorgs), Ma (his queen), and Junior (their son and only subject). The Gorgs, represented primarily by Junior, do their clumsy best to catch Fraggles when Fraggles attempt to get the radishes they eat (which grow in the Gorgs' garden). Also in the Gorgs' kingdom is Marjory, an oraclelike talking trash heap, and her two companions and sometime assistants—a pair of raffish, rodent-like creatures named Philo and Gunge.

Rounding out the cast are Gobo's Uncle Traveling Matt, who is busy exploring our world (which he calls Outer Space); Doc, the elderly inventor/tinkerer who lives in a workshop that abuts Fraggle Rock and provides the Fraggles with the means to enter our world; and Sprocket, Doc's inquisitive (Muppet) dog.

Each episode of *Fraggle Rock* features five young Fraggle friends—Gobo, Mokey, Wembley, Boober, and Red. The show often focuses on the problem of the moment faced by one or other of them and is framed as a parable with a strong moral. These parables, however, are always amusing and never ponderous. "We want to deal with situations that children encounter, and to work through them in a way that will be helpful and at the same time completely entertaining," was Jim's description of his agenda for the show.

In its very different way, the world of *Fraggle Rock* is every bit as rich as the worlds formulated for *The Dark Crystal* and *Labyrinth*. Mostly this is due to the conceptual skills of the creative team, but in addition *Fraggle Rock* displays a technical brilliance that is absolutely astonishing in the context of a television series, especially one made on a relatively low budget. In part, at least, this was a legacy of *The Dark Crystal*. That project had permitted Henson craftspeople to develop elaborate animatronic devices that could now be reapplied in this new context, thus providing *Fraggle Rock* with stunning production values.

As *Fraggle Rock* began its ninety-six-show production run, plans were also set in motion for another television series, *Jim Henson's Muppet Babies*. These infants had first seen daylight as puppets in *The Muppets Take Manhattan*, but now they were developed as animated characters for a CBS Saturday morning children's television show. The basic thrust of this show, as articulated by Jim, would be about the power of creativity and the use of the imagination in problem-solving.

The Muppet Babies go anywhere their hearts desire—but, like other babies, only in their imaginations. *Jim Henson's Muppet Babies*, however—far from being hamstrung by its characters' lack of mobility—takes bold advantage of it by creating a host of unusual animated adventures for its eight principal characters, all of which take place in their minds. In addition, the show departs from the standard Saturday morning format in that it uses old film footage and a variety of stills—sepia photographs, engravings, picture-book illustrations—as backdrops for the animated action. Since his student days, Jim had been experimenting with animation techniques, and now he had an opportunity to implement some of them. (In some ways this harked back to his experimental films of the sixties and to the mixed-media ideas he had hoped to integrate into Cyclia.)

As with *Fraggle Rock*, Jim had less hands-on contact with the day-to-day production of *Muppet Babies* than had been the case with his earlier shows. Nonetheless, his input was considerable and his influence apparent, both in terms of taste and technical approach. Most important, perhaps, Jim and his creative team stayed in close contact with the writers so that—even though the actual animation was contracted out to Marvel Productions, Ltd.—he was able to ensure that the series carried the Henson stamp when it came to quality and responsibility.

The same Henson hallmarks were amply manifested in the special titled *The Tale of the Bunny Picnic*, a story about a burrowful of fun-loving rabbits terrorized by a large dog who eventually becomes their friend.

Produced in 1986, *The Tale of the Bunny Picnic* came about as an incidental result of a trip Jim took with his daughter Cheryl.

"We were in Dresden for a puppet festival," she remembers, "and we had been talking about how nice it would be—after all the ambitious projects of the recent past—to do just a simple little puppet show again: a sweet little show for kids. In Dresden, we were strolling through a park when we came upon a puppeteer…wearing a green outfit and bunny ears. And his cart turned into a puppet theater. It was very charming, and…made me think out loud that it would be sweet to do a show with all these little bunnies—like Beatrix Potter, but different."

After further discussion, Jim asked Jocelyn Stevenson to develop the idea into a script and decided to go outside the usual Henson orbit to give the production a fresh but

A Man and His Dog

From its very inception, *Fraggle Rock* was planned as an international production. The basic plot of each episode—everything that takes place in the Fraggle world or the Gorg world, for example —would be shot in Toronto by the Henson team. But when a Fraggle ventured out into what we humans would call "the real world," then a local producer would take over for the different language versions. The "real world" might be a workshop in North America, a bakery in France, or a lighthouse in Great Britain, depending on where the show was being broadcast. This meant that a number of "Doc's" needed to be cast. Among them were Gerry Parks, the U.S./Canadian Doc, shown with Sprocket (Steve Whitmire), *above*; Fulton MacKay, from the English coproduction, who was known not as Doc but as the Captain (*inset*); Michel Robin, from the French coproduction (*below left*), in which Sprocket's name was changed to Croquette; and Hans-Helmut Dickow, from the German coproduction (*below right*).

Jim Henson's Muppet Babies: imagination and animation

From childhood, Jim Henson was always fascinated by animation. When he bought a Bolex movie camera from his *Sam and Friends* earnings, practically the first thing he did was to acquire a secondhand stand for it so that he could use it as an animation camera. He loved to explore a kind of freehand animation, in which paintings seemed to come to life, and later he adapted many of the techniques he had taught himself in order to provide little animated segments for *Sesame Street*.

Aside from *Sesame Street*, however, Jim did not become involved in animation as a form of television entertainment until the mid-1980s. By that time, television animation was beginning to improve somewhat, primarily because computers could now be used to make movements smoother without causing a huge escalation in cost. This improvement in quality was attracting more talent to the industry.

Even so, an animated show was not high on Jim's list of priorities when the subject came up in 1984. That was the year that the Muppet Babies first appeared in a scene in *The Muppets Take Manhattan*.

A musical novelty number was required for the movie, and the idea of building it around Muppet babies seemed like a very workable one. In the film, the scene that gave birth to the Muppet Babies begins during a romantic carriage ride, when Piggy fantasizes about what it would have been like if she and Kermit had grown up together—and the Muppet Babies appear in a "flashback." The number played beautifully on screen, and once the Babies had been realized as puppets it did not take much of a stretch of the imagination to picture how they might work as animated characters.

It was logical, network executives and others suggested, for the Henson organization to capitalize upon its prestige by producing a Saturday morning show. Why not center the show around the newly created Muppet Babies?

The more Jim thought about the idea, the more he liked it. The concept that evolved during a series of meetings and informal discussions was a cartoon series based on toddler versions of some of the most popular *Muppet Show* characters—Kermit, Piggy, Gonzo, Fozzie, Animal, Rowlf, and Scooter (Scooter's twin sister, Skeeter, was created for the show in order to provide it with another strong female character).

Muppet Babies would center around the way children—the Muppet Babies, in this case—use their imaginations to take them to fabulous and fascinating places that they're too young to visit—or can't visit at all, like outer space or back in time. The look of the show would be the responsibility of Michael K. Frith, who eventually became its executive producer.

Jim Henson's Muppet Babies made its debut on CBS Television in 1984 and was in production for eight years. It has received five Emmy awards, including four consecutive Emmys for Outstanding Animated Series (1985–1988).

---

coherent look. He settled on a well-known and highly respected illustrator of children's books, Diane Dawson Hearn, who had previously worked on *Fraggle Rock* books for the publishing division of Henson Associates.

Produced by Jim Henson and Martin Baker, *The Tale of the Bunny Picnic* was directed by Jim and David Hilliard with puppet staging in the able hands of Richard Hunt and Kevin Clash, who were also among the key performers along with other veterans like Steve Whitmire, Louise Gold, and Karen Prell. Jim Henson himself performed the dog, and the show turned out exactly as planned—old-fashioned children's entertainment presented with all the polished production values that by then could be taken for granted in any Henson television venture.

The following year, another outside illustrator, Larry DiFiori, was brought in to design *The Christmas Toy*, a charming special that was taped in Toronto and broadcast by ABC in the U.S. market. The two shows were to be part

WHEN THE MUPPET BABIES were first introduced in *The Muppets Take Manhattan*, they were a product of the adult Miss Piggy's imagination. The television show, too, does not pretend to reveal any of the characters' true origins. It simply places them together in a nursery, looked after by an adult character called Nanny who is only seen from the neck down—meant to represent the way kids view adults. The Babies take over from there, imagining a host of exciting adventures based on the everyday things that happen to them or the things that are around them—picture books, toys, leaky faucets.

The show reflects Jim Henson's imagination in some significant ways. The approach to animation, for example, displays his penchant for mixing genres and generally ignoring hard-and-fast rules. This is evident, for example, in the way that the animated characters sometimes interact with live-action backgrounds and with footage from old movies as well as with old photos, engravings, and more conventional hand-drawn backgrounds.

In addition to spawning a successful animated show, the Muppet Babies proved to be very popular with licensees. Michael K. Frith's drawing of Baby Fozzie as the Knave of Hearts in a Babies parody of *Alice's Adventures in Wonderland* (*left*) shows just how adorable the Babies can be.

THE CHRISTMAS TOY featured a furry tiger named Rugby, a curly-haired doll named Apple, a catnip mouse named Mew, and a host of other toys.

of an extended series of twelve "picture-book specials" that would have seasonal or holiday themes, but this project was eventually abandoned.

Among other Muppet series developed in the eighties was *Little Muppet Monsters*, of which only three episodes aired on CBS. The series involved a trio of young Muppet monsters living in a house that was also the ostensible home of Kermit, Miss Piggy, and other members of the classic Muppet troupe. These veterans would make occasional appearances, but mostly they would stay out of sight. The

younger Muppets would come across their elders' belongings—Miss Piggy's wardrobe, say—in the basement of the house. They would use these discoveries to create their own homemade television show.

"In a way what we're doing [with the Little Monsters] is talking about kids fantasizing about making television," Michael Frith explained at the time. "As Jim pointed out, a lot of people now have home video cameras and have grown up with computers, and *Little Muppet Monsters* tries to acknowledge this and imagine what kids' fantasies might

UNTIL JIM HENSON began to think about the movie project that became *The Dark Crystal*, Muppet design and styling was something that came out of the Muppet workshop. At first, Jim himself was the designer. Later, he worked in collaboration with Don Sahlin, Bonnie Erickson, Michael Frith, and other in-house stylists.

The Dark Crystal, on the other hand, was the result of a collaboration with an outside illustrator—Brian Froud—whose work Jim admired, and from that time on he turned to outside illustrator/stylists on several occasions. This was the case with *The Christmas Toy*, which was based on the drawings of Larry DiFiori (*left*).

To work with an outside artist provided a welcome challenge for both the Muppet workshop and for the performers, who could set aside their regular characters for a while and slip into new roles. In the case of *The Christmas Toy*, the production was like a children's book come to life, and involved devising characters like the toy robot seen at *right*.

THESE DRAWINGS for *The Tale of the Bunny Picnic* give some idea of how a character evolves from basic forms suitable for puppetry.

be like in a world where electronic toys can become creative tools."

In this respect, *Little Muppet Monsters* represented the fascination with new technology and its possibilities that was a constant in Jim Henson's life. Another passionate interest of his was the power of music. This is reflected in *The Ghost of Faffner Hall*—a thirteen-part series made in England for Tyne Tees Television and HBO in 1989, produced by Jocelyn Stevenson.

Each episode of *Faffner Hall* combines puppet ele-

ments with location segments featuring major musicians from a variety of fields, from jazz to pop to classical. The puppet segments are set in Faffner Hall, a stately Victorian pile built as a monument to music by the eccentric Fughetta Faffner. When her great-great-grandnephew Farkas, a music hater, inherits the house, Fughetta's ghost is forced to work overtime to defeat his philistine plans for the building. In this she is aided by various Muppet allies as well as the musical guest stars.

Another puppet series, created and produced by former

THE TALE OF THE BUNNY PICNIC was designed by children's book illustrator Diane Dawson Hearn (*illustration at left*). It was originally intended to be one of a series of twelve shows produced specifically for young children (the second of which was to be *The Christmas Toy*). Each of these shows would have a distinct, illustrative style, and each would also appear in print as a high-quality picture book.

The Tale of the Bunny Picnic centers around a young bunny character known as Bean (*right*), whose small size is more than made up for by his giant imagination. Bean's imagination gets him into scrape after scrape until it proves quite useful in the vanquishing of a large dog who is threatening the bunny community. Jim Henson himself performed the dog. Bean Bunny would later show up in *The Jim Henson Hour*; he also joined *The Muppet Babies* gang in 1990 and is one of the stars of *Jim Henson Presents Muppet∗Vision 3D*.

PUPPETMAN

Henson employee Roberta Kurtz and primarily directed by Brian Henson, was *Jim Henson's Mother Goose Stories*. The series won both an ACE award and a daytime Emmy.

Jim Henson's Mother Goose Stories consists of thirteen episodes, each of which brings three classic nursery rhymes to life. The nursery rhymes are not merely illustrated; rather they are enlarged on in various ways. It turns out, for example, that there is a good reason why "Little Boy Blue" keeps falling asleep, allowing the sheep to wander. As for "Hey

Diddle Diddle," this proves to be a rhyme about a cat who gets caught up in the strings of a violin.

A more ambitious project, and something of a departure for Jim Henson, was *Puppetman*—a situation comedy pilot produced for CBS by Henson Associates and the Brillstein Company. *Puppetman* featured Fred Newman as Gary, a puppeteer who performs a dragon on a fictional daytime puppet show called *Dragontime* in Madison, Wisconsin. In the pilot, *Dragontime* is suffering a dip in its ratings just as Gary's son, Zack, arrives to live with him. Gary must deal with *Dragontime*'s temperamental human star (played by Julie Payne) and a collection of eccentrics that includes a fellow puppeteer, portrayed by real-life Muppet performer Richard Hunt, and a pompous producer, personified by former *Muppet Show* producer Jack Burns.

Although *Puppetman* received generally favorable reviews in the trade magazines, it did not find a place in the CBS lineup. But it is significant in that it suggests how Jim Henson's imagination was reaching out in the latter half of the eighties toward new areas of television entertainment.

PUPPETMAN (*above*) was a 1987 pilot for a situation comedy developed by Jim Henson and Bernie Brillstein. Situation comedy was a new genre for Jim, but the premise of the show was one with which he could easily identify. Gary (Fred Newman), the show's principal character, is the host of a television puppet show. In the only episode made, he battles falling ratings and eccentric colleagues while coming to terms with being a single parent. *Little Muppet Monsters* (*right*) was an ambitious Saturday-morning project involving childlike Muppet monsters living in a house with familiar Muppets, like Kermit and Piggy, though these veterans are seldom seen. The basic idea was that the Little Muppet Monsters would find things such as Fozzie's magic kit and old props from the Muppet Theater in the basement and use them to create television programs of their own. Three shows aired on CBS before the series was canceled.

LITTLE MUPPET MONSTERS

eth anniversary of his actual debut as a television performer. An official thirty-year celebration of the Muppets was broadcast by CBS in January of 1986. It was one of several entertaining specials of the period featuring the classic Muppet cast—specials that included *The Fantastic Miss Piggy Show*, *The Muppets Go to the Movies*, and *John Denver and the Muppets: A Rocky Mountain Holiday*. Each of these specials served to keep the Muppet characters in front of their audience. But they were even more important in that they enabled the Muppets to be put into new situations on new TV shows—which was an effective way to keep the characters alive and growing. This was vital both for the Muppet performers and for the Henson organization as a whole.

For Jim Henson, though, working with the Muppets—no matter how satisfying that work was—was not enough. As always, he was restless and anxious to pursue new goals.

This period saw the usual quota of guest appearances by the more familiar Muppet characters. In 1986, Miss Piggy did a memorable vignette on *Life* magazine's fiftieth anniversary television special. In 1987, Kermit guested with Dolly Parton, and a whole group of Muppets—Kermit to the fore—joined Ted Koppel on *Nightline* to participate in a National Town Meeting devoted to Wall Street and the economy. The Muppets, and Jim himself, continued to receive awards from a variety of organizations, and on November 8, 1987, Jim Henson was inducted into the Television Academy's Hall of Fame.

In the summer of 1984, Jim had celebrated the thirti-

JIM HENSON'S MOTHER GOOSE STORIES (above) was a series of shows—each containing glosses on three well-known nursery rhymes—that aired on the Disney Channel. The show featured a Muppet Mother Goose, who told the backstories of these nursery rhymes to her three impatient, fluffy goslings. The show used both Muppets and children in starring roles. *The Ghost of Faffner Hall* (right) was a thirteen-part series developed by Jim and Jocelyn Stevenson in association with music educators, with characters designed by Ron Mueck. *Faffner Hall* encouraged children to appreciate all the different kinds of music around them and to value their experiences as listeners as well as performers. Its musical curriculum was developed in consultation with Professor John Paynter, head of music at the University of York, and Canadian composer R. Murray Schaefer, and it featured musical guest stars from Dizzy Gillespie to the Scottish Chamber Orchestra to Ladysmith Black Mambazo.

THE GHOST OF FAFFNER HALL

NIGHTLINE

JOHN DENVER AND THE MUPPETS:
A ROCKY MOUNTAIN HOLIDAY

**Muppet
Specials**

THE FANTASTIC
MISS PIGGY SHOW

JOHN DENVER AND THE MUPPETS:
A CHRISTMAS TOGETHER

THE FANTASTIC MISS PIGGY SHOW

**THE FANTASTIC
MISS PIGGY SHOW**

HE FANTASTIC MISS PIGGY SHOW

THE TONIGHT SHOW

Muppets, Muppets, Muppets!

On January 21, 1986, *The Muppets—A Celebration of 30 Years* was broadcast by CBS Television. In this show, Kermit, Miss Piggy, and other principal characters introduced highlights from the Muppets' three decades of entertainment for the benefit of (what else?) an audience of Muppets. Clips from *Sam and Friends, Sesame Street, The Muppet Show,* and *Fraggle Rock*—along with classic moments from commercials and movies—were put together to create a lively montage illustrating the scope of Jim Henson's achievement since the day he auditioned for WTOP in Washington, D.C., a little over thirty years earlier.

FOR JIM HENSON, the eighties was the decade of *The Dark Crystal* and *Labyrinth* and of television specials that introduced new characters and new technical challenges. This does not mean that the familiar Muppets of the *Muppet Show* era were not kept busy, however. In fact, they appeared in a number of remarkable specials and made some unforgettable guest appearances.

There was the memorable night in 1979, for example, when Kermit (shown at *near left* with Bernadette Peters) stood in for Johnny Carson as guest host of *The Tonight Show*, the very show on which the Muppets had made their network debut. There was another extraordinary late night outing when Kermit, Piggy, and some other Muppets joined Ted Koppel on *Nightline* for an electronic Town Hall Meeting about the state of the American economy. This show included Fozzie Bear's explanation of a bear market and a confrontation between Koppel and Miss Piggy over pork bellies.

More conventional specials included *The Muppets Go to the Movies, The Fantastic Miss Piggy Show* (in which John Ritter, shown *opposite*, dressed as a pig), *John Denver and the Muppets: A Rocky Mountain Holiday, Merv Griffin Salutes the Muppets,* and *A Muppet Family Christmas*. There were also numerous guest appearances—Miss Piggy with Anne Murray, Kermit as part of the special celebrating Bob Hope's eightieth birthday—and in *An American Portrait*, Kermit was called upon to honor naturalist Roger Tory Peterson.

CHAPTER NINE

In 1987, Jim Henson brought NBC's Brandon Tartikoff an ambitious and bold television project that would be, in a way, Jim's celebration of the television medium. The idea was to put together an hour-long package that would combine *Muppet Show*–like segments with other elements, including the last four tales from *The Storyteller* (which had not yet been seen in America), live action dramas, comedy sketches, and experimental puppet performances.

Jim would introduce each hour-long program himself, and there would be guest stars to add some of the spice of the old variety show format, though it was Jim's intention to vary the format from week to week.

The opening titles sequence of *The Jim Henson Hour* would be a compendium of optical effects, animatronics, and computer-generated imagery that was a vivid expression of Jim's fascination with the technology of film and television—guaranteed to dazzle the eye.

The show would be more or less centered around the conceit that the Muppets were now running a television station (called MuppeTelevision on the show). Kermit would be at the helm—deciding on programming and generally serving as the glue that held the station together—just as he had been at the Muppet Theater. The programming itself would consist of anything the Henson team felt like creating—including parodies of TV commercials, network series, and films, and even shows ostensibly broadcast from other planets.

Full of "backstage" business involving Kermit and his staff as well as skits and musical numbers, the first half of *The Jim Henson Hour* was not at all unlike *The Muppet Show*. Kermit's staff consisted of familiar characters like the Great Gonzo and unfamiliar ones, such as the surreal-looking Digit and the computer-generated Waldo C. Graphic. Even Miss Piggy and Fozzie made occasional appearances.

ON THE SET of *The Jim Henson Hour*, Jim Henson poses with Kermit and some of the new characters created for the show.

During the second half of *The Jim Henson Hour*, the audience would see the "show" that Kermit—in his role as station manager/head of programming—had ostensibly decided to air that week. These segments sometimes exhibited all the earmarks of a classic Muppet comedy, albeit with few of the familiar Muppet characters. *Dog City*, for instance, featured Rowlf in a guest-starring role, but was otherwise populated with new canine characters designed by artist Bruce McNally. Despite these newcomers, however, the humor in this spoof of Hollywood's film noir tradition was right out of the heyday of *The Muppet Show*.

The story follows Ace, the hero, through the nocturnal streets and back alleys of a Depression-era city where he is attempting to take possession of a tavern called The Dog House without paying protection money to a gangster named Bugsy. Inevitably, diners at The Dog House will find "cat of the day" on the menu, and you can bet that if a character is called Mad Dog he is an obedience school dropout with an encyclopedic repertoire of sociopathic bad habits.

Clearly Jim Henson had not forgotten his roots, and he directed *Dog City* with loving care and a sure sense of silliness that won him an Emmy for best direction. Beautifully produced and art-directed, *Dog City* can stand alongside Jim's best work. This is equally true of *Song of the Cloud Forest*, a celebration of the beauty of the rain forest and its varied creatures as well as a plea for endangered species and the preservation of their habitats.

Song of the Cloud Forest had been inspired by the brilliant colors of the rain forest's flora and fauna, as well as by the rhythms of Latin American music. Art-directed by Cheryl Henson with Jitka Exler, the show used computer-generated "paintbox" techniques to create a vivid animated background into which the puppet characters were electronically inserted. In its adoption of this technique, *Song of the Cloud Forest* pointed the way toward a future in which the puppet world and the electronic world will be able to interact more and more fruitfully.

FROM THE MOMENT the titles began to roll, *The Jim Henson Hour* had an electronic pizzazz about it that marked it as a full-blown product of the video era. Kermit was on hand to help out, but instead of the familiar surroundings of the Muppet Theater, he found himself in a high-tech video control room (*opposite*); and in addition to the old gang, he found himself driven slightly crazy by a new bunch of dubious helpers who ranged from the overly adorable Bean Bunny (*opposite, left foreground*) to an androidlike studio technician called Digit (*opposite, right foreground*).

This control room was treated as home base for what was basically a portmanteau show in which Muppet musical numbers might be juxtaposed with live-action dramas, comedy sketches, or animated segments. The structure of the show differed from week to week, with some episodes being devoted to a single theme.

As with *The Muppet Show*, guest stars were an important part of *The Jim Henson Hour*. In the pilot, for example, Bobby McFerrin (*above*) performed one of his amazing feats of vocal acrobatics against the background of a graffiti-covered wall while characters such as the three bizarre creatures seen in the *inset panel* climbed down from the graffiti and began to dance.

The Jim Henson Hour was inspired partly by Jim's interest in the way people were beginning to watch TV—jumping from channel to channel with their remote controls, rarely watching one show in its entirety. It also reflected his fascination with the relatively new field of cable television. The possibilities that cable offered—room for a multitude of programs produced at a much lower cost than network TV and thus able to support experimentation—greatly appealed to Jim. In fact, he may have felt that cable offered opportunities not unlike those he had had when he was producing his first low-budget, local TV shows in Washington, D.C.

Thirteen episodes of *The Jim Henson Hour* were created. But the show did not attract enough of an audience for NBC, and it was canceled after ten episodes aired. Perhaps the ambitious nature of the programs worked against them.

"In retrospect," says Alex Rockwell, who was Jim's creative assistant at the time, "I think that the public was perhaps hoping for something simple and straightforward from Jim at that point. Not just a reprise of *The Muppet Show*, exactly, but something that uncomplicated and entertaining.

"When the show was canceled, Jim was very disappointed…but he was not one to look back and indulge in recrimination. He had a way of picking up the pieces and moving on."

Moving on, in this case, involved an actual physical move. Except for *The Muppet Movie*—which in any case was produced by a British company—Jim had always worked outside the Hollywood orbit, at least so far as major projects were concerned. Now he made a radical decision.

THE JIM HENSON HOUR provided another opportunity to show off the craftsmanship and artistry of the Creature Shop. It was employed to especially good effect in *Monstermaker*, one of the shows within the show. Produced by Duncan Kenworthy, *Monstermaker* is the tale of a boy who becomes involved with an eccentric creator of special effects and is thereby forced to confront the fantastic and often frightening creations of his own imagination.

THE JIM HENSON HOUR took viewers into many and varied worlds. *Song of the Cloud Forest* (*far right*) was a vividly imagined and realized expedition into a tropical rain forest that combined music, puppetry, and computer-assisted animation to create a richly textured video tapestry. It was more than just an energetic entertainment, however. *Song of the Cloud Forest* was also an eloquent plea on behalf of endangered species and a protest against deforestation.

Waldo C. Graphic (*near right*) was something entirely new—a computer-generated puppet character. Jim had been interested in computer-generated characters for years; in fact, in 1983, he had begun to develop a TV special about computers starring the Muppets that would feature a brief appearance by a computer-generated Kermit. The show was finally abandoned, but the idea of creating such a character lived on.

Waldo made his debut on *The Jim Henson Hour* and achieved stardom in the 3-D film Jim produced and directed for the Disney–MGM Studios Theme Park at Walt Disney World.

Pictured *below* are Waldo and Kermit in the *Jim Henson Hour* control room.

THE JIM HENSON HOUR introduced viewers to a

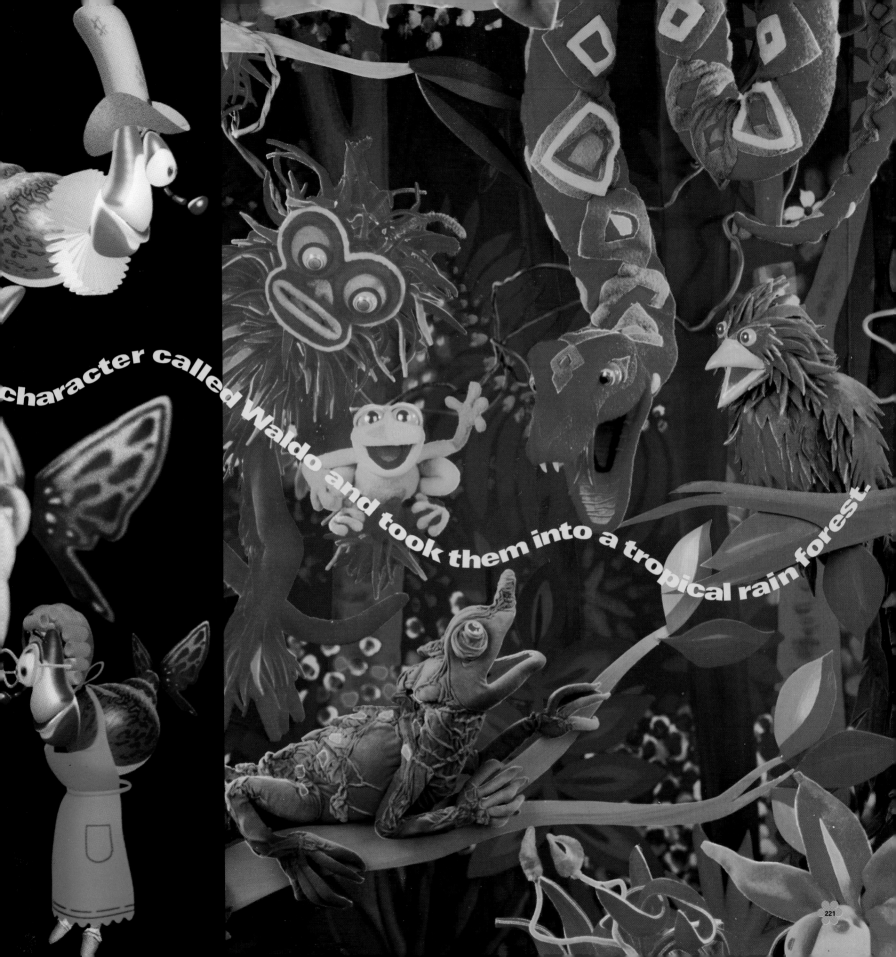

character called Waldo and took them into a tropical rain forest.

He would keep his New York and London operations intact, but he would move his headquarters to Los Angeles.

In Bernie Brillstein's opinion, the move made good sense. "It was time for a new beginning," he says. "I think Jim was ready to work within the mainstream for a while. Ready

DOG CITY (*above*)—another of the self-contained segments within *The Jim Henson Hour*—was a witty spoof of old Hollywood gangster movies. Directed by Jim Henson and written by Tim Burns, *Dog City* made use of Rowlf, who appeared as pianist and occasional narrator, but was mostly populated by entirely new canine characters designed by longtime Muppet illustrator and art director Bruce McNally (a watercolor of one of his characters, Officer O'Growler, is at *right*). Although anthropomorphic and fond of three-piece pin-striped suits, these characters were also somewhat naturalis-

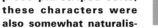

tic—very much in the tradition of *Emmet Otter*—and the show was notable for its imaginative sets and atmospheric cinematography. Jim won a prime-time Emmy for outstanding director in a variety or music program for the show. *Dog City* has since been adapted into a clever blend of Muppetry and animation (*opposite*) produced with Nelvana Entertainment.

to take advantage of the energy that's available in Hollywood."

As things turned out, Hollywood was ready and waiting for the move in an entirely unanticipated way. No sooner had Jim made his decision to move to the West Coast than he and Michael Eisner, chairman and CEO of The Walt Disney Company, began discussing the possibility of bringing Jim Henson Productions—as the company was now known—under the Disney umbrella.

Jim found the idea very attractive, though not without its drawbacks, and he entered into serious negotiations with Disney. At the time of Jim's unexpected tragic illness, however, no agreement had been reached, and under the changed circumstances it proved impossible to reach an accord with Disney.

Still, a couple of important consequences emerged from the protracted negotiations. One was that Muppet characters were eventually licensed to appear in the Disney–MGM Studios Theme Park at Walt Disney World in Orlando, Florida. The other was that Jim Henson began to produce a 3-D Muppet movie to be featured at a specially built theater at Walt Disney World. Jim approached this project—which would prove to be his last—with unbridled enthusiasm.

In one sense, the 3-D movie was a return to basics. It would be relatively short (approximately fourteen and a half minutes) and would rely upon gags rather than story line—precisely the kind of show with which Jim Henson had made his reputation. At the same time, though, it gave Jim a tailor-made opportunity to indulge his passion for advanced technical experimentation.

As early as *Sam and Friends*, Jim had learned how to use camera lenses to bring puppets alive on screen. Now he was being given the opportunity to use the most sophisticated optical equipment available to enable puppets to move in what would appear to be three-dimensional space. In almost every way imaginable, it was a dream project.

"For Jim," says Ritamarie Peruggi, Jim Henson Productions' producer for the movie, "it was a wonderful chance to have fun with special effects. I think he wanted the Disney people to see him at work there on the Disney lot—to let them see how he got things done. And that meant a lot of improvisation.

"There's a shot in the movie that involves a butterfly, and the Disney technical people said, 'That's going to be expensive to do. We'll have to do it as an optical effect.' But Jim said, 'I think we can just shoot it with a butterfly on a string. We'll give it a try, anyway.' And of course it worked beautifully."

It was characteristic of Jim that he would always use a simple effect if he thought it would work as well as an elaborate one. At the same time, he demonstrated a keen appreciation of the subtleties involved in creating the 3-D illusion. The optics involved dictate that the illusion is the most effective if characters or objects do not break the plane of the screen, which becomes in effect an invisible barrier between the audience and the action. Everything that happens behind that barrier is convincingly three-dimensional. Violate that plane, however, and the illusion is quickly destroyed. It is the expectation that a character or object *might* violate the plane that is the most startling.

Imagine, for example that a runaway car is coming directly toward the 3-D camera rig necessary to film the

3-D MOVIE

JIM HENSON PRESENTS MUPPET∗VISION 3D would prove to be the last production of Jim Henson's hugely prolific and illustrious career. Appropriately, it turned out to be a spectacular finale starring some of Jim's best-known characters—along with relatively new creations such as Waldo—in an astonishing montage of gags and special effects designed to delight and thrill audiences in a custom-built theater at the Disney–MGM Studios Theme Park near Orlando, Florida. Jim was inspired by the challenge of devising special routines to permit the Muppets to take maximum advantage of the 3-D format, and the movie was almost complete at the time of his death.

action. From the point of view of the audience, the car threatens to break out of the screen and invade the auditorium. In fact, that expectation is set up by what is perceived *before* the car breaks the plane of the screen. The illusion of motion through real space has been set up by the cameras, and the mind of the viewer then calculates what will happen as the car gets closer, based on his or her experience of reality. The less time the mind is given to adjust, the more effective the illusion will be.

©Jim Henson Productions, Inc.
©The Walt Disney Company

ALTHOUGH *Jim Henson Presents Muppet∗Vision 3D* **is enormously sophisticated from a technical point of view, in some ways it harks back to the kind of simple devices Jim Henson had employed in the days of** *Sam and Friends.* **He had discovered then that, with the help of a wide-angle lens, relatively modest arm movements could make a puppet appear to rush toward the camera from a great distance. The 3-D process offered an opportunity to build on that kind of illusion with the characters seeming to rush out into the auditorium. In the photo** *above,* **Jim stands by as Kermit sits on a fire-truck ladder that will shoot him forward "through" the screen and into the laps of members of the audience. Other, similar 3-D tricks in the film involve a squirting flower (enhanced by the actual water that is sprayed on the unsuspecting audience) and a paddleball wielded by the full-body Muppet character Sweetums.**

Jim Henson Presents Muppet∗Vision 3D has its fair share of spectacular moments, but it is at its best when the characters test the technology in understated ways, casually pushing up against the plane represented by the screen like kids pressing their noses up against the window of a toy store. A good example of this is the moment in which Sweetums, a full-sized Muppet character originally developed by Richard Hunt and currently performed by Jim's younger son, John Henson, bounces a paddleball directly toward the camera, making the ball appear to fly into the audience and back again. The whole thing happens so quickly that the 3-D illusion is vividly maintained.

This scene, in fact, turned out to be difficult to shoot for another reason. For the 3-D illusion to work, the paddleball had to hit precisely the right spot during shooting. John Henson had practiced hitting the ball correctly for days. But when he got into the Sweetums costume, which almost totally restricted his vision, he was completely unable to see the spot! Luckily, he hit it on the first take.

The 3-D movie makes full use of all the regular gang—Kermit, Piggy, Gonzo, and the rest—but it also takes spectacular advantage of Waldo, the digitally created character who first appeared in *The Jim Henson Hour.* Jim had previously experimented with a computer-generated character—a Kermit head—for a 1983 special about computers that was never produced. And an entire computer-generated set was later created for a project that was alternately called *InnerTube* and *IN-TV.*

But it was Waldo who was the ultimate expression of this technology.

Manipulated in real time by a performer using a glove-like servo-mechanism, Waldo was a puppet set free from normal puppetry constraints—a puppet who lived inside the cathode ray tube. Operating Waldo was a natural extension of the kind of video puppeteering that the Muppets had practiced to begin with—in which the characters reacted to each other on screen rather than in reality.

A basic system for doing this was devised by programmer Lance Williams. Jim then took the idea to several computer graphics companies and eventually selected Pacific Data Images to help refine the definitive Waldo, designed by Kirk Thatcher.

To perform Waldo, puppeteer Steve Whitmire wears an electronic "glove" that is connected to the computer that generates Waldo's image in "wire-frame" form on the screen. The performance is recorded by the computer, which then adds the color, texture, and detail of the "total" Waldo.

Waldo is nothing less than the world's first digitized puppet—a character who can be performed by a puppeteer using a remote control rig but who comes to life via a computer and a color monitor. Waldo is, in other words, a computer-generated image that can be manipulated by a puppeteer much as the figures in a Nintendo game are manipulated with a joystick. This enables the puppet to operate in real time and to interact with other, "real" Muppets.

In a sense, Waldo is a manifestation of the approach to puppetry Jim Henson embraced back in the fifties. For Jim, the reality on screen was the only one that mattered, and Waldo—*created* on screen—was the embodiment of that philosophy.

Waldo and 3-D were made for each other, just as Jim Henson and 3-D were made for each other. In the Disney World movie, the screen seems to burst with Muppets, props, fire trucks, and a blizzard of bubbles. At one point, the film appears to rip in the projector. At another, the theater seems to blow up and threatens to rain debris on the audience.

Jim Henson Presents Muppet⋆Vision 3D is the ultimate expression of Jim's fascination with the magical illusionism of film and television—which is what drew him into show business in the first place.

©Jim Henson Productions, Inc.
©The Walt Disney Company

MOST 3-D FILMS depend on dramatic illusions—stampeding elephants that seem to charge into the audience—which for the most part are outside the realm of puppetry. For his experiment with 3-D, Jim Henson did devise a few of these dramatic illusions, but mostly he relied upon more subtle effects that are more suitable to puppetry. To give a single example, there is one scene in which Statler and Waldorf are heckling as usual from their box (Statler and Waldorf are animatronic figures who sit in a real box built into one wall of the actual theater). Annoyed, Kermit (on film) leans forward to rebuke them. In doing so he barely breaks the plane of the screen, yet the illusion is as effective as if he had charged through the screen on one of those stampeding elephants. By means of such subtle tricks, Jim brought the Muppet gang to life in a new and exciting way. *Above*, the Muppets pose for a photo along with producer Ritamarie Peruggi (*left*).

Dear Freinds, May 17, 1990
I was sorry to hear about
Jim henson. I Love
The Muppets take
Manhatten.

My sister loves
Sesame Street
So do I.

Cookie monster

Bigbird

gra

ernie

Osc

Be

the
aracters.

My Sympathy
is to Jim
Henson

I Love Jim
Henson very much

me
nie.

da

228

CHAPTER TEN

On May 16, 1990, after a brief illness, Jim Henson died in New York Hospital. He had had himself admitted just hours earlier, not suspecting the seriousness of his condition until it was too late. Five days later, a packed memorial service at the Cathedral Church of St. John the Divine underlined the sense of loss felt by millions of people, as did a similar service in St. Paul's Cathedral in London, heartfelt tributes by the media, and the sacks full of letters that poured into Jim's Manhattan headquarters from ordinary people, especially from children around the world.

Jim had requested that no one wear black at his funeral and that there be a jazz band present, and so it was that at the huge, gothic St. John the Divine, a marching band played "When the Saints Go Marching In" and the interior was filled with songs and colorful costumes and hundreds of butterflies made in the Henson workshop. Still, the shock was very real, and so were the questions that surrounded the future of Jim Henson Productions.

Once the shock had subsided a little, negotiations with Disney were renewed, but after several months they were broken off. Eventually it was agreed that Muppets would remain in Walt Disney World for a period of time, and that the Muppet 3-D movie would find a temporary home there, too. Later it was announced that Disney would distribute Jim Henson Productions' considerable video library. The bottom line, however, was that there would be no merger. Jim Henson Productions would remain an independent company.

Jim Henson Productions had always drawn upon the talents of many people. And as Jim's five children came together to focus on how to successfully continue the company's operation, it was those people—Frank Oz, Jerry Juhl, David Lazer, Michael K. Frith, Duncan Kenworthy, Martin Baker, and all the others—who dedicated themselves to continuing the work that they and Jim had

WHEN JIM HENSON DIED, letters poured in from children all over, many decorated with likenesses of characters Jim had given the world.

so successfully accomplished over the years.

In some ways, this wasn't easy. Jim's personality, his talents, and his indefatigable energy had permeated every area of the company, from the Muppet workshops and the production arena to the accounting and business affairs departments. The thought of going on without him was painful at the very least.

But the thought of not going on was inconceivable.

On January 24, 1991, Brian Henson was named president of Jim Henson Productions, with Cheryl Henson to serve as vice president. In addition, Lisa Henson would actively consult for the company, and Heather and John would also continue to be involved with various projects in a creative capacity.

At that time, the prolonged negotiations with Disney had put many things on hold. The only continuing productions were *Sesame Street* (which had always been exempt from any acquisition by Disney) and *Jim Henson's Muppet Babies*. Another series—*Dinosaurs*—was about to go into production.

Dinosaurs was the result of an idea that Jim Henson and Alex Rockwell had pitched to executives of Disney's television division. It was Jim's notion to make a situation comedy about a family of dinosaurs—blue-collar dinosaurs—who live their lives while paying no attention to the signs that their world is on the brink of extinction.

Clearly this was a show that was reliant upon the Henson organization, since it would depend on the skills of the Creature Shop and the Henson repertory company of puppeteers. Unfortunately, Jim Henson had no time to realize the idea, but after his passing, Brian collaborated with veteran comedy producer Michael Jacobs to bring *Dinosaurs* to fruition.

Dinosaurs went into production in 1991 at CBS/MTM Studios in the San Fernando Valley—the lot where *The Muppet Movie* had been filmed thirteen years before.

Characters such as Earl Sinclair (described as "a forty-three-year-old bombastic Megalosaurus") and his daughter, Charlene ("a two-ton material girl"), called on all of the Creature Shop's ingenuity. The shop had by that time built the title characters for *Teenage Mutant Ninja Turtles* (for which production Brian Henson had been chief puppeteer and second unit director) and these served as a starting point for the Sinclair family of dinosaurs.

Like the Ninja Turtles, the Sinclairs would be "costumes" with people inside them; and like the turtles they would have animatronic puppet heads. But the dinosaur heads needed to be much more individual and expressive. Designed by Kirk Thatcher, they proved to be exactly that, and they were also provided with state-of-the-art remote control rigs that permitted puppeteers to operate them from a distance with almost the ease with which they would perform a hand puppet like Kermit.

Puppet performers on *Dinosaurs* included Kevin Clash, Steve Whitmire, David Greenaway, Dave Goelz, and Brian Henson himself. The first episode was broadcast by ABC in April of 1991 and received both good reviews and high ratings. Jim Henson Productions' first outing after the loss of the company's founder was a success, and the viability of Brian Henson as a successor to his father was established.

The company's first motion picture of the new era was

ALTHOUGH *Dinosaurs* did not go into production until after Jim Henson's death, it was based on one of his ideas. "We'd be on a plane," Alex Rockwell remembers, "and he'd start to talk about this family of dinosaurs, with a father who wore plaid shirts and had a Brooklyn accent. It always made him laugh." When The Walt Disney Company asked Jim if he had any ideas for situation comedies, he mentioned the *Dinosaurs* concept. After his death, the idea was developed by Michael Jacobs Productions in collaboration with Jim Henson Productions, with Michael Jacobs and Brian Henson as executive producers, and the Sinclair family of working-class dinosaurs was finally unleashed on audiences by ABC Television in the spring of 1991. The picture of Earl and Baby Sinclair (*opposite*) shows just how startlingly real these characters are—thanks to the Creature Shop and the latest developments in animatronics.

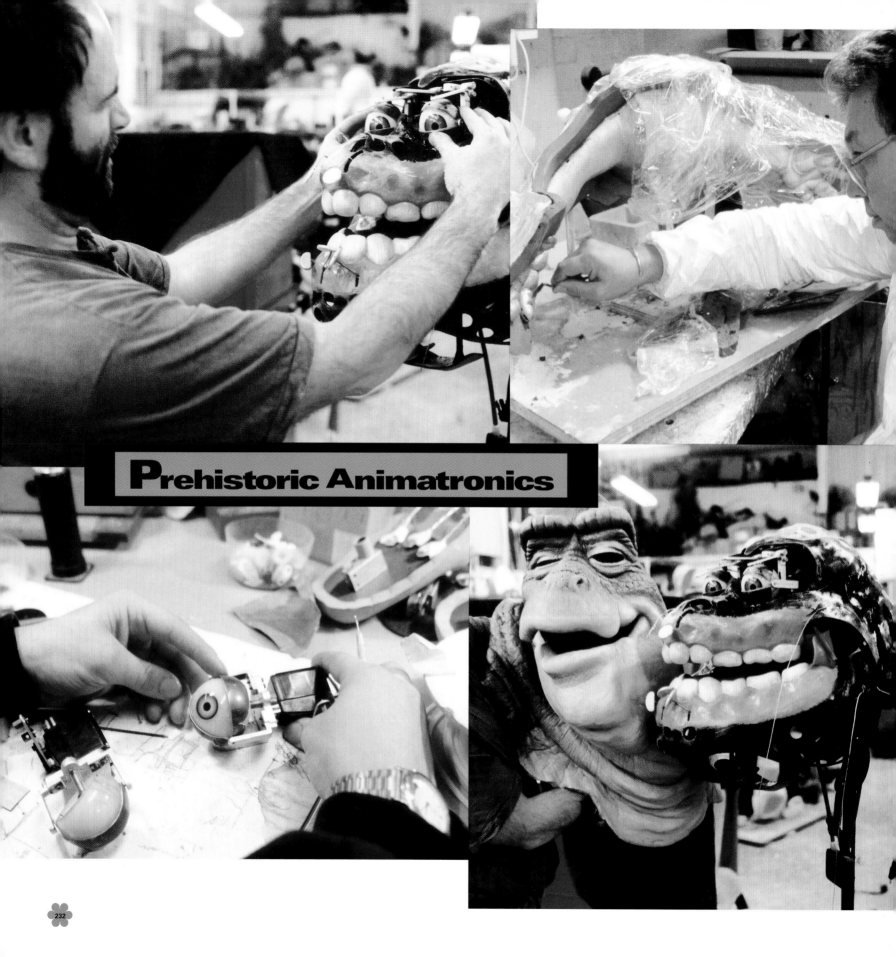

Prehistoric Animatronics

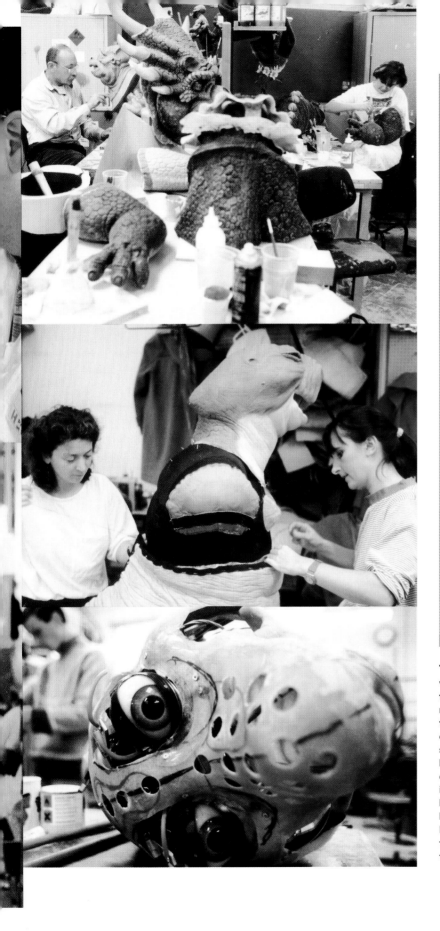

Brian Henson was only twenty-seven years old when he was named president of Jim Henson Productions, but by then he had been making valuable contributions to the company for a decade.

"[Jim] was my father and my mentor. We loved to work together, whether as a child doing yard work or as adults creating some complicated puppet effect. Work and play were really one and the same to him. 'If you can't find a way to really enjoy what you're doing, why do it?' That was a great outlook on life, and particularly attractive to me as a child.

"Of course, later on, I realized it was his ability to find something fresh and exciting in everything that made this outlook work. His energy was like some wildly addictive drug; hours and hours were lost in a cloud of frenetic enthusiasm."

BRIAN HENSON

THE CREATURE SHOP has always been an interesting place to visit, but never more so than during the development of the characters for *Dinosaurs*. When the project was first brought up, the shop had recently finished work on *Teenage Mutant Ninja Turtles*, and those famous warriors provided some degree of inspiration for the dinosaurs of the Sinclair family. But the Sinclairs would have to be much more subtle and expressive than Michelangelo, Donatello, Leonardo, and Raphael, and it would take all of the Creature Shop's artistry to produce characters that would be convincing in television close-ups. The images reproduced here hint at the complexity of these dinosaur heads, especially the eye and jaw mechanisms. However, building a head that could smile and crinkle its eyes solved only part of the problem. Beyond that it was necessary to devise *simple* remote controls that would enable a single puppeteer to animate that head at a distance without a team of helpers getting in the way.

DIRECTED BY Brian Henson (*above*, with the Great Gonzo), *The Muppet Christmas Carol* was the first feature film to star the Muppets since *The Muppets Take Manhattan* was released in 1984. The new movie presented many old favorites, including Gonzo (as Charles Dickens), Fozzie Bear, Rizzo the Rat, Bunsen, Beaker, Sam the Eagle, and Animal. Kermit (now performed by Steve Whitmire) was cast as Bob Cratchit and Miss Piggy made an exemplary appearance in the unforgiving role of Mrs. Cratchit. (Kermit and Robin, who played Tiny Tim, are shown at *left*.) Sharing the spotlight with the Muppets was Academy Award–winning actor Michael Caine as Scrooge (*opposite*).

Dickens's classic has, of course, lent itself to many cinematic interpretations, and in mood and spirit, the Muppet version is surprisingly faithful to the original. Needless to say, however, Muppet madness is allowed to peek through here and there and the result is a delightful entertainment that meets the high standards set by the Muppets' creator.

The Muppet Christmas Carol. Directed by Brian, the film differs from preceding Muppet films in that major Muppets are asked to portray characters other than themselves, characters who are already familiar to audiences around the world via Charles Dickens's classic story. Veteran British actor Michael Caine was cast as Scrooge, and Kermit (now performed by Steve Whitmire) fell into place as Bob Cratchit, with Miss Piggy rather astonishingly but effectively cast as the dowdy Mrs. Cratchit. Along with other Muppet favorites from Statler and Waldorf to the Electric Mayhem, they provide a sense of continuity on screen, with Brian's direction and Frank Oz's services as executive producer assuring the trademark Henson touch.

The Muppet Christmas Carol also represented a highly successful amalgam of the English and American halves of the company. It successfully combined the emotional content and the rich, fanciful period sets, lighting, and costumes more characteristic of the London productions with the brash, funny, quintessentially American Muppet characters. More important, though, it represented a rebirth of all that the company had stood for over the years. It was a reaffirmation—a critical demonstration that the Muppets woud not only survive but would continue to evolve.

Another new Henson venture was *Jim Henson's Dog City*, a Saturday-morning animated show produced with Nelvana Entertainment that features Muppet puppet wrap-arounds. This program evolved from the "Dog City" segment that originally appeared on *The Jim Henson Hour*. Not unlike *Jim Henson's Muppet Babies*, *Jim Henson's Dog City* focuses on imagination and creativity. In this case, these qualities are displayed by Muppet canine animator Elliot Shag, who, in various segments shown throughout the show, generates and solves the problems of the show's animated hero, Ace Hart.

And there is *CityKids*, which debuted as an ABC special in the winter of 1993 and became a series on that station in

THE MUPPET CHRISTMAS CAROL

the fall of the same year. *CityKids* is a hard-hitting show for preteens and teens that focuses on the problems and concerns of inner-city youth as represented by the New York outreach group known as CityKids. The television show attempts to encourage kids everywhere to take control of their lives and create positive experiences for themselves. But it also includes fanciful segments in which Muppet characters get to delve into the psyches of teenagers, discovering things like what makes an adolescent boy tick; how it might feel to be a rapping hot dog in a New York fast-food cart; and the way that prejudice is handled on the planet Koozebane.

Many other new Henson ventures are currently in development. Under the leadership of a vital creative and business affairs team that is headed by Brian and chief operating officer Charlie Rivkin, the company has created two new divisions: Jim Henson Video, which will distribute both existing television and film properties as well as new made-for-home-video releases; and Jim Henson Records, which will focus on both the extensive existing collection of Henson music and on new recordings and book/tapes. And, of course, there is *Sesame Street*, which is still going strong after twenty-five years of continuous production, having won over fifty Emmys during that time.

The endurance of Jim Henson Productions is a tribute to the many talented people who have joined the company over the years. But the reason they joined and then stayed on is mainly due to Jim Henson's own ability to welcome and nurture them. Jim was, in a sense, the best and most convivial of hosts. It was his generosity of spirit that both set the tone for the company and will allow it to continue to grow and prosper.

Once, when talking about the company, Jim said, "…in reality, we have a wonderful group of very creative people …that do all this work that I take the credit for." The atmosphere that resulted from this attitude was one in which innovation and independence were encouraged and therefore thrived; in which laughter was omnipresent; and in which lasting friendships flourished.

It is this attitude that Jim Henson Productions is intent on maintaining in the future.

A Pride of Puppeteers

Part of Jim Henson's legacy lies in the work of the Jim Henson Foundation, which is devoted to the encouragement of the art of puppetry around the world. In the past, the foundation has made grants to puppeteers to enable them to create innovative work with puppets, and in 1992 it produced the First International Festival of Puppet Theater. Held at the Joseph Papp Public Theater in Lower Manhattan, the festival successfully presented over seventeen companies from around the world.

Conceived as a way of making the American public aware of the richness of the puppetry world, the festival was first discussed by Jim and Cheryl Henson—who would produce the festival with Leslee Asch—when they were attending a Puppeteers of America festival in Boston in the late eighties. They began to think about how exciting it would be to present the very best of international contemporary adult puppet theater in a New York venue. The incredible variety and magic of this theater form was already recognized in Europe but virtually unknown to American audiences.

The Foundation continues to work to promote puppetry as an art form, to support young puppetry artists, and to strengthen the bonds between puppeteers all over the world through festivals, workshops, and conferences.

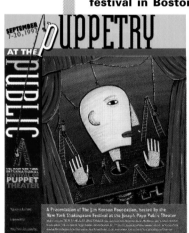

IT WAS ONE of Jim Henson's greatest aspirations to pass on his knowledge to younger generations of puppeteers and filmmakers. In July 1987, he taught a master class in puppetry at the Institute for Puppet Theater in Charleville-Mézières, France (*opposite*).

Other stuff that usually g

es in the back of a book

Turn, please

The following is excerpted from some notes written by Jim Henson in 1986. He had been asked to contribute some thoughts for a book that was to be called *Courage of Conviction*. The book was never published.

Over the years, I've evolved my own set of beliefs and attitudes—as we all have—that I feel works for me. I don't feel particularly comfortable telling other people how to think or live. There are people who know much more about these things than I do, but here goes...

I believe that life is basically a process of growth—that we go through many lives, choosing those situations and problems that we will learn through.

I believe that we form our own lives, that we create our own reality, and that everything works out for the best. I know I drive some people crazy with what seems to be ridiculous optimism, but it has always worked out for me.

I believe in taking a positive attitude toward the world, toward people, and toward my work. I think I'm here for a purpose. I think it's likely that we all are, but I'm only sure about myself. I try to tune myself in to whatever it is that I'm supposed to be, and I try to think of myself as a part of all of us—all mankind and all life. I find it's not easy to keep these lofty thoughts in mind as the day goes by, but it certainly helps me a great deal to start out this way.

I love my work, and because I enjoy it, it doesn't really feel like work. Thus I spend most of my time working. I like working collaboratively with people. At its best, the film and television world functions creatively this way. I have a terrific group of people who work with me, and I think of the work that we do as "our" work.

I don't know exactly where ideas come from, but when I'm working well ideas just appear. I've heard other people say similar things—so it's one of the ways I know there's help and guidance out there. It's just a matter of our figuring out how to receive the ideas or information that's there waiting to be heard.

I find that it's very important for me to stop every now and then and get recharged and reinspired. The beauty of nature has been one of the great inspirations in my life. Growing up as an artist, I've always been in awe of the incredible beauty of every last bit of design in nature. The wonderful color schemes of nature, which always work harmoniously, are particularly dazzling to me. I love to lie in an open field looking up at the sky. One of my happiest moments of inspiration came to me many years ago as I lay on the grass, looking up into the leaves and branches of a big old tree in California. I remember feeling very much a part of everything and everyone.

Working as I do with the movement of puppet creatures, I'm always struck by the

feebleness of our efforts to achieve naturalistic movement. Just looking at the incredible movement of a lizard or a bird, or even the smallest insect, can be a very humbling experience.

At some point in my life I decided, rightly or wrongly, that there are many situations in this life that I can't do much about—acts of terrorism, feelings of nationalistic prejudice, cold war, etc. —so what I should do is concentrate on the situations that my energy can affect.

I believe that we can use television and film to be an influence for good; that we can help to shape the thoughts of children and adults in a positive way. As it has turned out, I'm very proud of some of the work we've done, and I think we can do many more good things.

When I was young, my ambition was to be one of the people who made a difference in this world. My hope still is to leave the world a little bit better for my having been here.

It's a wonderful life and I love it.

243

1936 Jim Henson born.

1954 Appearance on the *Junior Morning Show*, WTOP/CBS, Washington, D.C., featuring Jim's first puppets, Pierre the French Rat, Longhorn and Shorthorn.
Jim Henson meets Jane Nebel in a puppetry class at the University of Maryland.

1955 Muppet appearances on *Afternoon with Inga* and *Footlight Theatre* on WRC-TV, Washington, D.C.
Sam and Friends begins airing live as five-minute shows at 6:25 P.M. and 11:25 P.M. nightly through December 15, 1961, on WRC-TV, Washington, D.C.

1956 Appearances on *The Arthur Godfrey Show*, *The Steve Allen Show*, and *The Will Rogers, Jr., Show*.

1957 First Wilkins Coffee commercial taped.

1958 Jim travels to Europe; produces *Hansel and Gretel* upon return.
Company incorporated as Muppets, Inc.
Appearance on *The Jack Paar Show*.

1959 Jim Henson and Jane Nebel are married.

1960 The Muppets appear for the first time on the *Today* show, hosted by Dave Garroway.
Lisa Henson is born.

1961 Jerry Juhl joins the company.
The Muppets begin regular appearances on the *Today* show. One appearance prompts a call from the William Morris Agency; Bernie Brillstein becomes agent for the Muppets.
Cheryl Henson is born.

1962 USIA show, Berlin, Germany.
Appearance in *Mad, Mad World* TV pilot.
Tales of the Tinkerdee taped in Atlanta.
Rowlf built by Don Sahlin for Purina dog food commercial.

1963 The Muppets and the Henson family move to New York, opening a small office on 53rd Street.

Frank Oz joins the company.
Don Sahlin officially joins the company.
Rowlf begins regular appearances on *The Jimmy Dean Show*.
Brian Henson is born.

1964 *Timepiece* begins production.

1965 The first meeting films are developed by Jim Henson and David Lazer for IBM.
Timepiece has first screening at the Museum of Modern Art, New York.
Hey Cinderella! pilot taped.
Appearance on *Perry Como Christmas Show*.
Jerry Nelson works with Jim for the first time on *The Jimmy Dean Show* and tour.
John Henson is born.

1966 Regular appearances on *The Ed Sullivan Show* begin, lasting until 1971. Appearances on *The Mike Douglas Show* and *The Hollywood Palace*.

1967 Incorporation of Cyclia Enterprises. Project abandoned in 1970.
First films made for IBM; Rowlf becomes mascot and salesdog.

1968 *Youth '68* begins taping to air on NBC Experiment in Television.
Muppets on Puppets TV special taped to air on PBS.
Hey Cinderella! filmed in Toronto.

1969 *The Cube* taped, to air on NBC Experiment in Television.
Sesame Street pilot and first show taped; first Big Bird created.

1970 *The Great Santa Claus Switch* taped.
First *Sesame Street* album, *Sesame Street Original Cast Album*, recorded.
Heather Henson is born.

1971 Muppet guest appearances on *The Flip Wilson Show*, *Pure Goldie* (Goldie Hawn special), *Tom Jones . . . at Fantasy Fair*, and a Dick Cavett special.
The Frog Prince taped in Toronto.
Muppets are featured in Nancy Sinatra's Las Vegas nightclub act and TV special.

1972 *The Muppet Musicians of Bremen* taped in Toronto.
Richard Hunt joins the company.
Muppet appearance on the *Perry Como Christmas Show*.

1973 Julie [Andrews] on Sesame Street taped at ATV Studios in London. *Muppet Valentine Special* (with Mia Farrow) taped at ABC in New York.

1974 Dave Goelz joins the company.
Muppet guest appearances on *The Tonight Show*, the *Today* show, *The Pat Collins Show*, *What's My Line?* (Jim Henson as Mystery Guest), and the *Herb Alpert Special* (first appearance of Miss Piggy).
First float with *Sesame Street* characters in Macy's Thanksgiving Day Parade.
The Muppet Show: Sex and Violence taped.

1975 First Muppet meeting films taped.
Muppet guest appearances on the *Cher TV Special*, *The Mike Douglas Show*, *The Julie Andrews Special*, *My Favorite Things* (ABC Afterschool Special), *The Andy Williams Special*, *The Tonight Show*, *A.M. America*, *The Peter Alexander Show*.
Jim Henson and Lord Lew Grade form an agreement to produce 24 episodes of *The Muppet Show*.
First Bert & Ernie placed in the National Museum of American History, Smithsonian Institution.
Michael K. Frith joins the company.
Saturday Night Live appearances. All-new Muppets created for regular appearances on the show. Characters include King Ploobis, Queen Peuta, Scred, Wisss, Vazh, and the Mighty Favog.

1976 *The Muppet Show*, season one, taped.
The Muppet Show Fan Club started.

1977 *Emmet Otter's Jug-Band Christmas* taped in Toronto.
Jim Henson and Brian Froud agree to work together on what will become *The Dark Crystal*.
The Muppet Show, season two, taped.
Kermit balloon in Macy's Thanksgiving Day Parade for first time.
New York City town house purchased.

1978 Steve Whitmire joins the company.
The Muppet Show Book is published.
Jim and Cheryl Henson, snowed in at Kennedy International Airport, write the story of *The Dark Crystal*.
The Muppet Show, season three, taped.

The Muppet Movie begins filming in Los Angeles. Development of Yoda for *Star Wars: The Empire Strikes Back*.

1979 1B Downshire Hill, Hampstead, London, is purchased. The building becomes headquarters for development of *The Dark Crystal* and will eventually become the home of Jim Henson's Creature Shop.
The Muppet Show, season four, taped.
The Tonight Show is hosted by Kermit the Frog.
The Muppets Go Hollywood special airs on CBS.
60 Minutes Report: Backstage at "The Muppet Show."
The Muppet Movie opens in the United States.
The Art of the Muppets exhibit opens at Lincoln Center.
Miss Piggy's first calendar published.
John Denver and the Muppets: A Christmas Together special taped and album recorded.

1980 *The Muppet Show*, season five, taped.
Muppet performance at UNIMA Puppet Festival, Kennedy Center for the Performing Arts, Washington, D.C.
Prototype Sesame Place play park opens near Philadelphia.
First arena show, *Sesame Street Live*, begins touring.
The Great Muppet Caper begins filming.
Muppet Stuff retail store opens in New York City.

1981 *Of Muppets and Men*, a TV special on the making of *The Muppet Show*, is produced in London.
UNIMA special *Here Come the Puppets* airs.
The Muppets Go to the Movies special taped in London.
The Dark Crystal filming begins.
First creative meeting about *Fraggle Rock* in London.
The Great Muppet Caper premieres.
"Pigs in Space" taped for NASA space shuttle.
Miss Piggy's Guide to Life published.
Muppets comic strip syndicated.

1982 Henson Foundation established to promote, develop, and encourage public interest in the art of puppetry.
Miss Piggy's Treasury of Art Masterpieces from the Kermitage Collection published.
The first season of *Fraggle Rock* begins taping in Toronto.

The Fantastic Miss Piggy Show TV special airs on ABC.
The Dark Crystal premieres.

1983
Muppet Magazine's premiere issue is published.
Fraggle Rock debuts on HBO.
John Denver and the Muppets: A Rocky Mountain Holiday TV special airs on ABC.
Big Bird in China, CTW special, airs on NBC.
The World of the Dark Crystal documentary airs on PBS.
The Muppets Take Manhattan filmed in Queens, New York.
Jim Henson Presents: The World of Puppetry begins taping.
National Wildlife Federation Public Service Announcements taped in Central Park with Kermit and Fozzie.
Don't Eat the Pictures, CTW special, taped.

1984
Dreamchild characters built at Jim Henson's Creature Shop, London.
The Muppets Take Manhattan premieres in the United States.
The *Sesame Street* movie, *Follow That Bird,* filmed in Toronto.
The Muppet Show on Tour arena show begins touring.
Jim Henson's Muppet Babies premieres on CBS.
The Bells of Fraggle Rock Christmas special airs on HBO.
Oral-B Muppet toothbrushes introduced.

1985
Principal photography begins on *Labyrinth.*
The *Sesame Street* movie *Follow That Bird* premieres.
Little Muppet Monsters taped.
The Muppets—A Celebration of 30 Years taped in Toronto.

Fraggle float appears in Gimbel's Thanksgiving Day Parade in Philadelphia.
Jim Henson's Muppet Babies' second season on CBS.

1986
The Tale of the Bunny Picnic taped in London.
Kevin Clash joins the company.
Labyrinth is released in the United States.
Inside the Labyrinth documentary produced.
The pilot for *Jim Henson's The Storyteller,* "Hans My Hedgehog," is filmed in London.
The Christmas Toy taped in Toronto.
Jim Henson's Muppet Babies' third season on CBS.

1987
The Storyteller, "Hans My Hedgehog" and "Fearnot," air on NBC.
Puppetman pilot is taped in Los Angeles.
Down at Fraggle Rock documentary airs on CBC in Canada.
Animals built by Jim Henson's Creature Shop in London for the film *The Bear.*
Jim conducts TV/Muppets workshop in Charleville-Mézières, France, at the Institute International de la Marionette.
Animated *Fraggle Rock* debuts on NBC Saturday mornings.
Jim Henson's Muppet Babies' fourth season on CBS.
The Muppets appear on Ted Koppel's *Nightline: A National Town Meeting on Wall Street and the Economy.*
Jim Henson inducted into the Television Academy Hall of Fame.
A Muppet Family Christmas airs on ABC.

1988
The Storyteller, "A Story Short" and "The Luck Child," air.
The Witches filmed in Norway under the direction of Nicholas Roeg.
Shooting begins on *The Jim Henson Hour* pilot in Toronto.
The Ghost of Faffner Hall begins production in Newcastle, England.
Jim Henson's Muppet Babies' fifth season on CBS.

1989
Sesame Street: 20 and Still Counting airs on NBC.
The Jim Henson Hour premieres on NBC. Episodes include *The Storyteller:* "The Heartless Giant," "The Soldier and Death," "The True Bride," and "Sapsorrow"; and "Dog City," "Song of the Cloud Forest," "Monster Maker," "Lighthouse Island," and "Miss Piggy's Hollywood."
Merger agreement between The Walt Disney Company and Henson Associates, Inc., is announced.
The Ghost of Faffner Hall premieres on HBO.
Jim Henson's Muppet Babies' sixth season on CBS.
The Teenage Mutant Ninja Turtles are built in London by Jim Henson's Creature Shop.

1990 Production begins on *Jim Henson's Muppet∗Vision 3D* for the Disney–MGM Studios Theme Park at Walt Disney World.
The Muppets at Walt Disney World taped.
Jim Henson dies.
The Witches premieres in the United States and the United Kingdom.
Jim Henson's Muppets Babies' seventh season on CBS.
The Muppets Celebrate Jim Henson airs on CBS.
Jim Henson's Mother Goose Stories air on the Disney Channel.
Henson Associates, Inc., and The Walt Disney Company agree to end merger negotiations.

1991 Brian Henson named president of Jim Henson Productions, Inc.
Dinosaurs' first season on ABC.
Jim Henson's Muppet∗Vision 3D officially opens at Walt Disney World's Disney–MGM Studios Theme Park.
Jim Henson's Muppet Babies celebrates its 100th episode as the show begins its eighth season on CBS.
Jim Henson is honored with a star on the Hollywood Walk of Fame.

1992 *Jim Henson's Dog City*'s first season airs on Fox.
Jim Henson's World of Television exhibit at the Museum of Television and Radio, New York.
Dinosaurs' second season on ABC.
Puppetry at the Public: The First New York International Festival of Puppet Theater, a presentation of The Jim Henson Foundation, is held at the Joseph Papp Public Theater in New York City.

Sesame Street, in its 23rd season, celebrates winning more than 50 Emmy Awards, including 12 Emmys for Outstanding Children's Show.
The Muppet Christmas Carol opens in the U.S. and U.K. The movie sound track is released on the newly formed Jim Henson Records label.

1993 Kermit appears at President Clinton's inaugural festivities.
Citykids special airs on ABC. Jim Henson Video line debuts. *Dinosaurs'* third season on ABC.
Jim Henson's Dog City's second season on FOX.
Citykids series premieres on ABC.
Sesame Street, for its 25th season, expands and goes "around the corner."
Dinosaur characters for *The Flintstones* feature film built by Jim Henson's Creature Shop.

ACKNOWLEDGMENTS

This book has been more than a decade in the making. Jim Henson first discussed it with me in the early 1980s, when the Muppets were at the height of their success. He emphasized, however, that it was a long-term project. He felt his career had not yet reached a point that justified such a book, explaining that there were too many things he still wanted to do. But he added that I should expect a call one day. He mentioned the project a couple of times over the next several years, but the call did not come until 1990. It arrived in the form of a telephone message that said, "I think this is the right time to do the book we talked about. I hope you'll be available in the near future and that we can get together soon to talk about it." Less than a week later, he was dead.

All this is touched on as a way of prefacing the fact that there is no easy way of assembling the acknowledgments for this volume, since it is a book I was researching in my head long before I formally began work on the manuscript. In addition, I wrote two earlier books —*Of Muppets and Men* and *The Making of the Dark Crystal*—that gave me the opportunity to spend time on the sets of *The Muppet Show* and *The Dark Crystal*, gathering much information that has found its way into this volume. Also, in connection with a Henson retrospective at the Museum of Broadcasting in New York and in preparation for another proposed retrospective that failed to materialize, I was able to interview Jim at length about his early career. This was an unusual privilege because he was always extremely reluctant to talk about his past. He preferred to think about his current project, or better still the next one.

In short, I have been squirreling away information about Jim Henson and his various enterprises for over a decade. During that period, I have talked to dozens of his associates, some several times, formally and informally. Better still, I have been permitted to act as a fly on the wall on television and movie sets, in workshops and offices, learning about the Henson way of creating entertainment.

Among the many people who have assisted me, members of the Henson family have been especially helpful. Jane Henson has been a vital source of all kinds of information, but in particular she has provided a wealth of detail about Jim's early career, which she of course shared. Cheryl Henson has been particularly close to this project and, along with providing her own insights, has made many valuable suggestions that have helped shape the manuscript. Brian and Lisa Henson have also been generous with their time, in terms of both submitting to interviews and reviewing the manuscript at various stages.

Two of Jim's oldest and closest associates also deserve special thanks. As Bert to Jim's Ernie, and Miss Piggy to Jim's Kermit, nobody understands Jim's performing skills better than Frank Oz. He has been extremely articulate in describing those skills for my benefit and has also provided a welcome commentary on the manuscript. As writer, producer, and performer, Jerry Juhl has been associated with the Henson organization for more than three decades. His memories of the early years have been invaluable to me, as have his insights into the Muppets themselves—insights that derive from his role in developing these characters as the head writer for *The Muppet Show* as well as in a variety of other capacities.

Over the years—going back to the days of *The Muppet Show* —I have also received special assistance from David Lazer and Michael K. Frith. As executive producer for *The Muppet Show*, David guided me through my early contacts with the Henson organization and has since been a constant and reliable source of information. As the key in-house art director, Michael became an expert at interpreting Jim's creative impulses and has been more than generous in sharing this expertise with me.

The Henson organization is made up of people with many different skills—writers, producers, art directors, puppet builders; but of primary importance to the entire enterprise are the performers. It has been my good fortune both to talk with many of them and to watch them work on projects ranging from *Fraggle Rock* to *Dinosaurs*. Among those who have been especially helpful, I would like to single out Dave Goelz, Jerry Nelson, the late Richard Hunt, Steve Whitmire, Kevin Clash, Kathy Mullen, Louise Gold, Dave Greenway, and Bobby Payne (whose association with the Muppets goes back to the 1950s).

The workshop personnel are the unsung heroes and heroines of the puppet world, and over the years I have conducted interviews or enjoyed less formal but no less useful chats with Caroly Wilcox, Franz "Faz" Fazakas, Amy Van Gilder, Rollin Krewson, Bob McCormack, Calista Hendrickson, Jan Rosenthal, Barbara Davis, Nomi Fredrick, Polly Smith, Wendy Midener Froud, Sherry Amott, Sarah Bradpiece, Tad Krzanowski, and Leigh Donaldson.

Other Henson associates, past and present, who contributed to my knowledge of Jim and the worlds he created are Al Gottesman, Duncan Kenworthy, Alex Rockwell, Harriet Yassky, Martin Baker, Bob Bromberg, Bruce McNally, Brian Froud, Gary Kurtz, Ritamarie Peruggi, Danielle Obinger, Craig Shemin, Chris Langham, David Odell, the late Don Hinkley, Ray Charles, and Derek Scott. For memories of *Sesame Street* and the exciting period that led up to it, I am indebted to Joan Ganz Cooney and Jon Stone, both of whom brought the beginnings of this ground-breaking show to life with a wealth of detail.

The worlds created by Jim Henson have always been visually inventive, and thus it is only appropriate that this book should be a feast for the eye. It is precisely that, due to the prodigious efforts of a Condé Nast team led by Rochelle Udell, Mary Maguire, and Sarah Parr, to whom I am greatly indebted and enormously grateful. Thanks are due also to designer Tina Strasberg and production editor Beth Pearson, and to David Rosenthal of Random House for his overall editorial guidance. The fine typesetting was done by DesignerType, and the excellent color preparation was done by Colotone Graphics.

It is with particular warmth that I thank all my friends at Muppet Press, especially Jane Leventhal, who has maintained her own high standards while serving as midwife to this project; Louise Gikow, who has brought clarity and perspective to the task of editing the manuscript; and Francesca Olivieri, who has responded to a thousand different requests with efficiency, tact, and intelligence. Thanks, too, to Karen Falk, keeper of the archives, for her quick, accurate, and gracious answers to innumerable questions.

Finally, I return to Jim Henson. Jim is the subject of this book, and he has also been my chief source of information. We taped our conversations on several occasions, but just as important were the lunches, dinners, and casual encounters when Jim talked freely about his achievements and aspirations. He encouraged me to sit in on production meetings and writers' meetings, and spent time with me in the editing room and on the set. And no matter how hectic his schedule, he always found time to answer my questions.

He was an extraordinary person, and I hope this book gives some idea of the magnitude of his achievements and the breadth of his generosity of spirit.

— CHRISTOPHER FINCH

Grateful acknowledgment is made
to the following for permission to reprint their copyrighted material.
Every reasonable effort has been made to trace the ownership
of all copyrighted pictures and works of art included in this volume.
Any errors that may have occurred are inadvertent and will be
corrected in subsequent editions provided notification is
sent to the publisher.

FRONT MATTER George Lange: title page. John E. Barrett: iv-v; David Dagley and Still Photographic Department of ATV Network Limited: ix, x, xiv, xv; George Lange: i, vi-vii, viii; Murray Close, David Dagley: xii, xv.

BEFORE CHAPTER ONE Ackard Photography: 7; Courtesy of Henson family: 2, 3, 4, 5, 6, 10, 11 top and bottom; Jim Henson original art: 1, 8 left and right, 9 left and right.

CHAPTER ONE Ankers, Anderson & Cutts Photographers, Washington, D.C.: 19 bottom/right, 22 top/left, middle/left, bottom/left, top/middle, middle/middle, 23 top/right, 24-25, 26; John E. Barrett: 17, 33 top/right, 36 bottom/right, 37 left, and bottom/middle; David Dagley and Still Photographic Department at ATV Network Limited: 36 left; Michel Delsol: 37 top/right; Courtesy of Henson family: 20-21; Jim Henson original art: 15, 28-29, 32, 33 bottom left, middle, and right, and middle/right.

CHAPTER TWO John E. Barrett: 41, Courtesy of the Ed Sullivan Estate: 45 bottom/right, 47 left; Jim Henson original art: 39, 44, 46 right, 48 top, middle/right, bottom.

CHAPTER THREE John E. Barrett: 52-53, 56 right, 57 top/left, 60 right, 61 top/middle and right, 67 top/right, bottom/left, bottom/right, 75, 78-79; Star Black: 64 top; Dwight Carter: 66 left; CTW: 50, 54, 55 top and bottom, 57 right, 61 middle/right, 62 top/left, top/right, middle/right, bottom/middle, 63 top/middle, middle/left, bottom/left, 64 bottom, 65 top/right, 66 bottom, 68 bottom/middle, 70 top, bottom/right, 72-73, 77 top/right, bottom/middle, bottom/right; CTW/Victor DiNapoli: 68 left; CTW/Randall Hagadorn: 77 bottom/left; CTW/Hal Martin Fogel: 68 middle/right; CTW/Richard Termine: 59, 62 top/middle, middle/left, middle/middle, bottom/left, bottom/right, 63 top/left, top/right, middle/middle, middle/right, bottom/middle, 66 top/right, 67 top/left, 68 top/middle, top/right, 69, 70 bottom/left, 74; Courtesy of Henson family: 76, 77 top/left; Jim Henson original art: 51, 56 bottom/left, 57 bottom/left, 61 bottom; Nancy Moran: 58 left and right, 65 left; K. C. Witherell: 62-63 (illustrations), 76-77 (illustrations).

CHAPTER FOUR John E. Barrett: 86-87 middle, 96, 110 bottom/right, 111 left, 115; Courtesy of Broadway Video Entertainment and NBC: 86 bottom/left. David Dagley and Still Photographic Department of ATV Network Limited: 85, 88-89, 90-91, 92-93, 98-99, 100 bottom, 102, 103 top/left, middle/middle, middle/right, bottom/left, bottom/right, 105, 106-107, 108-109, 110 left, 112-113, 116-117, 118-119; Michel Delsol: 97; Halston original art: 111 right; Jim Henson original art: 80, 81; Nancy Moran: 86 top/left, middle/left, 110-111 center; Charles Pike Roasan: 95.

CHAPTER FIVE Murray Close, David Dagley: 130, 131 bottom, 132, 133 top, bottom; John Davis: 136-137 (sketches, except on 136 top/left) Michael K. Frith drawing, Calista Hendrickson design: 133 middle; Kerry Hayes: 135, 136-137 (all photos), 138-139; Jim Henson original art: 121, 136 top/left; Nancy Moran: 120, 124-125; *Playbill*R: 134 top (*Playbill*R is a registered trademark of Playbill Incorporated, New York City. Used by permission); Marcia Reed, Sidney Baldwin, John Shannon: 126-127, 128-129; Drew Struzan: 125 top, 131 top.

CHAPTER SIX Jaime Ardiles-Arce: 156 top/left, top/right, 157 middle; John E. Barrett: 140 bottom, 143, 146 top/left, 147 top/right, 148-149, 150-151 (all photos), 154-155, 156 bottom/left, 156-157 top/center, 162; Marianne Bernstein: top/right; Susan Berry: 163; William Coupon: 157 top/right; Jim Henson original art: 141, 142 bottom/right, 160-161; Guy and Brad Gilchrist 150 top ■ MAGAZINE SPREAD, 144-145: *American Cinematographer:* Courtesy of *American Cinematographer* magazine; *Animation Magazine:* Courtesy of *Animation Magazine;*